IMMERSED IN GOD

IMMERSED IN GOD

BLESSED JOSEMARIA ESCRIVA, FOUNDER OF OPUS DEI, AS SEEN BY HIS SUCCESSOR, BISHOP ALVARO DEL PORTILLO

Interview by
CESARE CAVALLERI

[An English translation of *Intervista sul fondatore dell'Opus Dei*, a cura di Cesare Cavalleri (Milano, Edizioni Ares, 1992), by Dr. Gerald Malsbary.]

Scepter Publishers
Princeton, NJ
and
Sinag-Tala Publishers
Manila

This edition of *Immersed in God* is published in the United States by
Scepter Publishers, Inc., PO Box 1270, Princeton, NJ 08542; and in
the Philippines by Sinag-Tala Publishers, Inc., Greenhills PO Box 536,
Manila 1502.

Scepter Publishers   ISBN: 0–933932–85–5
Sinag-Tala Publishers   ISBN: 971–554–000–7

First printing, April 1996
Second printing, August 1996

Library of Congress Cataloging-in-Publication Data

Portillo, Alvaro del.
    [Intervista sul fondatore dell'Opus Dei. English]
    Immersed in God: Blessed Josemaría Escrivá, founder of Opus Dei,
as seen by his successor, Bishop Alvaro del Portillo / interview by
Cesare Cavalleri.
    p.   cm.
    Includes bibliographical references.
    ISBN 0–933932–85–5 (pbk.)
    1. Escrivá de Balaguer, Josemaría, 1902-1975. 2. Blessed—Spain—
Biography. 3. Opus Dei (Society)—History. 4. Portillo, Alvaro del—
Interviews. I. Cavalleri, Cesare, 1936– . II. Title.
BX4705.E676P6518 1996
567'. 182'092—dc20
[B]   95–50940
                                             CIP

Italian Original © 1992 Edizioni Ares
© 1996 Scepter Publishers

CONTENTS

	Foreword	vii
	Preface	ix
1	A Son of the Church	1
2	Citizens of Two Cities	15
3	What the Father Was Like	31
4	His Upbringing	43
5	The Founder	53
6	A Family and an Army	64
7	Means and Obstacles	86
8	Outlines of Interior Life	99
9	The Bread and the Word	109
10	Devotions	123
11	Virtues Lived to a Heroic Degree	141
12	A Reputation for Sanctity	174
13	June 26, 1975	191
	A Chronology of the Life of Blessed Josemaría Escrivá	213
	Bibliographical Note	244

Foreword

THE ORIGINAL, ITALIAN EDITION OF THIS BOOK was published shortly after Pope John Paul II beatified Msgr. Josemaría Escrivá on May 17, 1992. Bishop Alvaro del Portillo himself died only a little over a year later, on March 23, 1994, just after returning from a pilgrimage to the Holy Land; he said his last Mass on earth in the Church of the Cenacle in Jerusalem—traditionally believed to be the site of our Lord's institution of the Holy Eucharist. His successor as Prelate of Opus Dei is Fr. Javier Echevarría, who worked closely with Msgr. Escrivá during the twenty-five years before his death, and who was secretary general (and later vicar general) of Opus Dei for the almost nineteen years during which Bishop del Portillo served as successor to the founder. The current Prelate was ordained a bishop by Pope John Paul II on January 6, 1995.

The interviewer, Cesare Cavalleri, who was born in northern Italy in 1936, has been the publisher of the theological journal *Studi Cattolici* since 1965, and a columnist and television critic for the Italian newspaper *Avvenire* since its beginnings in 1968. His column, "Persone & Parole" ("Persons and Words"), gave rise to his book of the same name, published in 1989. He has also published a version in Italian (in poetic form) of *Libro de la Pasión*, by the Chilean poet and theologian José Miguel Ibáñez Langlois, and is a professor of communications arts at the University of Genoa.

Preface

FIRST OF ALL, I would like to express my profound thanks to the late Bishop Alvaro del Portillo for his generosity in sharing with me his personal recollections, together with relevant letters and documents, which cast light on little-known features of the personality of Opus Dei's founder, whom, as of May 17, 1992, the Church venerates as Blessed.

Having lived for forty years at the side of Msgr. Escrivá, Bishop del Portillo was a privileged—even more, a unique—witness to the founder's holy life and his untiring and heroic activity for the good of the Church and all souls.

This book is relatively brief, covering only some aspects of the founder's personality and correspondence to God's initiative. It is by no means exhaustive. His spiritual richness was such that even a much longer book could scarcely do it justice. The founder's message—a practical spirituality—is, in my opinion, most clearly shown through a combination of anecdotes, specific deeds, and personal experiences. This book is not, therefore, presented as any kind of substitute for the biographies of Opus Dei's founder. An acquaintance with them would, in fact, provide a historical context for the information contained herein, much of which has never before been published.

Carrying out this interview was a most gratifying professional and spiritual experience. Gaining a deeper knowledge of so beloved a man of God through the living experience of his closest son was the source of a deep joy.

There only remains for me to express my hope that the readers of these pages will be moved by Blessed Josemaría's life and virtues, so faithfully reflected in the words of his first successor, Bishop Alvaro del Portillo.

1. A Son of the Church

The decree on the heroic practice of virtue lived by Msgr. Jose-maría Escrivá, the decree promulgated by Pope John Paul II on April 9, 1990, situates the founder of Opus Dei in a definite context within the Church: that of the call to holiness of all baptized Christians, which in the words of Pope Paul VI is "the most characteristic element of the conciliar magisterium, and, so to speak, its ultimate purpose." Msgr. Escrivá, who ever since October 2, 1928, had dedicated all his energies to proclaiming the universal call to holiness, had clearly been in "prophetic congruence with the Second Vatican Council."

The founder's love for the Church and his desire to serve her are an evident feature in all his writings, his preaching, and his life itself. I would like to begin with this question: How did Msgr. Escrivá express personally his deep conviction that he was a son of the Church?

I shall never forget his first arrival in Rome. It was June 23, 1946. The Father was then forty-four years old. I had been in Rome since February of that year, because he had assigned me several tasks related to the gaining of pontifical approval of the Work. Since certain features of Opus Dei represented a complete innovation relative to the canon law then in force, I worked to the best of my ability to follow the exact directions of the founder. However, I was told, among a number of other things, that it was not yet possible to obtain an approval for Opus Dei; that we had been born—and these were the exact words—a century too early. Finding myself in such an apparently insuperable difficulty, I decided to write to the Father to tell him that his presence was needed in Rome.

1

At that time he was suffering from diabetes. His condition was, in fact, so serious that his physician, Dr. Rof Carballo, refused to take any responsibility for his life should he undertake the journey. Nevertheless, on June 21 the Father sailed from Barcelona on an old steamer, the *J. J. Sister*, having consulted with the General Council of Opus Dei and having entrusted himself to Our Lady of Mercy.

After a voyage that was quite harrowing because of an exceptionally violent Mediterranean storm, the ship reached the port of Genoa on June 22, a little before midnight. In the meantime, I had come to meet him from Rome, together with another member of Opus Dei, Salvador Canals. Salvador and I stopped at a modest inn beforehand, to book rooms for the night. I recall that we ate a very frugal dinner—we were still very much in the postwar period—and for dessert we were served some Parmesan cheese. I was not acquainted with this type of cheese; but I tasted it, and I liked it so much that I saved the rest of it for our founder. I had no idea that this would turn out to be the first food he had had in forty-eight hours. The Father afterward would often tease me about that little present!

Next day the founder celebrated his first Mass on Italian soil, in a church badly damaged by bombing. The drive to Rome, in a small rented car and along ruined roads, was a quite uncomfortable one, and seemed to go on forever. But the Father was full of joy and made no complaint; he was delighted that one of his greatest aspirations, *videre Petrum* [to see Peter], was being fulfilled. During the whole ride he prayed fervently for the pope.

At nightfall on June 23, we arrived in Rome. At the first glimpse of St. Peter's from the Via Aurelia, the Father, deeply moved, said the Creed. We had rented some rooms on the top floor of a building at 9 Piazza della Città Leonina; there was a balcony from which St. Peter's Basilica and the pontifical palace could be seen. When he went out on this balcony and saw the rooms occupied by the Vicar of Christ, the Father said he wanted to remain there awhile; and so he did, staying recollected in prayer while the others, exhausted, went straight to bed. Out of love for the pope, made all the more palpable by this proximity to the papal apartments, and without a thought for his fatigue, for his diabetes and the intense thirst which this must have been causing him, or for the toll taken on him by the hardships of his long sea voyage, the Father spent the whole night in prayer, on that balcony.

This episode gives us some idea of the intensity of the founder's love for the Church and especially the pope. And yet, though he had an intense longing to pray at the tomb of St. Peter, so great was his spirit of mortification that he waited several days before crossing the threshold of St. Peter's.

On June 30, the Father was able to write to his sons in the General Council (which at this time was still located in Spain): "I have a signed photograph of the Holy Father addressed to 'the Founder of the Priestly Society of the Holy Cross and Opus Dei.' What a great joy! I have kissed it a thousand times. We are living in the shadow of St. Peter's, next to the colonnade."

On August 31, the founder was able to return to Madrid with a legal document from the Holy See in "praise of the objectives" of Opus Dei; such a document had not been granted for nearly a century. The difficulties were beginning to be overcome.

On October 22, 1946, the founder returned to Barcelona to thank Our Lady of Mercy. On November 8, he again left Madrid for Rome, the city which would be his habitual residence until the day, almost thirty years later, when God called him to himself.

> *Our Father was well received in the Roman Curia, especially by the then undersecretary of the Vatican Secretariat of State, Msgr. Montini (later Pope Paul VI). But he met with difficulties from some churchmen. Sometimes he said he lost his innocence after coming to Rome . . .*

Nevertheless, his own responses were always characterized by a profoundly supernatural outlook. He often visited St. Peter's to recite the Creed before the tomb of the Prince of the Apostles. He used the version taught to him by his mother when he was a little boy; and when he reached the words "I believe in the holy Catholic Church," he added the adjective "Roman," and then, parenthetically, he added "in spite of everything." He once confided this custom of his to Msgr. Tardini* (I was there at the time, but I don't remember if this was before or after he became cardinal secretary of state), and that prelate asked him, "What do you mean, 'in spite of everything'?" The Father replied, "I mean, in spite of my sins and yours."

He did not, of course, intend this as any disparagement of Msgr. Tardini. If, as we know, nobody is exempt from sin ("the just one falls seven times a day" [Prv 24:16]), our founder meant only to emphasize the need for those who assist the pope to be very holy and filled with the Holy Spirit, in order that there be more sanctity throughout the Church.

As he often said, the Church, inasmuch as she is the bride of Christ, is without blemish; therefore, while he recognized the reality of human limitations, he would not accept or justify the false humility of certain ecclesiastics who seemed perennially disposed to be ashamed of the Church; what he called the attitude of "mea-culpism" was most distressing to him. He was convinced that the recognition of human failings should never be allowed to cloud over one's faith in the objective sanctity of the Church.

Our Father met three popes. What was his relationship with the first of them, Pope Pius XII?

Pope Pius received the Father in audience many times. He showed his own esteem for the Work by granting the first two papal approvals: the *Decretum Laudis* in 1947, and the definitive approval in 1950. To express his affection for the Holy Father, our founder did all kinds of things, even offering him simple little gifts. For example, he once brought him some oranges which he had received from Spain, at a time when we could hardly afford to

---

*In Italian and some other languages, bishops are commonly referred to as "Monsignor." Since in some cases it is not clear whether or not the person was a bishop at the time of the incident mentioned, we have in those cases simply kept the Italian usage. Msgr. Escrivá, of course, was not a bishop.

buy food for ourselves; another time, knowing that the Holy Father liked a certain Spanish wine, he obtained some bottles of that wine and gave them to him as a present.

There is another episode that shows the affection our founder had for the Holy Father. During an audience, at a certain point he wished to kiss the feet of Pope Pius. The Holy Father permitted him to kiss only one foot—not the other. But the Father, with filial insistence, prevailed by reminding the Holy Father that he was from Aragón in Spain, and stubborn like all the Aragonese.

Pope Pius XII expressed his personal appreciation for the founder of Opus Dei on many occasions. He once confided to Cardinal Gilroy and his auxiliary bishop, "He is truly a saint, a man sent by God for our times." (It was that same auxiliary bishop, Bishop Thomas Muldoon, who recorded this reminiscence, in a testimonial written after the death of the Father.)

> *In a magazine interview* (Conversations, *No. 22) our Father himself recalled having made the following remark to Pope John XXIII, encouraged by that pope's affability and fatherly charm: "Holy Father, in our Work everyone is welcome, whether Catholic or not—I did not learn ecumenism from Your Holiness." Pope John was moved to laughter; he was well aware that from 1950 on, Opus Dei had had authorization from the Holy See to enlist non-Catholics and even non-Christians as cooperators.*

That episode took place during the first audience that Pope John XXIII granted the founder, on March 5, 1960. The simple and disarming manner of the Holy Father encouraged confidence and sincerity in his visitors. Furthermore, the Father, when he was received at papal audiences, and even when he had to bring up important matters, always made a point of relating news that might bring cheer to the pope. I remember one time, a few days after his arrival in Rome, when he was received by Msgr. Montini, who at that time was undersecretary of the Vatican Secretariat of State. The Father spoke to him at some length about the Work and used as illustration several anecdotes about our apostolic activities. Msgr. Montini assured him that he would pass these on to Pope John. "All we usually get here," he said, "are pains and sorrows. The Holy Father will be very happy to hear about all the good things you are doing."

At the end of that first audience, Pope John confided to our founder that his explanations of the spirit of the Work had opened up for him "unsuspected horizons of apostolate."

I was not present at the private audience granted him by Pope John on June 27, 1962; Fr. Javier Echevarría accompanied the Father. It was a tête-à-tête meeting between the Holy Father and the founder of Opus Dei. I do know that they spoke a long time about the spirit and activity of the Work in the world, and that a few days later, on July 12, 1962, the Father wrote a letter to his sons and daughters the whole world over, asking them to be united with him in the gratitude that he justly felt toward Pope John XXIII for the Holy Father's having offered him once again "the honor and joy of seeing Peter." I should add that our founder spoke to me many times, with great admiration, about the priestly virtues of Pope John XXIII.

During the painful illness of Pope John, Msgr. Angelo Dell' Acqua informed the Father (they were very close to one another) about some of the particulars of how he was caring for the ailing pope. For example, when Msgr. Dell'Acqua was standing by his bedside, the Holy Father would take his hand, and if he made any sign of moving away, he would exclaim, "Angelino, don't leave me!" The Father was grieved at the thought that the Holy Father might feel abandoned, and he wholeheartedly thanked Msgr. Dell'Acqua, who, with the most intimate associates of the pontifical family, was taking care of Pope John with such affection during his last days.

From the foregoing remarks one can infer that Pope Paul's appreciation of Opus Dei and its founder dated from before his elevation to the papacy.

It suffices here to recall that once papal approval for Opus Dei had been obtained, I felt the time was right to request from the Holy See (in my capacity as procurator general and on behalf of the General Council of the Work) that our founder be named monsignor. The then Msgr. Montini not only approved my initiative, but took it up himself. This was at the beginning of 1947.

Well aware of the humility of the Father, I arranged everything without saying a word to him about it. In the spring of that year, a letter from Msgr. Montini arrived, with the document naming the founder of Opus Dei as a monsignor; it was dated April 22, 1947. Msgr. Montini expressed praise for Opus Dei and for its founder, and added that the Work was a bright prospect for the Church.

The Father was very grateful, but told me he did not want to accept. He thought he should return the document, with all due gratitude, to Msgr. Montini, explaining that he wanted no honors. However, Salvador Canals and I asked him not to do this. The argument that convinced him was that the title [which is given only to secular priests] would make the secular nature of Opus Dei more obvious than ever. So he changed his mind and wrote a letter to the undersecretary of the Secretariat of State, expressing his gratitude for this sign of the Holy Father's and Msgr. Montini's affection. We afterwards learned that Msgr. Montini had paid the fee for the nomination out of his own pocket.

I was privileged to see in a very special way the affection of Pope Paul VI for the Father when I was received by him after my election as the founder's successor. Pope Paul spoke to me of his admiration for the Father and expressed his conviction that he was a saint. He assured me that he had been reading *The Way* daily for many years, with great profit to his soul, and asked me how old the founder had been when it was first published. I replied that he had sent it to the press when he was thirty-seven years old, but that actually the core of the book had already seen the light of day in 1934, under the title of *Consideraciones Espirituales,* and had been written a couple of years earlier than that— in other words, when the author was only about thirty years old. The Holy Father became pensive for a moment, and then remarked: "So, he wrote it in the maturity of his youth!"

*I still have a very vivid memory of the visit of Pope Paul VI to
the Centro ELIS on its opening day, November 21, 1965. The
great complex that stands in the working-class Tiburtino district of Rome was begun on the initiative of Pope John XXIII,
who had decided to devote a sum of money (collected from
Catholics all over the world to celebrate the eightieth birthday
of Pope Pius XII) to the creation of a social-work center in
Rome. He entrusted the planning, realization, and management
of the project to Opus Dei. The result was a multipurpose
structure comprising a residence for student workers, a center
of professional training for crafts and trades, a library, an ath-
letic center, and a school of hotel management that incorporated
many activities for the advancement of women. Next to the
ELIS was built the parish church of San Giovanni Battista al
Collatino—a parish entrusted to priests of Opus Dei. The pope
stayed well beyond the time planned for the visit. He celebrated
Mass, blessed a statue of our Lady for the University of Navarre,
and attentively visited the various parts of the center. When the
visit was over, he embraced our founder and exclaimed, with
visible emotion, "All this is Opus Dei!" Since, at that time, papal
visits were rare, this was a sign of great regard for the Work
and for the Father. Pope Paul wanted the opening of the Centro
ELIS to take place during the concluding phases of the Second
Vatican Council, to facilitate the participation of many conciliar fathers in the ceremony; and this wish was fulfilled.*

    *Can you describe the last meeting between Pope Paul VI
and the founder?*

Yes. It took place on June 25, 1973, and it had a special and
unforgettable quality. The Father spoke to Pope Paul about very
supernatural matters, and brought him up to date on the development of the Work and on the God-given fruits it was bearing
throughout the world. The Holy Father was very pleased with
what he heard. From time to time he would interrupt with some
words of praise or simply to exclaim, "You are a saint!" I know
about this because I couldn't help noticing afterwards that the
Father had a very pensive, almost sad look on his face. I asked him

why. At first he refused to answer me. Then he told me what Pope Paul had said to him, and he said that he had been overcome with shame and grief for his own sins, so much so that he had made a filial protest to the pope: "No, no! You do not know me, Your Holiness—I am just a poor sinner." But Pope Paul had insisted, "No, no—you are a saint." At this the founder, full of emotion, had replied, "On this earth there is only one saint—the Holy Father!"*

Then there is the testimony of Msgr. Carlo Colombo, theological advisor and a close friend of Pope Paul VI, that the Holy Father himself encouraged him to write a postulatory letter for the opening of the cause for beatification of the founder of Opus Dei. This is what he said: "In the course of a meeting with Pope Paul VI, in which various topics were discussed, I had an opportunity to express to him my intention of writing a postulatory letter requesting the opening of the canonical process to introduce the cause of Msgr. Escrivá de Balaguer, the founder of Opus Dei. I felt an obligation to tell the Holy Father that I was intending to address a postulatory letter to him, a letter which I would not have written had I not had a serious personal motivation to do so. Given the great confidence which I enjoyed with the Holy Father, it would have constituted a betrayal of trust not to tell him. Pope Paul gave me his full assent and approval, based on the great esteem which he had for this servant of God. He knew the good desires which had guided Msgr. Escrivá—his burning love for the Church and her visible head, and his ardent zeal for souls."

> I was present with a group of members of Opus Dei, from various countries, at the Mass which Pope John Paul II celebrated for us on August 19, 1979. He delivered an unforgettable homily. Among other things, he said: "Your ideal is truly great. From its very beginnings it anticipated the theology of the laity that was later to characterize the Church of and after the council." All of us present were moved at hearing this praise of our spirituality, and of our realization of

---

*There is a play of words here, in Italian, between "saint" (*santo*) and "Holy Father" (*Santo Padre*).

*"being Church," from the lips of the successor of St. Peter.
Our thoughts immediately went to our founder, who never
had the opportunity to meet the future Pope John Paul II, a
pope whose name is linked to the history of the Work.*

*The founder of Opus Dei, then, was considered a pre-
cursor of the Second Vatican Council, although he did not
personally participate in the council.*

The Father was very pleased at the convocation of the
Second Vatican Council. From the moment it was publicly announced, he sent Pope John XXIII a letter full of gratitude. He
intuited, among other things, that this council would fill in some
theological gaps concerning the role of lay people in the Church—
which is, in fact, what happened.

He thought that he might be summoned to attend in his
capacity as president general of a secular institute, which was the
juridical form of Opus Dei at that time. In such a case he would
have had to participate as a council father, together with other
superiors of institutions that were included in the "state of perfection" category. Despite his great desire to take an active part in the
council assemblies, he did not judge it fitting for him to participate
as president of a secular institute. While that might not have
meant the actual acceptance of a juridical status inadequate to the
Work, it could in some way have set a precedent unfavorable to a
future revision of the juridical framework of Opus Dei. He
explained to the Curia his reasons for not considering it prudent
for him to participate in the council, and his decision on this matter was well understood.

He was then invited to participate as a *peritus* (expert ob-
server) of the council. This invitation was transmitted to him by
Msgr. Loris Capovilla, on behalf of the Holy Father John XXIII.
The founder asserted once again his total and unconditional avail-
ability; but after expressing gratitude for the invitation, he explained why he would prefer not to accept it, while making it clear
that he would in any event do whatever the pope wanted.

In short, this was his reasoning. On the one hand, he would
not have been able to dedicate to this task all the time it would

have taken to accomplish it properly. On the other hand, various sons of his who were bishops were council fathers; so it would have seemed strange for him to take part as a simple *peritus*. There was no vainglory in this; he was simply trying to avoid misunderstandings with the Holy See. Had he accepted the role of *peritus*, after having declined being named a council father, some people might have thought he was trying to operate "behind the scenes." At the same time, others who did not know the background might have seen this as meaning that Opus Dei was not considered to have any real importance in the Church.

Nevertheless, our founder offered to the appropriate ecclesiastical authorities the active cooperation of the Work as a whole and that of individual members—quite a number of whom, as it turned out, did participate, both in the preparation of the council and in the council itself.

As for me, he encouraged me to accept appointments to various commissions of the council, and to dedicate myself to this work with all my energy. At the beginning of the activities I was named a *peritus* of the council and secretary of the Commission for Discipline of the Clergy and the Christian People. In this latter capacity I found myself having to play a very active role.

> *That was the commission which worked on the decree* Presbyterorum Ordinis . . .

Yes. In addition, I was named a consultor to three other conciliar commissions—one for bishops and diocesan administration, one for religious, and one for Catholic doctrine. I also served as a consultor to the Mixed Commission for Associations of the Faithful, and to the Commission for the Revision of the Code of Canon Law. Once the proceedings of the ecumenical council were finished, I was appointed consultor to the postconciliar Commission for Bishops and Diocesan Administration.

During the sessions of the council, along with the positive and encouraging results which were to find expression in the definitive documents, there were also certain disagreements and confusions, and these were often exaggerated by the newspapers.

The resulting tensions made Popes John XXIII and Paul VI suffer, as Msgr. Dell'Acqua confided to our founder. I ought to clarify that the trust which Msgr. Dell'Acqua felt in our founder (a trust that is evidenced by the considerable correspondence which took place between them at that time) was not simply a fruit of their intimate bond of friendship. Actually, it was the Holy Father himself who encouraged the undersecretary of the Secretariat of State in this, thus ensuring that there was always a direct channel of communication between himself and our founder.

In the three years of the council, not to mention the preparatory period, our founder met with many council fathers, *periti*, and other participants. Sometimes he would invite them to dine at our central residence. On other occasions, he would go to see them in the houses where they were lodging—nearly always to return visits they had made to him. There were days on which he would receive over half a dozen of these visits. And it was certainly not easy for him to take time away from his duties of governing Opus Dei in order to receive the various cardinals, archbishops, bishops, nuncios, theologians, and so on, and to do so in a suitable manner.

I was present at many of these meetings, and was able to observe the simplicity and affability with which the Father treated those who came to meet him. Archbishop Marty (at that time archbishop of Rheims, and later cardinal archbishop of Paris) later wrote the following: "At the time of the Second Vatican Council, I had the occasion to meet several times with Msgr. Escrivá de Balaguer, the founder of Opus Dei. From these conversations I retain the memory of a man who spoke only about God. A time spent speaking with him was like time spent in prayer. And this was quite in keeping with his good humor, with his supernatural outlook, and with his affectionate charity." And Bishop del Campo, of Calahorra, left the following testimony: "I believe sincerely that Josemaría contributed in a decisive way to the clarification of many doctrinal points, for which the light given him by God, along with his extraordinary pastoral experience in the world of work, was virtually indispensable. There were many council fathers who profited from their friendship with him by receiving appropriate counsel."

I would imagine that some of this counsel had to do with the defense of Catholic orthodoxy at that time, when a misunderstood "spirit of the council" was sowing some confusion . . .

The testimony of Msgr. Barabino, who at that time was the secretary of Cardinal Siri and is now bishop of Ventimiglia, is especially significant on this matter. He writes: "His defense of orthodoxy did not stem from a spirit of conservatism, from narrowmindedness, or from a rigidity of character. He was, indeed, clearly concerned to preserve orthodoxy and the vital, divine structures of the Church; but his open, innovative spirit was equally evident. I found it truly inspiring to hear him speak about how necessary it was for each one of us, while remaining in his place and keeping faithfully to his own proper charism within the Church, to further the impulse of sanctifying grace which is poured out by the Holy Spirit upon the People of God, upon each and every member of the faithful, all of whom are called to the fullness of the Christian life. As part of his bold openness, he emphasized the missionary character that the Church has in all environments, even the most difficult. For him it was a reality which he experienced every day, in line with the fundamental idea that was his point of departure: namely, the universal vocation to sanctity; a powerful idea which he constantly applied, with a truly admirable flexibility, to the needs of the times and to the Church's development among all peoples."

It must have been very moving for our Father to see the intuition entrusted to him by the Lord on October 2, 1928, affirmed by the council, and to see it become the heritage of the entire Church . . .

Very much so—in fact, shortly after the closing of the council, I heard him say many times: "My children, we must be very pleased at the outcome of this council. Thirty years ago some people accused me of being a heretic because I preached aspects of our spirit which have now been proclaimed in a solemn way by the council." And in an interview granted to *L'Osservatore della*

Domenica in 1968, he stated: "One of my greatest joys has been just this: to see how the Second Vatican Council has proclaimed with such great clarity the divine vocation of the laity. Without a trace of presumption, I have to say that, with regard to our spirituality, the council has not represented an invitation to change, but has, rather, confirmed something which, by the grace of God, we have already been living and teaching for many years. The principal characteristic of Opus Dei is neither a certain technique or method of apostolate, nor any particular structure, but rather a spirituality which leads precisely to the sanctification of ordinary work" (*Conversations*, No. 72).

2. Citizens of Two Cities

*According to the Second Vatican Council, secularity is "proper
and peculiar to the laity"* (Lumen Gentium, *No. 31), and this
applies also to the correct exercise of the rights of citizenship—that is, we should be true Catholics, without being
either clerical or bigoted, and at the same time be true citizens who do not forget in moments of decision that we are
Catholics. This was a constant teaching of our Father. Can
we hear some examples taken directly from his life?*

Secularity can be seen as the harmonious union of a "priestly
soul" with a "lay mentality." The Father wanted all the members
of the Work—priests and lay people, men and women—to have
this; and it was always lived by him personally, as an integral element of his character, of his very being. Evident in his own lively
sense of justice and in the exercise of his rights as a citizen, which
he never neglected, this was what led him to devote a chapter of
Furrow to "Citizenship."

Among the many episodes which could be cited, let me mention one from his student days. Beginning in the academic year of
1922–1923 (when he had already been named a seminarian-superior
at the seminary of Saragossa and had received the clerical tonsure),
he was enrolled as a student in the law school of the University of
Saragossa. In June of 1924 he presented himself for the examination
in Spanish history. This was a subject which he knew very well from
his secondary school courses and from his wide reading; he had
always had a liking for history, and had a deep grasp of the subject.
However, because Josemaría had not attended classes during the
year—he was not a student following the official track, and he was
very busy, both with his theological studies and with his duties as

seminarian-superior—the history professor let him know, by way of some common acquaintances, that he might as well not show up for the examination, because he intended to fail him. Young Josemaría was taken aback, since he knew quite well that he was not required to attend classes. And so, in order to defend a right which was his by academic regulations, and feeling confident of his knowledge of history, he showed up for the examination. The professor failed him without asking him a single question.

After some calm reflection, Josemaría wrote a letter to the professor, explaining politely that he had committed an injustice and had a moral obligation to make up for it. Josemaría added that he wanted to take the examination again in September, and that he would like to be sure of receiving fair treatment.

In those days, professors enjoyed complete autonomy and had full responsibility for making up the examinations and grading them. It was not easy for students to defend their legal rights, even if they did so in the most respectful manner. But when September came, the professor acted very properly. He acknowledged his error, and the student passed.

There was also a very secular simplicity in the way Josemaría, who always wore his cassock, got along with his university colleagues. Sometimes, when classes were over, his companions would invite him to go for a drink in an establishment much frequented by students: the Abdón Bar, near Constitution Square. Josemaría would occasionally accept the invitation, thus making friends in a very natural way. His behavior was at once so priestly and so down-to-earth that as soon as he was ordained (in 1925), some of these friends chose him for their regular confessor.

A lawyer and a priest. Were there times when our Father exercised both of these professions?

His legal studies helped him, among other ways, by enabling him to offer private lessons. These helped support his family, both at Saragossa and during his first years in Madrid. However, since he wanted to be a priest one hundred percent, he never made use of his degree in civil law.

A revealing incident took place during the Spanish Civil War. At a certain point the Father saw that in Madrid he could not exercise his priestly ministry. The atmosphere was becoming unbearable; he was in constant danger of death. There were mass arrests and executions. Churches and convents were burned. It was religious persecution in the full sense of the term. The Father was left with no alternative but to try to cross the Pyrenean border and then enter Spain's liberated zone by way of Andorra; the point of departure would be Barcelona. Our founder happened to read in a newspaper that a colleague of his from the University of Saragossa, Pascual Galbe, was now serving as a magistrate in the Barcelona law courts, representing the government of the autonomous region of Catalonia. They had been great friends before, but in these new circumstances it was not easy to predict how Galbe would react. Therefore the Father sent word by way of Tomás Alvira, who had been a classmate of Galbe's in secondary school, that he was in Barcelona and that he wanted to see him. "Not in the courthouse," was the reply. "It would be better for him to come to dinner at my house."

As soon as he saw the Father, Galbe embraced him warmly. "You don't know how much I've suffered—I thought you had been killed . . ." To help him escape the danger, Galbe suggested that he take a job in the law courts of Barcelona. Galbe was a very influential man, and the courts at that time had a real need for graduates with degrees in law. But the Father refused the offer. "If," he said, "when the clergy and the rest of the Church were not being persecuted, I chose not to pursue this profession because I wanted to devote myself entirely to the priesthood, I will certainly not seek to use it as a means of survival now, serving an authority which is persecuting my Mother, the holy Church." Pascual Galbe tried to convince him otherwise. "If they catch you," he warned him, "they will very probably kill you." But the Father replied, "I don't care. I live for my priesthood, and I don't care if they kill me."

It seems to me that the question of his title of nobility is also of interest in this respect . . .

This is a point worth spending some time on, because it brings out clearly the great humility of the Father.

As we came to recognize what the founder of Opus Dei was, both for us, his sons and daughters in the Work, and for the Church in general, we began, prudently and with filial love, to gather up all the information we could about his family. One way we did this was to take good advantage of the trips made by members of the Work, for professional or apostolic purposes, to places where the family of our founder had lived, and where his ancestors had come from.

In the 1960s we gave all the collected information to a noted genealogist in Aragón, who confirmed that there were titles of nobility still in existence which had come down in a direct line to the family of the founder. In my capacity as secretary general of Opus Dei, I decided that we should have the genealogist do a detailed study. I then suggested to the Father the possibility of asking that these titles be called out of abeyance. We were thinking about how much the family of our founder had labored and suffered for the Work. At first the Father avoided the issue; afterwards he realized that it was not a purely personal matter, but that it affected his brother and his brother's children—all the descendants of his parents. He meditated about this for a long time, in the presence of the Lord. In his private life, the Father always made a distinction between, on the one hand, his duties and rights as a Christian and as a priest, which he sought to fulfill and exercise heroically at every moment, and, on the other hand, those duties and rights of his as a citizen which were not in conflict with the former. Although his priesthood embraced his whole existence, this did not mean that he renounced his obligations and rights as a member of his family or as a citizen. With regard to those also he gave example to his spiritual children and to others with whom he came in contact.

Along with his desire to compensate his family in some way for the sacrifices and sufferings involved for them in the founding and development of Opus Dei, there was also his sense that he could not make his family pay a second time for his own detachment from human honors. As the firstborn son and in accordance with the Spanish legislation then in force, only he was eligible to recover the family's rights of nobility. I must stress that these honors meant nothing to him personally. But he did come to the conclusion that he could not deprive his brother and his brother's children of any of their rights of lineage, through some kind of false humility—or, still less, out of a fear of criticism and defamation. The solution, then, was to reclaim the rights and then transfer them to his brother.

Even so, he knew very well that his gesture could be misunderstood; and so, before coming to a final decision, he sought the counsel of a number of persons, including some not in the Work. Among others, he turned to Cardinal Dell'Acqua, Cardinal Marella, Cardinal Larraona, Cardinal Antoniutti, Cardinal Bueno y Monreal (archbishop of Seville, and a good friend of long standing), and the Most Reverend Casimiro Morcillo (archbishop of Madrid, and also a friend of many years).

All of these prelates were in favor of the plan and encouraged him to carry it out. Cardinal Larraona, who was an outstanding canon lawyer, explained to him that not only did he have the right to reclaim those titles, but also, as founder of the Work, he had an obligation to do so. "You have always taught your children," he said, "to fulfill their own civil obligations and to exercise all their rights as citizens; therefore, if you don't do this, you will be setting them a bad example." Indeed, the cardinal believed that if the founder renounced this right, not only his sons and daughters in Opus Dei but also many other good Catholics would probably follow this example of "humility" and renounce rights that they had no right to renounce.

Our founder also informed the Vatican Secretariat of State; everyone there agreed with his intentions. Furthermore, he had the assent of the competent civil authorities. However, he knew perfectly well what was likely to happen: he would be severely criticized by poorly informed people, by some who were, perhaps, ill-willed or envious, and by others who were loose-tongued and stirred on by the devil. He saw with absolute clarity that he would be offering to all of them—as if on a silver platter—an opportunity to insult him.

Just as the founder foresaw, criticism and gossip were not lacking. But that just made his heroic and profound humility all

the more evident. Just as he had exercised his own rights and carried out a duty of justice in order to give an example to his children, so also did he make sure they understood clearly that the
thing in itself was of no importance.

On July 24, 1968, the title of Marquis of Peralta was officially
restored; a controversy immediately broke out, and lasted for
some time. Some of the Father's friends asked him for an explanation; others simply assured him of their support. He dealt with the
matter clearly and, when appropriate, with humor.

Afterwards, when at last the gossip had died down and the
issue could be considered more or less settled, he quietly ceded
the title to his brother, as he had planned to do from the outset, so
that his brother could hand it on to his children.

> *Our Father also detested any form of clericalism that in-
> volved a presumption of entitlement to special treatment.
> This is why he did not approve of the custom, widespread in
> many ecclesiastical circles, of seeking free services from cer-
> tain professionals, such as Catholic lawyers, doctors, engi-
> neers, or dentists; he always insisted on paying their fees.*

Yes—even at the University of Navarre, when he, the chan-
cellor of the university, needed a physical examination at its medical school, he paid the usual fee.

On the other hand, he also insisted that work be carried out
in accordance with the demands of justice. An illustrative episode comes to mind. When the oratory of the General Council of
Opus Dei was being planned, it was decided that the floor should
be made of marble; the slabs were to have geometric shapes, and
each of them was to be cut from a single stone. An estimate for
this work was agreed upon that stipulated this condition. But
after the marble worker finished his polishing and said his work
was done, the Father noticed that the individual designs had
been made by the joining together of smaller pieces of marble,
and the joints were clearly visible. Such shabby work was intoler-
able to him, especially in a place of worship; he consulted with
me and with others and decided to have the floor taken up again

and replaced. The reasons were clear: the estimate had been approved with certain stipulations, and the bill had already been paid. To accept the poorly done job would not have reflected a true spirit of poverty; those who came after would have received a disedifying example of carelessness in things which pertain to the Lord.

> *With regard to the rights of citizenship, the teaching of the founder was always very clear, even in the matter of political activity: the members of Opus Dei, in politics as well as in all other temporal activities, have the same freedom, the same rights, and the same obligations as other Catholic citizens. This is an aspect of his teaching that has often been misunderstood, especially in view of the Spanish situation. Can you recall some incidents, beginning with an explanation of the founder's attitude towards communism and Nazism?*

With regard to communism and Marxism, the Father was always faithful to the very clear teachings of the Church's magisterium about these ideologies. He would state his position, in public, whenever the circumstances required it. His view was not based on the sufferings which he personally experienced under the communist dictatorship in Spain—he had forgiven those responsible, from the very beginning—but was based, rather, on his awareness of the atheistic foundation and the inhuman and antireligious nature of their doctrine.

From the early sixties on, especially in his catechetical activities on the Iberian peninsula and in Latin America, and in response to the wide diffusion among the faithful of currents of opinion which tried to reconcile Marxism and Christianity, the founder echoed repeatedly the teachings of Pope Paul VI, as well as the condemnations contained in documents issued by the relevant departments of the Roman Curia.

This passage from a homily given in 1963 illustrates very clearly his attitude toward communism: "For this reason, it is urgent to repeat (and here I am not speaking politics, I am simply pointing out the Church's teaching) that Marxism is incompatible with the Christian faith. Can there be anything more opposed to the faith than a system which is based on eliminating the loving presence of God from the soul? Shout it aloud, so that your voice is clearly heard, that in order to practice justice we have no need whatsoever of Marxism. On the contrary, because of its exclusively materialistic solutions, which know nothing of the God of peace, this most serious error raises all kinds of barriers to the achievement of happiness and understanding among men. It is within Christianity that we find the good light that will enable us to answer all problems: all you have to do is to strive sincerely to be Catholics, *non verbo neque lingua, sed opere et veritate*, not with words or with the tongue, but with works and in truth [1 Jn 3:18]. Speak up fearlessly, whenever the occasion arises (and, if necessary, look for such opportunities), without being in any way shy" (*Friends of God*, No. 171).

By the end of the thirties, the majority of Spaniards, having lived through the unfortunate experience of the civil war, had deep reservations regarding communism. The same thing did not happen with regard to Nazism. As a matter of fact, not only did the official propaganda, for one reason or another, conceal the crimes of National Socialism, but the Spanish government even prohibited publication of the papal document condemning Nazism. Hence, our founder had to speak out against Nazism, on a number of occasions, as part of his priestly ministry. Precisely because the regime in Germany was looked upon with sympathy in some governmental circles, he felt it his duty to put on guard those who were overlooking the aberrations of Nazi ideology. He warned against not only its totalitarian nature, but also its discrimination against—and persecution of—Jews, Catholics, and others, and the paganism so characteristic of Nazi racism. He made great efforts to make known the contents of the papal document condemning Nazism, and to spread it privately.

> *And yet some newspapers have recently spoken of the "Nazi sympathies" of our founder, though the accusations were immediately rebutted.*

That this is a patent falsehood should go without saying. However, I would like to bring up a testimony which has come to my attention in connection with that slanderous campaign carried on by the press. (And let me add, in passing, that we follow in all such cases the sound guidelines which the Father left us: to forgive these attacks from the very beginning, to pray for the slanderers, to reaffirm the truth, and always "to drown evil in an abundance of good," knowing with certainty that the truth will eventually win out.) Well, on January 9, 1992, a man by the name of Domingo Díaz–Ambrona wrote to me from Madrid: "I knew the future saint during the Spanish Civil War. At that time I had taken refuge, with my wife, in the Cuban embassy. While we were there, she gave birth to our daughter Guadalupe, on September 3, 1937, in Riesgo Hospital, which no longer exists, but which at that time was under the protection of the English flag. Due to the situation our country was in, we could not have our baby baptized, and we mentioned this to a dear friend of ours, José María Albareda.

"A few days later, José María told me that a priest friend of his would come on a certain day to administer baptism to the little one. Trusting in the security afforded by the English flag, I invited the godparents and some other friends to the ceremony. The priest arrived at five in the afternoon, two hours ahead of schedule, stayed just long enough for the baptism, and left. Everything happened so quickly that we didn't even ask him his name. It was only afterwards that I found out it was Fr. Escrivá. His behavior was a lesson in prudence for all of us in those difficult circumstances. I tried to get him to stay, but he replied, 'Many souls have need of me.'

"I afterwards learned that throughout that time, even though his papers were not in order, and the social and political climate was very risky for any priest, he carried out an intense apostolic activity. He heard many confessions—sometimes risking his life in the process—and gave courses and retreats, constantly changing his residence; he also gave spiritual guidance to a group of nuns who were suffering the effects of the persecution.

"As I said before, at the time I didn't know who he was. I learned that much later, from a chance meeting in a train on the

Madrid–Avila line, in the month of August, 1941. I was traveling with my wife and our four-year-old daughter; Fr. Josemaría happened to see us, and he recognized us. He came to our compartment and said, 'I baptized this child.' We exchanged greetings, he identified himself, and we spent some time discussing the historical situation we were involved in. We knew we were living at a decisive moment in European history—I remember being anxious to reach our destination at Navas del Marqués, so I could hear the latest radio reports about the advance of German troops into Russia.

"I mentioned to him that I had just returned from a trip to Germany, and that I had noticed how afraid Catholics were to express their religious convictions. This was giving me some doubts about Nazism, although, as was the case with most Spaniards, the negative aspects of the Nazi political system and philosophy had escaped me. That was because of the deceptive propaganda which made Germany appear to be the power which would finally annihilate communism. I asked him his opinion.

"For the reasons I have given, I was profoundly surprised at the time by the decisive answer he gave. Here was a priest who had accurate information about the position of the Church and of Catholics in Germany under Hitler's dictatorship. Fr. Escrivá spoke very forcefully to me against that anti-Christian regime, and with an energy that clearly showed his great love of freedom. It is necessary to explain that it was not easy, in Spain at that time, to find people who would condemn the Nazi system so categorically or who would denounce its anti-Christian roots with such clarity. And so that conversation, taking place as it did at such a historically significant moment, before all the crimes of Nazism had been revealed, continues to impress me profoundly.

"Afterwards, when I told my friend José María Albareda about this meeting, I learned that I had spoken with the founder of Opus Dei.

"I am not a member of Opus Dei, but my personal experience leads me to state that anyone who has anything contrary to say about the thought of Josemaría Escrivá de Balaguer on this matter is only trying, in vain, to obscure the sanctity of life of this future saint: he was a passionate lover of freedom."

That is an incontrovertible testimony that only confirms what common sense would have told us anyway. The Father did, of course, make all the necessary distinctions between Nazism and the German people. In fact, he always had a special affection for that nation—it was a sentiment he had inherited from his father—and he was profoundly grieved to see it subjected to that aberrant dictatorship. His grief became all the greater when World War II broke out.

How about his relationship with Francoism?

Before answering this question, I think it imperative to underline a truth that is already well known: that the activity and purpose of Opus Dei are exclusively spiritual, and so were the mission and priestly ministry of its founder. The government of a nation—of whatever nation—and Opus Dei are realities which operate on totally different planes. The Prelature encourages its members to exercise their rights and diligently carry out their own duties as authentic Christians, but leaves them in complete freedom with regard to their concrete decisions in temporal matters. In fact, the Prelature urges them to exercise such freedom; the only stipulation it makes is that they should follow whatever guidelines may be given by the Church hierarchy in such matters.

In the case of Francoism, it is necessary to recall that the end of the Spanish Civil War signaled the rebirth of the life of the Church, of religious associations, of Catholic schools . . . The hierarchy, understandably, did come out in favor of General Franco, whose rise to power was considered by many to be providential. It is enough to remember how at the end of the civil war, the façades of cathedrals and parish churches all over Spain were plastered with the symbols of the Falange and the following inscription: "All those who died for God and Spain—forget them not!" ["Caídos por Dios y por España. ¡Presentes!"] The founder of Opus Dei protested against this abuse many times.

In those circumstances, although the Father acknowledged Franco's achievements in bringing peace to the country, he had to counteract two dangers: on the one hand, a manipulation of the Catholic faith, an attempt on the part of certain groups to monopolize the representation of Catholics in public life; and, on the other hand, a tendency in some Catholic circles to use public power as a kind of secular arm; in short, two versions of clericalism.

The Father always recognized that it was for the hierarchy alone to provide guidance to Catholics on political matters; he refrained from doing this himself. Now, the hierarchy did openly encourage Catholics to support Franco—so much so that members of Catholic Action and other religious organizations had representatives serving in Franco's cabinets. Clericalism was so pervasive that some people even asked for (and, of course, obtained) the permission of their bishop before accepting a ministerial post.

When, in the fifties, some members of the Work became ministers in Franco's government, the Father neither approved nor disapproved; they were exercising their freedom as Catholic citizens, and showing respect to the hierarchy. However, there were people who tried to attribute the use of political pressure or interference to the Work as such. We experienced no end of difficulties and misunderstandings on this account.

Already in the forties, for example, some members of Opus Dei presented themselves for the qualifying examinations for university professorial positions. Thanks to their thorough preparation, and without seeking any recommendations, they succeeded brilliantly. There then came a violent reaction from some enemies of the Church, members of a group which ever since the end of the previous century, by means of the Institución Libre de Enseñanza [Free Institution of Education], had been in control of the university. A rumor was circulated—it was absolutely slanderous—that the members of Opus Dei had passed their examinations in an irregular way. Actually they never enjoyed any advantages whatsoever; if anything, they were discriminated against in favor of members of other Catholic institutions which had the backing of the ministers of education then in office.

But it was not only the enemies of the Church who opposed or did not understand Opus Dei. In 1947, when the founder returned briefly to Spain to prepare for the transfer of the government of the Work to Rome, he had a meeting with Martín Artajo, the minister of foreign affairs, who, before he took this position, had been president of Catholic Action in Spain. To the Father's astonishment, as he later told us, Artajo said that he could not understand "how it was possible for someone at the same time to be consecrated to the Church, with a bond of obedience, and still serve the state." The Father explained that he himself would have no problem with this, because the *matter* of the obedience owed to the Church was the same for him as for all other Catholics, whether or not they were consecrated to God; the obligation was on an equal *level*, though it might take a different form. But Artajo apparently could not understand this clear and obvious truth; he gave orders that members of Opus Dei, or those thought to be such, were not to be admitted to the diplomatic corps, even if they had passed the qualifying examination. This completely unjust ruling was applied in several specific cases.

> *Since other Catholic organizations were openly and directly supporting the Franco regime, some people could not imagine the attitude of Opus Dei as being any different. Yet our Father always vigorously defended the freedom of opinion of his children, and it was only natural that among the members of the Work there would have been some who supported Franco, and others who took part in the opposition.*
>
> *I recall a film of one of the catechetical get-togethers of the founder, in which he told the story of how he did not hesitate to go in person to a "very powerful" personage to defend the freedom of opinion of one of his sons. I would like to hear a bit more about that.*

It happened that a member of the Work had written an article against the Franco regime. The reaction of the authorities was very harsh, and he had to go into exile. On this point the Father had nothing to say, since it had to do with questions into which he did not enter; issues in which his children were involved as free and responsible citizens. However, among other insults thrown at that member of the Work, it was said that he was "a person without family." At that point our founder reacted, literally, like a father defending his own son. He returned immediately to Spain, where he requested (and immediately received) an audience with Franco. Without going into any kind of political discussion, he just stated quite clearly that he could not tolerate a son of his being spoken of as "without family": this young man had a supernatural family, the Work, and our founder considered himself his father. Franco then asked, "And what if they put him in prison?" The Father answered that he would respect the decisions of the judicial authorities, but that if they did take him to prison, nobody could keep him from bringing to that son all the spiritual and material assistance he would need. He said the same things to Admiral Carrero Blanco, Franco's right-hand man. And I have to add that both of them, showing themselves to be gentlemen with Christian sensibilities, recognized that our founder was right.

> *Many attacks on the Work and on the freedom of its members proceeded directly from institutions of the regime, such as the Falange . . .*

In this connection, the letter which our founder wrote on October 28, 1966, to the minister José Solís, the head of the Falange, is very revealing:

"Most esteemed friend:

"Word has reached me about the campaign which the press of the Falange, which is in Your Excellency's control, has been so unjustly waging against Opus Dei.

"I repeat to you once again that the members of Opus Dei— each and every one of them—are personally utterly free, as free as if they did not belong to Opus Dei, in all temporal matters and in those theological matters which are not of faith, which the Church leaves people free to disagree about. It therefore makes no sense to publicize the fact that a particular person belongs to the Work, when it comes to political, professional, or social matters—just as it would make no sense, when speaking of the political activities of Your Excellency, to bring in your wife, your children, your family.

"This misguided policy governs the publications which are connected with your ministry. As a result, they accomplish nothing other than to offend God by creating confusion between the spiritual and the temporal orders. It is obvious that the directors of Opus Dei can do nothing to hinder the legitimate and complete personal freedom of its members, who, for their part, never hide the fact that each one of them assumes full responsibility for their own actions. Consequently, the plurality of opinions among the members of the Work is, and always will be, just one more manifestation of their freedom, and one more proof of their good spirit, which leads them to respect the opinions of others.

"In attacking or defending the thought or public action of any of your fellow citizens, let your publications have the decency—which justice demands—not to make any kind of reference to Opus Dei. This *spiritual family* does not intervene, nor can it ever intervene, in any political or earthly affair in any field whatsoever, precisely because its ends are *exclusively* spiritual.

"I hope that you have understood my surprise, both at the announcement of this campaign of denigration and at seeing it carried out. I'm sure that by now you must be aware of the blunder which is being made, as well as of the responsibility in conscience which those involved in this campaign are assuming before the tribunal of God. This blunder involves the denigration of an institution which does not—and cannot—influence the use which its members scattered over five continents make, as citizens, of their personal freedom, while not evading their personal responsibility for their actions.

"I beg you to put an end to this campaign against Opus Dei, since Opus Dei has done nothing to deserve it. Otherwise, I will have to conclude that you have not understood me, and it will then be clear that Your Excellency is not able either to understand or to respect freedom, *qua libertate Christus nos liberavit* [the freedom with which Christ has freed us], the freedom of Christian citizens.

"Fight when you must (though I am no friend of fights), but do not commit the injustice of bringing into such conflicts something which is above human passions.

"Let me take this opportunity to convey to you my best wishes and to bless you and your family.

In Domino . . ."

If I may be allowed to express a completely personal opinion, it seems to me that those members of the Work who freely collaborated with the government of Franco, on their own responsibility, worked for the good of their country; they achieved successes, unanimously recognized today, in improving the economy and in ending the isolation of Spain by turning her towards the rest of Europe. While he refrained from intervening in political matters, and even from expressing publicly any opinion on them, was there any aspect of them that particularly concerned the Father?

He was concerned about the problem of the succession to Franco. He did not hesitate to make his concern known to Franco himself, and he did seek to bring this sensitive issue to the attention of the Spanish bishops who came to see him. But our founder was wise enough to resist any and all hints, some of which came to him from the Vatican, suggesting that he take initiative in this regard. He refused to act as an intermediary for certain individuals, because it was not his mission to get involved in politics. He made his position on this matter quite clear, in a manner that left no room for misunderstanding, in a letter of conscience he addressed to Pope Paul VI on June 14, 1964.

I now understand better why he had such a great devotion to St. Catherine of Siena . . .

3. What the Father Was Like

Father, you lived for forty years in the company of our Father. I realize that it is practically impossible to describe the personality of our founder, a personality so rich in terms of both natural and supernatural gifts. On the other hand, who could do this better than you?

His personality had so many facets that it would be difficult to describe it in general terms. In addition, he received so many graces from our Lord that, when it comes to examining his behavior, one finds it difficult to distinguish between the natural qualities of his character and that which came as a consequence of the grace of God and the ascetical struggle. I purposely use the word "distinguish," rather than "separate," because one of the fundamental traits of his personality was its unity: there was a complete interpenetration of the human, ascetical, and apostolic aspects of his life. It would be impossible to separate these out.

He always taught us that the natural virtues are the foundation of the supernatural virtues; and those who had the good fortune of living with him saw actualized in his own behavior that "unity of life" which he so passionately preached.

In general terms, I suppose you could say that both through his supernatural virtues and through his natural gifts (of intelligence, empathy, and character), the Father possessed the perfection of an instrument prepared by the Lord for the mission of founding Opus Dei.

To understand the character of our founder, one must keep in view this basic quality which pervaded everything else: his dedication to God, and to all souls for God's sake; his constant readiness to correspond generously to the will of the Lord. This

31

was the aim of his whole life. He was a man in love, a man possessed of a secret he would later spell out in point No. 1006 of *The
Forge:* "With crystal clarity I see the formula, the secret of happiness, both earthly and eternal. It is not just a matter of accepting
the will of God, but of embracing it, of identifying oneself with
it—in a word, of loving the divine will with a positive act of our
own will. This, I repeat, is the infallible secret of joy and peace."

His dedication was never something cold or formal. It sprang
from love, and so it expressed itself in sincere demonstrations of
affection and understanding: he had a great and noble heart. He
was open to all. He loved the world passionately, since it was created by God. Every human reality attracted him. He read the newspapers, he watched the television news, he liked love songs, he
prayed for the astronauts who went to the moon—he was very affable. He knew how to instill confidence and be welcoming to others.

> *Speaking of songs, our Father loved singing, and in reference
> to the many apostolic journeys he had undertaken for the pur-
> pose of preparing the "prehistory" of Opus Dei in various
> countries, he used to say that he had sown Europe with Hail
> Marys and songs . . .*

Yes, he often sang, in that baritone voice of his that was so
refined and pleasing. He was not at all a gloomy or aloof man; on
the contrary, he was rich in humanity, warmth, good cheer. He
taught us that a smile is often the best mortification, since our
mortifications are not supposed to annoy those around us. And
he was the first to adhere to this teaching. His own life of prayer
and penance, far from dampening other people's spirits, transmitted a genuine joy—both natural and supernatural—to those
who were near him.

> *Let's turn now to the Father's temperament . . .*

I can assure you that all his life, he was the very paradigm of
a man who knows how to love with his whole heart, who wants to
serve others and make them happy.

He was endowed with a keen, agile intellect that was complemented by a lively interest in all branches of knowledge, by a remarkable juridical mentality, and by a most refined aesthetic sense. His personality was vibrant and vigorous; his temperament was courageous and impetuous, strong and energetic; and he managed to acquire a remarkable degree of self-mastery. More than once he told me about an incident that had happened when he was a young priest. In reaction to a serious setback, he had for the moment lost his serenity. "I was angry," he told me, "and afterwards I was angry at myself for having become angry." He was walking along a street in Madrid in this state of mind when he came upon one of those automatic-camera booths where one can get six passport-type pictures for a few coins. The Lord gave him to understand that he now had a good opportunity to humble himself and receive an ascetic lesson on cheerfulness. He went into the booth and got himself photographed, and sure enough, "I looked really funny with that angry face!" Afterwards he tore up all the snapshots but one. "I carried it in my wallet for a month," he said. "From time to time I would look at it, to see that angry face, humble myself before God, and laugh at myself. I would say to myself, 'You fool!'"

> Our Father taught us to dress properly and with a certain elegance, in accordance with the social circumstances of each person. That was a "secular" way of understanding poverty in this context—one in which he also led by example.

The Father usually had two cassocks, which he wore on alternate days so that they would last longer. But sometimes—during the years 1941 to 1944, for example—he only had one, and if it got torn, he had to stay in his room until his sister, Carmen, could mend it for him. Even in Rome we occasionally had to ask his daughters to mend his cassock, while he waited in his room in shirtsleeves.

Every evening he brushed his cassock and sprinkled some water on it if there were any spots: I often helped with this by holding the cloth tight. When it needed cleaning, he handed it over to his daughters who looked after the household. With this kind of care, his cassocks lasted quite a long time.

Before the founding of Opus Dei, the Father possessed the usual clerical clothing, one set for winter and another for the summer. Every year (when he was still in Saragossa), he switched to the winter clothing on October 12, the feast of Our Lady of the Pillar, and to the summer clothing on March 7, at that time the feast of St. Thomas Aquinas. This meant he would sometimes be too warm in October, and cold in March and April. From the time of the foundation of Opus Dei, however, he decided to use the same type of clothing the whole year round, as a further expression of sobriety and poverty.

He disliked wearing an undershirt, and had not done so since his boyhood. But on November 27, 1949 (we happened to be in Turin at the time), the weather was very chilly and he caught a bad cold. So I bought him a woolen undershirt and politely asked him to wear it. He agreed, but not being used to wearing one of these, he cut off the sleeves. Years later, when the doctors suggested that he use knee pads to alleviate his rheumatism, he used those sleeves for that purpose.

Could you tell us a bit more about his daily life?

The Father loved personal cleanliness, but didn't use any cologne, as he was convinced that the best smell for a priest to have is none at all. It was only years later that he took our advice to use an aftershave to disinfect an occasional shaving cut.

For many years he had us help him cut his hair at home, and at one point he asked us to buy him one of those combs with a built-in razor, designed for giving oneself a haircut. However, the amount of money he was saving was so small— and the results were so unsatisfactory—that at last we persuaded him to go to a barber.

Because he was so heroically detached from himself, he did not have anything superfluous. For instance, from the forties until 1970 he used the same glasses, even though they became quite old-fashioned. He finally decided to change them, but only when Fr. Javier Echevarría and I insisted that he do so.

From 1953 on, the Father slept in a small, cold room with a tiled floor, in our central residence. One day in 1973, when he got up in the morning, he fell on the floor and for a little while lay unconscious on those cold tiles. When I learned of this, I was concerned, for one thing because I knew how susceptible he was to bronchial ailments. Not long before, something similar had happened to one of the cardinals of the Roman Curia, Cardinal Larraona, and he had gotten pneumonia and died soon after. And so in 1974, taking advantage of one of our founder's trips, we installed wall-to-wall carpeting. When he returned, he was annoyed that we had taken it upon ourselves to do this, without even telling him. He accepted it only when we told him we had done it on medical advice.

I know that our Father didn't smoke. He gave up smoking when he entered the seminary, and gave his pipes and tobacco to the doorman.

Nevertheless, he always lived with people who smoked, and he never complained. In fact, he would sometimes receive as a gift from a visitor a box of cigars, and he would go out of his way to preserve them for the others. He kept them in a closet in his bedroom, with a little jar of water which he would periodically refill to keep them properly humidified. On feast days he would bring them out for the family get-together after lunch, with great delight, and would light a candle from which the smokers could light their cigars.

From these anecdotes one can glimpse something of the simplicity, the tactfulness, the spirit of service, the good-natured character of our Father. And while we're on the subject of our founder's daily life, could you sketch for us an outline of his typical day?

One could not really speak of a "typical day" in the life of the Father, since everything he did was in response to what the Lord was asking of him: to serve all souls out of love. All that was truly typical of our founder was his eagerness to go along at every moment with the wishes of God.

It is true that throughout his time on earth, he subjected himself to a plan of life with certain fixed points of reference: mental
prayer, the holy Mass, praying of the Breviary and of the holy
rosary, and other pious practices. In fact, contrary to what a person
might think who had only heard him speak of the sanctification of
work, without fully understanding the spirit of the founder, he
constantly drove home this fundamental truth: "The weapon of
Opus Dei is not work, it is prayer. That's why we transform work
into prayer, and have a contemplative soul."

But though these essential reference points were always
maintained, the Father's day followed very diverse patterns in the
various stages of his life. For example, his daily agenda in the thirties, when he was carrying out an intense and direct pastoral
activity throughout Madrid, was quite different from that of the
sixties, in Rome, when his basic occupation was the governance
and guidance of Opus Dei.

> *Could you, then, describe a typical day of our Father's life in
> Rome, during those later years?*

Toward the end of the sixties, in obedience to his doctor's
orders, the Father rested for seven and a half to eight hours each
night; he was so faithful to these instructions that even when he
woke up much earlier, he did not get out of bed until he was called
by one of his *custodes* [Latin for "custodian" or "guardian"], Fr. Javier
Echevarría (I was the other *custos*). Before he was given this medical
advice, it was his custom to get up as soon as he awoke, or as soon as
the alarm clock went off, even if he had gotten only two or three
hours of sleep. He never stayed in bed beyond the prescribed time,
and never took a siesta. Since he didn't want us to worry, he didn't
like to speak about his long hours of insomnia, which he spent in
prayer. Often, when someone asked him in the morning if he had
slept well, I was amused to hear the Father reply, "Thank you very
much, and the same to you." Thus he gave the impression that he
had answered, while in fact he'd just neatly evaded the question.

As soon as he woke up, he lived the heroic minute: he
jumped out of bed, kissed the floor, and eagerly pronounced the

aspiration "Serviam!" ["I will serve!"]. He would then offer his whole day to the Lord. Tracing the sign of the cross on his forehead, lips, and heart, he would say the following prayer: "Out of love I offer you all my thoughts, all my words, and all my deeds of this day, O Lord, together with my whole life." Then he would kiss the crucifix and the image of our Lady which he kept at his bedside.

While he shaved, he would repeat the prayers he had learned in childhood from his parents. Often, and especially after he got a room to himself (at the beginning of the fifties), he said these prayers out loud, and even sang them. After bathing and getting dressed, he took care to clean the sink and shower and to tidy his room and leave everything in order, out of consideration for the people who did the housecleaning, and to make their task easier.

Immediately afterwards, continuing the prayer which he had begun during the hours when he lay awake in bed, he devoted a further half hour to mental prayer, in preparation for holy Mass. At times he would preach a meditation for those of us who were with him in the oratory. I must admit, we all looked forward to those moments when the Father would open his heart and confide to us, in the presence of God, something from his interior life. For us it was a real present from God. More often, however, and especially in the last few years, he made use of the volumes of *Meditaciones,* a collection of meditations which had been written under his direction.

When it comes to the holy Mass, we would need a long time . . .

> *Perhaps we could return to this subject, Father, with a specific question I would like to ask when we discuss the sacramental life of our Father.*

All right, we can postpone that for now. Well, his breakfast was quick and frugal, because of his deep spirit of mortification and because of the strict diet prescribed for him at the onset of his diabetes. It consisted of a cup of coffee with milk but without sugar and, in place of bread, some fruit, usually an apple or a pear. He

kept to this same diet after he was cured of the diabetes, except for
having a little piece of bread instead of the fruit. The coffee was not
very strong, and he used nonfat milk.

After breakfast, the Father devoted a few minutes to reading
the newspaper. First he divided the pages into two sets, so that he
and I could pass the paper back and forth (I ate breakfast with
him). You could see that while he read, he was praying about all
these great problems in the world and in the Church. In his last
years, you could say that he didn't really succeed in reading the
daily paper, because more often than not, he would hardly have
begun to read it when suddenly he would be drawn away from the
news story, his mind instantly and completely immersed in God.
He would rest his forehead on his right hand, close his eyes, and
pray, taking advantage of the fact that he was alone with me. As I
looked at him, and saw him so absorbed in God, I also prayed.

After the Breviary, which he usually said with Fr. Javier
Echevarría and me, and before getting down to work, he dedicated some time to the meditative reading of the New Testament.
As he read, he often made notes of phrases which he could use
afterwards in his preaching, writing, or mental prayer. I am certain
that he always gleaned at least one thought on which to meditate
during the day, in the presence of God.

The morning's work normally began with matters connected with the administration of Opus Dei. In his work of government our founder always saw souls behind the papers. To
keep himself aware of the presence of God, he used little devices
such as frequent glances at the crucifix on the wall, or at the
image of our Lady which stood on his desk. Occasionally, while
moving something on the desk, I would accidentally knock this
picture over; I was always struck by the affectionate way he
would immediately give it a kiss.

Then came time for the mail. The Father liked to open all
envelopes personally, though he would afterwards hand them over
to me—and in the last years, to Fr. Javier as well—so that we could
help him with reading the contents. He separated business letters
(those addressed to the General Council) from personal letters. If
we could tell that there was something confidential in a letter, we

handed it back to him immediately, without reading it. I am certain that the Father never read a letter without praying for the person who wrote it, and about the problem discussed in it.

After reading the mail, he recited the Angelus, at noon. This was an important moment in the Father's day, because, in addition to being a filial conversation with our Lady, it signified as well the point at which his Eucharistic devotion "changed tracks." He had spent the morning in thanksgiving for the Mass which he had just celebrated; starting with the Angelus, he began to prepare himself for the Mass which he would celebrate the next day.

Then began the time reserved for receiving visitors. These came in great numbers, and at times from very distant lands, to see the Father and obtain counsel and encouragement from him. He gave instructions that, apart from exceptional cases, every visit would last ten minutes. This was done for two reasons: for the sake of good order, as there were many who wanted to see him; and for the sake of mortification, since this kept him from spending more time with the ones whose company he might have found more enjoyable. Of course, whenever it was appropriate, the Father would give people all the time they needed, and did not hesitate to make additional appointments for them.

After taking leave of the last visitor with his priestly and fatherly blessing, the founder would recite, with the members of the General Council, the prayers of the Work. As is the custom in Opus Dei, he would kiss the floor and say "Serviam!"—renewing interiorly the total self-offering which he had made at the beginning of the day. After this he would recite invocations of praise and supplication to the Trinity, to Jesus Christ, to our Lady, to St. Joseph, and to the guardian angels. He prayed for the pope and (when he was away from Rome) for the bishop of the diocese he was in, for unity in the apostolate, for the benefactors of the Work, for his own sons and daughters, and for the dead. He then concluded with a prayer to the Holy Spirit and with invocations to the six patrons of Opus Dei: the three archangels and the three apostles Peter, John, and Paul.

Once the prayers were finished, the Father made a brief examination of conscience about the half-day he had just spent, and considered in particular how he had fulfilled the resolutions he had made in the examination of the previous evening. If he saw that he needed to ask someone's forgiveness about something that had happened that morning, he went right away to seek out the person concerned.

Usually only Fr. Javier and I would join him for lunch [the main meal of the day], for the simple reason that the Father did not want his austere eating habits to inhibit his younger sons, who generally needed to eat more than he ate. Out of the same kind of concern, whenever he did receive visitors at this time, he took care to hide his frugality so as not to make his fellow diners uneasy. At this meal, as at breakfast, he followed the diet prescribed by his doctors, but sought to add to each dish the condiment of mortification. He began with boiled greens, without salt; next he had some meat or fish, usually grilled, with little garnishing; for dessert he had a piece of fruit. He had neither bread nor wine. He did drink a glass or two of water, but even this was only because of doctors' orders; left to his own preferences, he tended to mortify his thirst severely. It was also out of mortification, as well as common courtesy, that he always waited for Fr. Javier and me to be served before he began eating.

First thing after lunch, the Father made a visit to the Blessed Sacrament. Then he enjoyed a get-together with his sons, for thirty or forty minutes of conversation. This was a custom which our founder practiced every day, ever since members of Opus Dei began to live as a family in our respective centers; he expressly directed that it become part of the daily life of every center of the Work. In the simple and hospitable atmosphere of the living room, as in that of the typical truly Christian family, the conversation would turn upon everyday events, and on our apostolic ventures, or sometimes on things which might have amused us. The Father used this opportunity to form in us a sound doctrinal understanding, to give a supernatural tone to the news of the day, and to allow his sons to relax. On many occasions he opened his heart to us in confidence—he transmitted his spirit—and thus contributed to the spiritual formation of all who were listening. It always filled me with admiration to see how the Father—even if he was overcome with fatigue, had been enduring nights of insomnia, or had suffered some difficult setback—would completely forget all this and give himself so generously in these get-togethers.

Once this family gathering was over, he would do his spiritual reading, typically from one of the classical treatises on asceticism, and then go back to work. (He never had any use for the siesta; in fact, he directed that members of the Work should not sleep in the early afternoon, except on doctors' orders.) He then continued the work of the morning, and would frequently call in some member of the General Council so that they could work out some specific problem together. He dedicated a considerable amount of time to writing letters to us, in the spare moments of the morning or in the first couple of hours in the afternoon.

During the time of work which preceded his half hour of afternoon prayer, he would prepare himself for this appointment with the Lord. Afterwards, before resuming his work, he would have a teatime snack; this consisted of a piece of fruit, which he often shared with Fr. Javier or me, and a glass of water.

Every day, he recited and meditated on the three parts of the rosary. He distributed them over the course of the day, ending, after the afternoon prayer and snack, with the mysteries of the particular day, and then the litany of the Blessed Virgin Mary.

His supper was even more frugal than his lunch: it consisted of some broth or vegetable soup, without bread. In the last years, his doctor ordered him to eat also a little cheese, or an omelet, as well as some fruit.

After supper, the Father would sometimes watch the television news; and even in these moments, he would make use of some device for living in the presence of God. For example, whenever the image of the world turning on its axis appeared on the screen, he took this as an opportunity to pray for the Church's work of evangelization all over the world, and in particular for the apostolic work of Opus Dei. I can affirm that the Father, especially in his later years, would pray very intensely while watching the news: he commended to the Lord the events which were being reported, and prayed for world peace.

After the news, he returned to his work until nine-thirty, at which time he sat down again with his sons for a get-together like the one at midday. When it was over and he was leaving the room, he would pause, almost imperceptibly, before going through the doorway—"to let my two angels go before me," he told me. This was a tiny detail, unnoticed by the others, which showed how he lived in relationship with his guardian angel and ministerial archangel. There was nothing theatrical about it; one had to watch very closely and be "in the know" to observe it.

Immediately after this get-together with his sons, the Father retired in profound silence to make his examination of conscience and recite his last prayers of the day. Every night, just before going to bed, he would recite the *Miserere* [Psalm 51], prostrate on the ground; then, on his knees and with his arms stretched out, as on a cross, he would pray three Hail Marys, begging for purity for all souls, and especially for himself and for his children in Opus Dei. He had a habit of keeping a crucifix in the pocket of his pajamas; before going to sleep, he would kiss this crucifix again and again—while repeating aspirations, making a spiritual communion, and in his imagination keeping company with the Lord present in the tabernacles of distant countries.

4. His Upbringing

Our Father always described himself as having been an ordinary child who grew up in a family that was profoundly Christian but not exaggeratedly devout. Could you tell us something about our Father's childhood?

Josemaría was for most of his childhood a strong, healthy lad; but when he was about one and a half, he was stricken with a very serious infectious disease.

The family doctor, Ignacio Camps Valdovinos, who was a close friend of Josemaría's father, José Escrivá, went so far as to say, "Look, Pepe [José's nickname among his friends], I have to tell you the truth. Your little boy is going to die; he won't outlast the night."

The parents reacted like the good Christians they were. They prayed a lot, abandoned themselves to the will of God, and even made a promise that if the boy got better, they would take him on a pilgrimage to Torreciudad. This was a shrine high in the Pyrenees, and not easily accessible, where an ancient image of our Lady, very dear to the inhabitants of Barbastro, was venerated.

The next morning, Dr. Camps came to the Escrivá residence and asked, "When did the baby die?" José replied, "He not only didn't die, he is perfectly healthy! Can't you hear him talking?" Dr. Camps went into the boy's room and saw him standing up in his crib, holding on to the bars, jumping and whooping it up. (Speaking of this crib—his mother told me that little Josemaría was so lively that once, while jumping up and down in it, holding on to one of the bars, he took such a jump that he somersaulted right out of the crib and fell on the floor!)

His parents did keep their promise; they made a pilgrimage of thanksgiving to Torreciudad, where there is now a large shrine dedicated to our Lady.

His parents taught him his first prayers, which he continued to say all his life, even after he turned seventy—he began then to say that he was only seven years old, as a way of pointing out the advantages of the life of spiritual childhood.

When speaking of his childhood, he sometimes said, "I remember a little boy who, when reciting the act of contrition, instead of saying 'resolve to amend' [*propósito de la enmienda*] would say 'resolve to almond' [*propósito de la almendra*]. He didn't know what 'amendment' was, but he knew well enough what almonds were, because he liked them so much. That child was myself. And that prayer did show a real willingness to please God and to act well: to offer the 'almond' of not sinning anymore. They must have begun to teach me this prayer when I was about three years old, and now that I have reached the age of 'seven,' I have still not gotten past the 'almonds' stage. I thank God for this."

Even as a small child, Josemaría had an assertive personality. We know, for example, that when his mother would ask him to give some acquaintance a kiss, he would sometimes reply that he didn't have any "ready-made kisses."

The atmosphere of Barbastro was very devout. When one of the first airplanes was being exhibited at a country fair, José Escrivá took his son to see it. Our founder remembered with amusement that he had overheard some nuns asking one another, "If the airplane flies over the convent, will that mean a violation of our enclosure?"

When he was a little older, Josemaría would occasionally go hunting with his father, who was an enthusiastic hunter. In the courtyard of the house there was a cage where decoy birds, for quail hunting, were kept. This was a small cage that had a removable floor, so that when it was placed on the ground, the birds could walk about and feed themselves directly from the ground. Mr. Escrivá preferred hunting quails and partridges, but he would also shoot thrushes, if they came within range. Like all hunters, he loved to tell stories of his exploits, and years later his son remembered many of the details.

Little Josemaría was very observant, and he liked visiting the kitchen. There he noticed that the cook would calculate the time for hard-boiling an egg by reciting the Creed twice.

Which calls to mind something else that's both amusing and significant . . .

On the subject of boiled eggs—yes. I remember that in the sixties, a director from Kenya told the Father that when they boiled eggs, they calculated the boiling time according to the local custom: they would dig a hole in the ground and throw some water into it; when the water had all drained away, the time was up. Upon hearing this, our founder realized that things were so financially tight there that they didn't even have a kitchen timer. He was moved by this, and decided on the spot that that daughter should be given the alarm clock that we had in our center.

But let's return to the childhood of the Father. He played with his companions and did his share of getting into fights, but he could not tolerate cruelty. As everyone knows, children can be cruel at times, and the children of Barbastro were no exception. Some of them would catch bats and pin them to a wall, and then kill them by throwing stones at them. One day Josemaría was an involuntary witness to one of these brutal scenes; he remembered it for the rest of his life. Ever inclined to reflect on the things he saw, he got from this incident an insight into how far human cruelty can go—and, from a certain perspective, even a glimpse into the inconceivable behavior of our Lord's executioners, in nailing him to the wood of the cross.

Our Father attributed to his Aragonese heritage his frankness and sincerity of manner, as well as his constancy and tenacity of purpose.

These are qualities which he possessed from childhood. I heard him tell how, as a child, he would sometimes get embarrassed when he heard people talking about "the scribes and the Pharisees," and how the same thing happened to his sister, Carmen. The explanation is simple: many people used to write the name "Escrivá" with a "b," since in Spain "v" and "b" are pronounced the same way. And so, when their classmates would hear about the scribes [*los escribas*], they would look at the Escrivá children and smile. In reality, of course, nothing could have been more foreign to the character of the Father than hypocrisy or any kind of pretense. I might add that while he often spoke of his childhood faults, he never referred to his virtues or successes. For example, he never mentioned the fact that in elementary school he had won a prize for hard work and good conduct. I learned about this after his death, while looking through the diocesan records.

> *From the time he entered secondary school, the founder was a brilliant student. That period began in Barbastro and ended in Logroño; his father moved the family there at the end of 1915, after the failure of his business. Mr. Escrivá, who had generously borne the consequences of a business associate's unethical behavior, had found a new occupation in a textile business in Logroño. The family now had to adjust to a new lifestyle. They bore with great dignity all its initial hardships. But young Josemaría certainly had to keep in mind the needs of his family when thinking about his own professional vocation . . .*

He wanted to become an architect. He was inclined to this choice by his interests in the arts and humanities, as well as by an aptitude for mathematics and design. At that time, the students who got the highest grades sat in the first row and had to answer the teacher's questions when the other students were unable to do so. In his fourth and fifth years of secondary school, Josemaría sat in the first row in three of his classes: algebra, trigonometry, and literature.

His parents were pleased with his career choice, even if his father would sometimes gently tease him about it, saying he was going to be just a "glorified bricklayer."

Like all mothers, Mrs. Escrivá would keep a watchful eye on the friendships of her adolescent son. On more than one occasion the Father repeated to me, with amusement, this piece of advice his mother had given him—as there was nothing to indicate that he wouldn't get married—about the choice of a wife: "Ni guapa que encante, ni fea que espante" ["Neither so beautiful that she bewitches, nor so ugly that she causes twitches"].

Actually, things turned out quite otherwise . . .

Yes. As a matter of fact, the Father began to have "premonitions of Love" (he was always using this expression, "barruntar el Amor") at a very precise moment.

Around the end of December 1917 and the beginning of January 1918, there was a heavy snowfall in the region of Logroño. According to the local newspaper, *La Rioja* (replaced in the fifties by a different paper, *La Nueva Rioja*), the snow kept falling for about a month. The temperature went down to sixteen or seventeen degrees below zero [centigrade; about zero degrees Fahrenheit], and several people died from the cold. Communications were paralyzed. One morning Josemaría saw in the snow some footprints—made by the bare feet of a Discalced Carmelite. Immediately he felt a profound uneasiness in his soul, and he asked himself, "Others are making such great sacrifices for God and neighbor; will I not be able to offer anything at all?" He became aware, with an absolute certainty, that our Lord was asking something of him, and since he did not know what it was, he began to turn to the Lord with the prayer of the blind man Bartimaeus, "Domine, ut videam!" ["Lord, that I might see!" (Mk 10:51)], and with a similar prayer: "Domine, ut sit!" ["Lord, let it be!"]. He also had recourse to the Blessed Virgin Mary, asking that God's plans for his life should be fulfilled: "Domina, ut videam!" ["My Lady, that I might see!"], and "Domina, ut sit!" ["My Lady, let it be!"].

He intensified his prayer life, and went daily to Mass and Communion. As a result of this devotion, he came to see that if he became a priest he would be in a better position to ascertain what the Lord more specifically wanted of him. He therefore decided to enter, as a nonresident student, the seminary in Logroño. His parents did not oppose this, even though it meant a radical change in the family's plans. Mr. Escrivá brought his son to speak with

Fr. Antolín Oñate, the abbot of the collegiate church at Logroño, a holy priest who was a veritable institution in the city; and this priest encouraged the boy's vocation.

> *Nevertheless, given the quite Christian but at the same time definitely lay character of the Escrivá family, Josemaría's transition into the environment of the seminary of Logroño— and later, in 1920, into that of Saragossa, where he did his theological studies—could not have been easy.*

Josemaría's parents had always taught him to venerate the priesthood, but before the episode of the footprints in the snow, he had never thought of becoming a priest. At school he had even had an initial aversion to Latin, which he expressed by saying, "Latin—that's for priests!" Afterwards, when he got into the subject and developed an enthusiasm for Latin, he felt as if he needed to make up for the lack of interest he had shown in those early years. He called his previous attitude foolish, and went on to say, "I can never be thankful enough for the good they did me in school, when they made me study Latin. I remember how they made us fill up our notebooks with declensions and verb conjugations, both regular and irregular. We also had to get the accents right. As a result I've never had to be corrected for saying, for example, '*legerem*' instead of '*legerem*.'"

But let's get back to what you were saying. No, it wasn't an easy transition. Most of Josemaría's companions at the seminary in Saragossa came from a rural background and were not familiar with the habits of hygiene and the good manners which he had learned at home. He never claimed to be a model of etiquette or refinement; indeed, he would have liked to pass unnoticed among his fellows, whom he always described as excellent young men. But it could not be. As I once heard him explain it, "There were no washbasins in the rooms, so in order to wash myself from head to toe, I had to fetch three or four buckets of water. Perhaps this was what some of them found scandalizing!"

Whenever he spoke about his days in the seminary, all that the Father recalled about his companions was how virtuous they were, and how desirous of serving the Church. But he did suffer from being misunderstood when, against his wishes, the others began to notice his efforts to cultivate a life of piety. He did his best not to stand out; ever since childhood, he had had a strong aversion to ostentation and idiosyncrasy. And yet he lived up to the counsel he would later give us: "Don't be afraid if your effort to be devout is noticed."

He spent long hours of prayer in the chapel of the seminary (San Carlos) in Saragossa, just as he had done in Logroño. And once again, though he tried not to attract attention, these long visits could not go entirely unnoticed. Some of his companions used to say, loud enough for him to overhear, "Look, here comes the dreamer!" [In Genesis 37:19, this expression is used by Joseph's brothers, just before they sell him as a slave to the Egyptian merchants.] He gave no importance to such barbs, but instead just tried to get the others to pray more.

Neither did it go unnoticed that every day, on his way home from the university, Josemaría would step into the Basilica of Our Lady of the Pillar—to honor "my Mother," as he put it. Some of the seminarians started teasing him about this by calling him "Mystical Rose." This nickname did hurt him, but mostly because it showed—even if this was unintentional—a lack of reverence for our Lady. It also saddened him to have his friends make fun of behavior that should have been seen as completely normal, not just for someone studying for the priesthood, but for any Christian.

> *Nevertheless, there must have been some reality and depth to the respect he was shown by both his professors and his fellow students when Cardinal Soldevilla, the archbishop of Saragossa (who was assassinated not long afterward), expressed his own high regard for Josemaría by appointing him seminarian-superior of the seminary; which meant, among other things, that the clerical tonsure had to be granted to him ahead of schedule.*

This was, indeed, an acknowledgment not only of the well-rounded maturity which he had attained at this early age, but also of all that he had put into the achieving of it. Since his early years he had invested prodigious effort in all aspects of his formation: doctrinal, spiritual, apostolic . . . He had been very demanding of himself, both in his ascetical struggle and in his studies. His companions from childhood, from secondary school, and from the seminary have retained a vivid memory of his affability and his readiness to serve.

> *Our Father was ordained a priest on March 28, 1925. His joy was shared by his mother, by his sister, Carmen, and by his six-year-old brother, Santiago. However, the occasion was not so happy as it might have been, because the family was still in mourning. Just four months before, on November 27, José Escrivá had suddenly died, leaving his children with the bittersweet memory of an exemplary father.*
>
> *The first priestly assignment of Father Josemaría was to fill in for a couple of months for a parish priest in the village of Perdiguera.*

It was a difficult situation. This priest, the pastor of the parish, had abandoned his post under circumstances that never were fully explained. The reason officially given was illness; and presumably there was at least some truth in that, for this priest died suddenly a month later, in May.

The Father lavished priestly zeal on that village of eight hundred inhabitants. In those smaller communities it was normal for a priest to have a good deal of time left over after fulfilling his ministerial duties. Once these were finished, he would get together with the local "powers that be"—the mayor, the doctor, the pharmacist, the town hall clerk—to play cards. But Fr. Josemaría had plenty of other responsibilities besides his priestly duties and keeping up his prayer life. He had a widowed mother and a sister and a brother to support, and he needed to finish his studies for his licentiate in law. And over and above all else, he felt clearly that the Lord wanted a special something of him, even if that something was still wrapped in obscurity. Therefore, neither then nor at any time thereafter did he ever allow himself the luxury of getting bored; he didn't have the time. I heard him say it very often, up to the last day of his life: "I have never been bored."

And so, while he was at Perdiguera, instead of taking part in leisure activities with the "powers that be," he dedicated himself to the catechesis of children and of adults, either in groups or, when necessary, on a one-to-one basis. He went from house to house, and although he was careful not to do so when the men were out working in the fields, within less than two months he had visited all the families of the village, to rekindle in their hearts the love of God.

When the people were taking their siesta and it was not possible to engage in any pastoral activity, the Father made good use of the time by taking long walks in the countryside, by praying, and by disciplining his body through mortification.

He made sure that everybody knew that he was always at their service and that they could call on him at any time, for any kind of need.

This behavior was criticized by some people. The nickname that was given to him in Saragossa reached Perdiguera as well. Because of this and because of his conduct as a priest, some of his fellow priests in the region began to call him "the Mystic."

The Father never said a word in protest, never showed any resentment at being the object of such a slur. Of course, it grieved him a great deal, not so much because it was directed at him personally, but because it showed a lack of respect for the priesthood.

As soon as he was ordained, our Father began to refine his priestly skills, both in his preaching and in the administration of the sacraments. How did he acquire that incisive style of preaching which we were privileged to hear, and which can still be appreciated in his published homilies?

The Father's preaching was always grounded in doctrine, but as applied to the concrete realities of everyday life. It was very rich and varied. He often spoke about the nearness of God, about his presence in our midst, with such faith and conviction that he seemed to be engraving in the hearts of his listeners those words of the Lord, "Regnum Dei intra vos est" ["The Kingdom of God is within you" (Lk 17:21)]. He really lived with God at all times, was totally immersed in him—his preaching was simply the overflowing of a smitten heart.

I can attest that the founder preached as if he were praying out loud, and so he said whatever our Lord put into his heart to say at any given moment. Nevertheless, he always prepared his sermons with care, even when dealing with a subject which he knew backwards and forwards and on which he had already preached many times. He did not just follow the notes he had prepared for some other occasion: he always adapted them to the circumstances or specific situation of those who were listening. And he counseled our priests to do the same. He would often remind his priestly sons not to follow the example of Friar Gerundio de Campazas—a well-known character in Spanish literature, created by Fr. Francisco José de Isla—who laid aside his books and started preaching sermons which were eloquent but totally lacking in substance. He also advised us not to imitate "the talent of Fr. Stupendo, who preaches in the morning what he's just got through reading the night before." The only thing, he said, that will really convince anybody is our own life, a life truly consistent with the Gospel. And in this, too, the Father led by example.

5. The Founder

On October 2, 1928, our Father "saw" Opus Dei; he always used the verb "see" to describe the event. It was something very personal between himself and God. But it was also of vital importance for us, and for the life of the whole Church, since the sanctity of our Father was structurally inseparable from his charism as the founder. We know that on that day he was in Madrid, making a retreat. The whole event was clearly part of a providential plan.

As the Father himself later explained on many an occasion, his attitude was never like that of a chess player, who in making one move is already thinking what moves to make next. He lived in serene abandonment to the divine will, and sought, in every way, not to hinder it with a lot of useless rushing about. With the permission of his Ordinary, the archbishop of Saragossa, he moved to Madrid in order to pursue a doctorate in law at the Universidad Central. He arrived in the city on April 20, 1927, and just a week later enrolled in the program of studies in the history of international law. Afterwards, at the end of August, he also enrolled in the philosophy of law program.

But his plan altered with the founding of the Work. On October 2, 1928, the Lord changed the course of his life and made him see with noonday clarity that his particular mission on earth would consist of doing Opus Dei. "Madrid was my Damascus," I sometimes heard him declare, with deep gratitude in his tone of voice. I don't know how soon he decided that he would have to establish himself permanently in the capital, where the Work was born and where prospects for its development seemed most favorable, but I do know that from the very beginning he had the approval of the local Ordinary.

On that October day in 1928, the founder saw opening before him the horizons to which the Lord was calling him by entrusting him with the establishment of Opus Dei. This was to be a mobilization of Christians in every part of the world, Christians of every social class, who, by way of carrying out their professional work with freedom and personal responsibility, would seek their own sanctification while sanctifying, from within, all their temporal activities, in a daring movement of evangelization aimed at bringing all souls to God. This was, after some decades of anticipation, the message of renewal of the Church given by the Second Vatican Council, which proclaimed the universal vocation to sanctity for the salvation of the world, with all the pastoral consequences which derive from this task. These consequences, in fact, delineate the ecclesial function of Opus Dei, and will continue to do so for as long as, in the words of the founder, "there are people on earth who work."

To whom did the founder speak about this—apart, that is, from his confessor?

One of the first to know was one of his teachers at the state university of Saragossa, Dr. José Pou de Foxá, a well-known professor of canon law. In the early thirties, this professor wrote to him: "Tell me what's going on—why I find you so changed. You always write with a lot of joy, and I see that you are still happy, but you seem now to be rather reserved. Something has happened to you. Are you suffering some sorrow?" It is likely that in his reply, the Father told him in some way about his special calling. As a matter of fact, in his next letter Dr. Pou states that after learning the news, he understood very well why his correspondent seemed so immersed in God and so eager to fulfill his most holy will. He adds: "You say you are a useless and inept instrument. It is not so bad if you say that, because otherwise you would be doing your own thing and not God's. Since you are disposed to consider yourself inept, God will do everything, and everything will be of God." Our founder did not speak to anyone else about the mission he had received from our Lord, except for those who came close to the Work, and (after the middle of 1930) his spiritual director, who assured him many times, "This is all from God."

Didn't he speak of it to his own family? Together with his mother were his sister, Carmen, who was a little more than two years his senior, and his brother, Santiago, who in 1928 was nine years old.

Not until 1934 did the Father speak explicitly about the Work to his mother and sister, who, in spite of his precautions, had become aware of the growing intensity of his mortifications—a clear sign that something important had come into his life. They themselves told me about this. There is also a letter, dated September 20, 1934, in which the Father relates the conversation he had with them about the Work. He says: "Fifteen minutes after my arrival in this village (I'm writing from Fonz, though I'll be mailing this letter tomorrow from Barbastro), I spoke about the Work, in general terms, to my family. How much I had pestered our friends in heaven, in anticipation of this moment! Jesus caused everything to go very well. I will tell you word for word what their responses were. My mother: 'Fine, my son—but don't beat yourself, and don't wear a long face.' My sister: 'That's what I thought! I even said so to Mama.' And the little one: 'If you have sons . . . they'll have to treat me with a lot of respect, because I am . . . their uncle!' And right away, all three of them saw it as entirely natural that their money should be used for the Work. Glory be to God, their generosity is so great that if they had millions, they would give that money just as freely."

Where did the name "Opus Dei" come from?

In his earliest autobiographical notes, the Father always spoke of "the work" or "the work of God" when referring to what had been founded, but he hadn't yet thought of an actual name. A little later, he became convinced that this latter expression should be the actual name. In a detailed handwritten report dated June 14, 1948, describing an episode which took place toward the end of 1930, he wrote: "One day I went to have a talk with Fr. Sánchez, in a parlor of the residence at La Flor. I spoke to him about my personal affairs (I only spoke to him about the Work insofar as it related to my own soul), and at the end, the good Father Sánchez asked me, 'How is that work of God coming along?' Afterwards, as I walked along the street, I began to think: 'Work of God. Opus Dei! *Opus, operatio . . .* God's handiwork. This is the name I've been looking for!' And after that it was always called Opus Dei."

> *A young priest with very limited means, in a tense political situation which not long afterward would erupt into the civil war . . . Opus Dei was born small, but right from the start it had a universal scope.*

I remember very well, for example, how from the beginning of my vocation, in 1935, the Father encouraged me to study Japanese—which I did, though not with very encouraging results. Our founder had a particular predilection for the Far East, and after the war, when it was finally possible to initiate the Work there on a permanent basis, he was delighted. When the first letter arrived from his sons in Japan, he wrote on the envelope: "The first letter from Japan! *Sancta Maria, stella maris, filios tuos adiuva!* [Holy Mary, star of the sea, help your children!]" From then on, whenever correspondence was being handled, if a letter from Japan arrived he would open it first and set it aside. All the other letters would get stacked up, and he would read them together with me afterwards, but the first letter that he read was always the one from Japan. His children in Japan had a special place in his heart, because they lived in such a marvelous land, with so difficult a language, and where the great majority of the people did not yet know Christ.

He put this universal spirit into action as soon as conditions permitted it—that is, after the Spanish Civil War, and especially after World War II. The Father himself prepared the soil for the expansion of the Work with his frequent travels, and the seed sprouted abundantly.

I can think of only one country where this "prehistory" of the Work carried out by our founder was not followed immedi-

ately by a stable apostolic activity, and that is Greece. The Father
went there in 1966, together with Fr. Javier Echevarría, Javier
Cotelo, and me. He wanted to start the Work there as soon as
possible, and sowed the divine seed in abundance. We set out
from Naples on February 26. In Athens and Corinth we visited
the places where, according to tradition, St. Paul is supposed to
have preached. The Father did not give too much credence to
that popular tradition. On his return, he explained: "The actual
places may or may not have been those; but we don't gain or
lose anything either way. In the final analysis, you win out regardless, if you just make use of the occasion to come closer to
God. We made a spiritual communion there, and prayed for the
future apostolic activity in Greece. If St. Paul was really in this
or that place, fine, but if he wasn't, that's fine too—it's really a
very incidental matter."

We also saw various Byzantine churches. At times we happened to be there when liturgical ceremonies were taking place, at
which a few of the faithful were present, mostly women. The
Father prayed for the Greek people, most of whom are separated
from the Church of Rome. We went to the Catholic cathedral and
to the University of Athens. On March 13 we returned to Rome.

We later came to the conclusion that for us to set up apostolic activities in Greece was not going to be feasible any time
soon. One reason was that the Catholics there were such a small
minority. Our founder put it this way: "My impression is that
there is, humanly speaking, little possibility for us to work
there. It's as if everything there is on a very small scale . . . I
don't know how to explain it. Though for the Holy Spirit, nothing is impossible." In any event, he never gave up the hope of
sending some of his sons and daughters there when the circumstances became more favorable. In this connection he once said,
"Apostolic activity will not be easy, but neither will it be difficult; it will be as it is everywhere. It will come as the fruit of the
prayer, and mortification, and work, of everyone."

*The spirituality and apostolic methods of Opus Dei remain
consistent with those of its founder. I would like it if you could*

explain these in a little more detail, though I realize it won't be possible right now to go into all aspects of them.

The list will indeed be incomplete, since the spirituality of Opus Dei seeks to bring about a unity of life—that is to say, a union of action and contemplation—through the practice of all the virtues, both the natural ones and the supernatural ones.

Observing our Father's spiritual life, we find that its basis—as he himself said many times—was "the sense of divine filiation, which expresses itself in an ardent and sincere desire, both delicate and profound, to imitate Jesus Christ, the Son of God the Father, as one's own brother." This filial spirit led him to keep himself always conscious of the presence of God, to live with absolute faith in Providence, and to respond serenely and joyfully to the divine will.

If all of us, regardless of our condition or situation, are called to sanctity—and Opus Dei helps us to become aware that we are, and to act upon this truth—then we are all called to participate in the life of Christ. And if that is the case, then the life of the Christian is to be centered in the Eucharistic sacrifice, which is where we find the closest possible union with Christ.

The spirituality of the founder had a solid foundation: a profound awareness of the richness contained in the mystery of the Incarnate Word. Our Father understood that with the incarnation of the Word, all good human realities were raised to the supernatural order. Working, studying, smiling, crying, getting tired, resting, developing friendships—all of these things, among so many others, became divine actions in the life of Jesus Christ. They could, therefore, mesh perfectly with the interior life and the apostolate: in a word, with the search for sanctity. And this is why, in the founder (and, thanks to his example, in so many others as well), the effort to attain human perfection in the carrying out of one's obligations became transformed, through the operation of grace, into prayer, into a path of sanctification, a way of exercising the supernatural virtues, and at the same time into fruitful service to others in the courageous fight against the enemies of the soul.

Because of all this, our founder did all his work with a contemplative spirit. He offered each task to the Lord at both the start and the finish of it; he sprinkled it with aspirations; in short, he transformed everything into prayer.

As both source and consequence of this unity of life, he nourished himself, without interruption, with an awareness of the presence of God, and transformed his whole day into prayer. He would explain, as I mentioned before, that "the weapon of Opus Dei is not work, it is prayer. That's why we turn work into prayer." He was a contemplative soul *nel bel mezzo della strada*—an expression [meaning "right in the middle of the street"] that he liked to keep in Italian, no matter what language he was speaking. He was also fond of saying that for the ordinary Christian, "your cell is the street." He could take his cue from any event; there was nothing he couldn't elevate to the supernatural order and make the subject of a conversation with God. His plan of life also included what he called "always norms," that is, certain acts of piety that penetrated every moment of his day and nourished his intimacy with our Lord: recollection of the presence of God, meditation on divine filiation, spiritual communions, acts of thanksgiving, acts of reparation, and aspirations, together with mortifications, study, work, orderliness . . . and all of it permeated with the joy of knowing that he himself was a son of God.

The spirit of the founder was also distinguished by his attentiveness to the little things. It was marvelous that one with a heart so big, with a soul that could fly so high and that took part in such immense divine undertakings, could immerse himself with such intensity in what, as he used to say, "can be perceived only by pupils dilated by love."

Other components of our founder's spiritual personality included his doctrinal piety, a piety nourished by the study of our revealed faith and by personal practices of prayer, sacrifice, and penance; his tender devotion to our Lady, St. Joseph, the holy guardian angels, our patron saints, and our holy intercessors, to the Church and particularly the pope; and his profound respect for the legitimate freedom of others. In our Father's life, prayer and mortification (the prayer of the senses) and work and apostolate were all united. Apostolate truly was for him what he taught us that it should be for all of us: "an overflow of the interior life." I can vouch for the fact that he made use of all possible occasions to speak about God. He would often insist that he didn't want—that he didn't even know how—to speak about anything else.

He was convinced that the most important and effective part of the apostolic activity of the Work is the personal apostolate that the members each carry out, by word and example, in their daily relationships with friends and colleagues, in their own family, professional, and social life.

> *On November 28, 1982, with the apostolic constitution* Ut Sit, *Pope John Paul II established Opus Dei as a personal prelature. In line with its founding charism, the Work was thereby recognized by the Church as a secular jurisdictional structure, of a personal character (that is, not territorial), consisting of a Prelate, of priests incardinated in Opus Dei, and of laity. The establishment of the Prelature brought to a conclusion a juridical odyssey which had gone through many stages. In 1941 the Work was approved by the bishop of Madrid as a pious union; in 1943 the establishment, at the diocesan level, of the Priestly Society of the Holy Cross allowed for the ordination of men who had been lay members of the Work. With the 1947 and 1950 approvals as a secular institute of pontifical right, it was given the international character necessary for the expansion of its apostolate.*
>
> *How did the founder, who did not live to see its definitive canonical form come into effect, experience these various juridical stages?*

The canon law then in force did not provide any juridical framework adequately suited to what the Lord wanted for the Work —nor even a glimpse of a possibility of new paths being opened up. This is why, at the beginning, our founder did not take the risk of obtaining a formal approval from the ecclesiastical authorities; if he had, Opus Dei would have been squeezed, as it were, into an ill-fitting juridical suit. Accordingly, he limited himself to keeping the bishop of Madrid informed about everything; he was careful not to take a single step without the bishop's permission and blessing.

The first approval in writing goes back to 1941. It was, in good measure, prompted by a terrible campaign of wild accusations that was unleashed against our founder just after the end of the Spanish Civil War. To quell these attacks, Bishop Leopoldo Eijo y Garay, the bishop of Madrid, who had already intervened repeatedly by spoken word in defense of Opus Dei and its founder, decided to put his own authority on the line and, in order to put an end to any misunderstanding, to give a written approval of the Work. But in order to do this, he needed to ask the Father for a copy of its regulations.

Now, from the very beginning, the founder had been unwilling to use the term "constitutions" with reference to the regulations, statutes, or particular law of the Work. In ecclesiastical usage, the word "constitution" was used to signify legislation proper to the religious, to what was called "the state of perfection"; Opus Dei was a completely different kind of ecclesiastical reality.

Some months passed, and the founder had still not set about drawing up the list of regulations which the bishop had asked him for. Finally, now in 1941, it occurred to him one day that even though he had always tried to obey the ecclesiastical authorities very faithfully and in every particular, in this matter he was not being obedient to Bishop Eijo y Garay. He immediately asked to see him, and on being received by the bishop, he said to him, "You must pardon me, Your Excellency, because, without realizing it, I have been disobeying you. You told me to present those papers, and I haven't done so. The reason I haven't done so is that I haven't felt moved by God to do so, and that's because I so much fear that an approval which does not respect the theological, ascetical, and juridical nature of Opus Dei could bring it great harm. But you know what? When I realized that I was putting up a passive resistance to this approval, I was filled with joy, because I realized then that something unusual is happening here. Ordinarily, any founder who saw his own bishop so ready to approve his foundation would just naturally hasten to get together the documentation and present it to him. If I have not done so, it must be because the Work is not mine, but God's. So if, when the time comes to give it a juridical niche, Your Excellency is not there to approve it, then it will be approved by your successor." (Our founder told me about this episode, in these words, on several occasions.)

Nevertheless, the bishop insisted on the need for himself to provide some official support to the Work in order to defend it against the attacks being made on it. And so the Father did submit to the will of his Ordinary. Shortly afterwards, on February 14, 1941, he presented to him the text of the regulations, so that the Work could be recognized as a pious union.

It was with this same attitude of adherence to the will of God that the founder accepted the later juridical configurations of the Work, always knowing how to "give way without giving in, and with an eye to later recouping the losses."

While faithfully obeying the ecclesiastical authorities, he resolutely went on defending the foundational charism. And I can vouch for the fact that the definitive solution—which it fell to me, as the first successor of our founder, to see through to its completion—corresponds exactly to the specifications he left behind, down to the last detail.

> *The chief difficulty which the founder had to overcome was that of making clear the fully secular character of the Work, which in no way was to be confused with, or assimilated into the category of, religious orders, congregations, and associations. This implied no disrespect for them, but simply a realization that the Work, though it is not at all exclusivist, is an essentially different kind of entity.*

Our founder always loved and respected members of religious orders, and helped them in every way he could: by preaching retreats for them; by encouraging people, when they sought his counsel, to enter religious life if they seemed to have such a vocation; and by generously working for unity (which does not mean uniformity) in the apostolate—an intention for which the members of Opus Dei pray daily.

The Father never permitted the least criticism of other persons or institutions in the Church. From the time I first got to know him, I often heard him say, in these or similar words: "I will never lift a finger to extinguish a light which has been lit in Christ's honor—that is not my mission. If the lamp oil isn't good, it will go out by itself."

Among the thousands of episodes I could cite, there is one that stands out in my mind. Sometime around 1940, a girl came to our house on Diego de León Street in Madrid and told us she needed a certain sum of money for a dowry, to enter a convent. After ascertaining that her intentions were sincere, and after speaking with me, the Father asked Isidoro Zorzano, who kept the books, how much money we had in the house, and then gave it all to that future novice.

It should also be mentioned that religious have always understood the pastoral originality of the Work. Sister Lucia, the surviving seer of Our Lady of Fatima, took an enthusiastic interest in the establishment of our apostolic activity in Portugal, and has always prayed for the Work. In 1972 I accompanied the founder when he went to see her. On that occasion, Sister Lucia gave him thousands of booklets containing reflections on our Lady and the rosary; the Father was delighted to distribute them.

6. A Family and an Army

Blessed Josemaría, who used to call the fourth commandment "the sweetest precept," taught us by his example to love our parents and other relatives with tenderness, but also with the detachment appropriate to those who have given themselves entirely to God. He was brought up in a profoundly Christian home that was characterized by a noble dignity, even in the midst of financial difficulties. From his family he learned certain customs which he quite naturally carried over into the centers of the Work.

His father, José Escrivá, died suddenly, at the age of fifty-seven, on November 27, 1924. How did our Father conduct himself at that time?

His father's death was a very severe blow, all the more so since it was totally unexpected. On that November morning, Mr. Escrivá had gotten up at his usual time, not feeling bad at all; or if he was, he didn't say anything about it. After breakfast he went and prayed on his knees in front of a pilgrim statue of Our Lady of the Miraculous Medal. (It was the custom to take this statue from house to house, and at this time it was in the Escrivá household.) Then, as he always did just before leaving for work, he stopped to play with his little boy, Santiago, who was then five years old. Suddenly, at the front door of the house, he felt faint. He leaned against the doorpost and then fell to the floor, unconscious.

On hearing the thud, his wife, Dolores, and his daughter, Carmen, came running. They immediately called the parish priest and the doctor and then carried his inert body into a bedroom. The doctor told them nothing could be done. Two hours later, José Escrivá died, without recovering consciousness, but having received the last sacraments.

Our Father, who was at that time in the seminary at Saragossa, received a telegram asking him to come at once because his father was not feeling well. Actually, the founder knew right away what had happened, because, as he told us years later, Bishop Miguel de los Santos Díaz Gómara, the auxiliary bishop of Saragossa and head of the seminary, broke the news to him as soon as the telegram arrived.

With the rector's permission he caught the first train for Logroño. Waiting for him at the station was Manuel Ceniceros, who was employed at the clothing store, called La Gran Ciudad de Londres [The Great City of London], where Mr. Escrivá had found work after his own business at Barbastro had closed down. Manuel Ceniceros—he was the one who had sent the telegram—confirmed at once that Josemaría's father had died. Years later the Father told me that he'd then hurried home, grief-stricken, and that as he went he kept praying for the repose of his father's soul, and he placed himself in the hands of God and began to think about how he could support his family. He was the one that took charge of preparations for the funeral and burial.

A priest friend, Fr. Daniel Alfaro, lent him the money for the funeral expenses. As soon as possible he paid it back, with profound gratitude, and he never forgot the generosity of that friend. He prayed for him and for his intentions every day, in the Memento of his Mass. When he later came to hear of his friend's death, he commended his soul to the Lord in every one of his daily Masses, up to and including that of June 26, 1975. I could see for myself how moved our Father was whenever he recalled the selfless charity of that brother of his in the priesthood.

The burial took place the following day. The cemetery of Logroño was on the other side of the river, by the road to Mendavia. On his way home, absorbed in his grief and in the realization that the weight of responsibility for the family now rested entirely on his shoulders, our Father was crossing the bridge over the river, the Ebro River, when he suddenly remembered that he had in his pocket the key to the coffin; it had been given to him by the undertaker, for a keepsake. He thought, "What am I doing with this key, which could turn, for me, into an attachment?" He then quickly cast it into the Ebro, offering to God this separation from his dearest friend, his father.

This gesture, which he made with great serenity and interior peace, united him even more closely with the divine will. God had decided to take his father to himself, and our founder was accepting, without any reservations, being left on this earth without that tangible base of support. He had learned, once and for all, to live free of detachment even to what might seem indispensable.

Our Father also saw the hand of the Lord in his already having received the subdiaconate, on June 14 of that year. Thus bonded forever to God, he had every reason to put all his trust in the divine will—including now, when the whole responsibility of looking after his family fell upon him, as the eldest son.

After spending some time comforting his family, he returned to Saragossa, to continue with his studies for the priesthood. Three weeks later, on December 20, 1924, he received the diaconate in that city, the capital of Aragón.

> *Our founder learned from his father the importance of being very honest in one's work, and of practicing a charity that goes far beyond the narrow confines of justice. I have always thought, too, that his profound devotion to St. Joseph took shape from his meditations on the virtues of his father. As for his mother, Dolores Escrivá (who is known in the family of Opus Dei as "the Grandmother"), she also had the opportunity of collaborating directly with the Work.*

Our Father's commitment to the priesthood couldn't help but have some repercussions on his family. Here's one little example. In those early years, about 1927 to 1936, Mrs. Escrivá still had quite a youthful appearance. So whenever they went out to visit a certain family, some friends of theirs, our founder would say: "Mama, we can't go down the street together. It's not exactly written on my face that I am your son—I just don't want to take a chance on anybody getting scandalized. You go on ahead, and I'll meet you there."

Mrs. Escrivá had for years been tinting her hair, to conceal a premature graying. After the Spanish Civil War, the Father suggested to her, with great delicacy, that it might be better if she discontinued doing so. She had no problem agreeing to this, though it did mean quite a sacrifice for her—it did go against all her womanly instincts.

But the Grandmother willingly made much greater sacrifices for her son and for the Work. As I have already mentioned, the founder openly discussed Opus Dei with his mother, with his sister, Carmen, and with his brother, Santiago, in September of 1934. If up to that moment his mother had always been a sure source of support for her son, from then on she collaborated with him in an even more effective, though unobtrusive, way. She seconded his wishes, intuiting the ones he left unstated; she subordinated all her plans, for herself and for her family, to those of God; she placed at her son's disposal all the resources she had.

During the Spanish Civil War, when our founder was finally compelled to go over to the national zone, Mrs. Escrivá remained in Madrid with her other two children and, at the risk of her life, took care of the archives and all the documents of the Work. She hid them inside a mattress, and whenever the militia men came to make a search, she took to her bed as if she did not feel very well—which certainly was the truth!—and in this way succeeded in keeping safe the records and personal papers of her son. Among these were real treasures, such as some notes our Father had written about his interior experiences and other graces he had received from God, some early thoughts and plans regarding the development of the Work, and many other very precious texts.

After the war, when the residence on Jenner Street was initially being fitted out, the founder gave his mother a book describing the life of St. John Bosco. "Now you wouldn't by any chance be hoping," she said, "that I'm going to act like the mother of Don Bosco? Because I don't have the slightest intention of doing any such thing." "But, Mama," he replied, "you already are!" And his mother, who knew that as well as he did, burst out laughing. "And I will continue to do so," she said, "with great pleasure." His sister, Carmen, did exactly the same. She too renounced a life for herself and put all her energies into serving the Work—at first, perhaps, mostly just out of affection for her brother, but always with great love of God.

> *The Grandmother and Aunt Carmen took care of the domes-*
> *tic administration of the centers of the Work until such time*
> *as the women of Opus Dei were able to take over.*

They transmitted the warmth that had characterized the domestic life of the Escrivá family to the supernatural family our founder was creating. We learned to recognize this in the good taste exemplified in so many small details, in the delicacy with which people treated each other, and in the way the material things of the house were cared for, which implied—and this is the most important thing—a constant concern for others and a spirit of service characterized by vigilance and renunciation. We had observed all this in the character of our Father, and now we saw it confirmed in the Grandmother and in Aunt Carmen. We could not fail to treasure all this, and so, with spontaneous simplicity, family customs and traditions took root in us which even today live on in all the centers of the Work: family portraits and photographs, which help to make a house a home; a special dessert for someone's name day [or birthday]; the affectionate and tasteful placing of flowers in front of an image of our Lady, or in some other appropriate place in the house . . .

The family atmosphere that is so characteristic of Opus Dei comes basically, of course, from our founder. But if he succeeded in setting up such a lifestyle for our centers, it was not in virtue of his founding charisma alone, but also because of the way he himself had been brought up. And it is only right to point out that his mother and sister helped him immensely.

> *The news of the death of his mother came to our founder at a*
> *significant moment, while he was preaching a retreat for priests.*

It was on April 22, 1941. Ever since the end of the war, the founder of Opus Dei had been doing a great deal of apostolate in

Madrid and in other places throughout Spain. Among other things, he preached many retreats for priests. In April 1941 he was to give one of these for the bishop and all the priests of the diocese of Lérida.

Some days before the departure of our founder for Lérida, his mother had been with some of us on an outing to El Escorial, and she came down with a mild bronchial infection. It kept her in bed the whole next day, yet didn't seem to be anything really serious. But just to be on the safe side, our Father did ask the doctor if there was any reason he shouldn't leave, and the doctor assured him there was no need to worry. So he went to take leave of his mother, and as he was saying good-bye he asked her to offer her illness to the Lord for the priests who would be taking part in the retreat. Mrs. Escrivá, who was perhaps the only one to suspect the seriousness of her illness, agreed to do that, but as our founder was leaving the room, she whispered, "This child of mine!"

The sickness seemed to follow a normal course, but then, in the afternoon of April 21, her condition suddenly took a turn for the worse and she developed an acute case of pneumonia. The last sacraments were administered, and she died in the early hours of the following day. I immediately tried to telephone our founder. In those years it could sometimes take hours before the telephone exchange could get through to another town. When I finally did get through, I was told that our founder was giving one of his talks. So I spoke first with the bishop.

I heard, later on, that the bishop's concern was written all over his face—it had gone very pale—when he told our Father that I was on the phone, wanting to speak with him. I gave him the news in these few words: "The Grandmother is dead." I learned afterwards that at the time of my call, he had been preaching on the vital role a mother has in the life of a priest. Among other things, he had said that a mother is like a guardian angel to a priest, and that ideally she should die a day after her son.

Our founder immediately went to the chapel, prostrated himself before the tabernacle, and prayed, "Lord, you have seen fit to arrange things this way, so obviously I was wrong. Whatever you want is always best. I accept with all my heart your will, your having taken to yourself my mother." As soon as he could, he returned to Madrid. He wept and prayed before her body, turning to the Lord with the heartfelt outburst of a son to his father. "Lord," he said, "why are you doing this to me? The way you treat me!" I remember also that he took me aside and said to me, "My son, help me to pray a Te Deum." And so we did. He got through the whole funeral service with a great serenity. He was even able to console his sister and brother.

How did our Father come to the decision that he should ask his mother and sister to help in the running of the first centers of the Work?

I remember this very well. One day toward the end of 1938, when our founder was in Burgos, living at the Sabadell Hotel, he asked me, as he had done on other occasions, to accompany him on a walk along the Arlanzón River. While we were walking, he put to me a question that shows the heroic, absolute detachment with which he served God. He asked me if I thought it would be a good idea for him to ask his mother and sister to take care of the domestic administration of our centers—to look after the cleaning, the cooking, all those services essential to the running of a good household.

Obviously such a help would be invaluable for our supernatural family, so I replied that it seemed to me a wonderful idea. But that was a rather thoughtless reply, because I was not taking into account what this would do to his mother, his sister, and his little brother. No longer would they have a house of their own. Instead they would have to live in a small section of a residence for students, and, what is more, try their best to be unobtrusive. Our founder, after thinking this over very carefully in the presence of God, did ask his mother and his sister, notwithstanding all these difficulties, to offer this service to the Lord.

Their willingness to help out in this way made all the difference in the world to Opus Dei, especially in those early days. Carmen always confronted with a profound sense of responsibility this work that she had now freely made her own. She set up

the domestic administration of many centers of the Work, courageously putting up with the discomfort and problems of the initial stages. Once everything was working well, she would step
aside. She never became flustered, never let herself get agitated,
worried, or overwhelmed, never lost her temper. She always appeared serene, possessed of an interior peace and a confidence in
God which multiplied her effectiveness. I remember, for example,
when she started setting up the administration of the first two retreat houses—La Pililla, in the province of Avila, and Molinoviejo, near Segovia. At first we did not even have any electricity.
Carmen, as always, acted like it was no problem at all for her to
take care of this work until conditions were such that the women
of Opus Dei could take over.

We have to bear in mind that Carmen never belonged to the
Work. She did not have a vocation to it. Yet every time the founder
asked his sister for some help with the Work, she responded generously.

On April 2, 1948, our Father, who had by then been living
in Rome for some time, went to Madrid, and a few days later, on
April 15, Carmen herself moved to the Eternal City. Her brother
had asked her to come and lend a helping hand to the household
employees who were doing the domestic services and to the
women who were directing that work. She cheerfully said yes, as
she did any other time that she was asked to sacrifice herself for
the Work.

Carmen afterwards returned to Spain, and in the early 1950s,
with Santiago, rented an apartment on Zurbano Street in Madrid.
Finally, after so many years, she had a home of her own and was
able to lead an independent life according to her own tastes. But
this break lasted only a few months. Before she had finished deco-
rating the place, the founder asked her if she would take charge of
the domestic administration of a property which had been bought
in Italy, at Salto di Fondi, near Terracina. Carmen accepted at once
and returned to Rome in July 1952.

She remained at Salto di Fondi until the summer of 1953—
that is, until the work of reconstruction was completed and the
women of Opus Dei could move in. But instead of returning to

Spain, this time Carmen stayed in Rome, with Santiago, in a small house on the Via degli Scipioni. There she spent the last four years of her life. She made the decision to stay because she wanted to be readily available, in the best possible position to do whatever the Lord might ask of her by way of her brother. She really saw his requests as expressions of God's will.

It should be pointed out that Carmen did not lack the opportunity to have a family of her own; actually, she could have married very well. There was at one time a suitor, a man of distinction—a titled nobleman, in fact—who formally asked for her hand. Our Father later told me of the conversation he'd had then with his sister. Carmen said, "Josemaría, right now I don't feel anything for him. If I spent more time with him, maybe I could grow to love him—in fact, I probably would. But I'd rather stay with you and do all I can to help you."

Our founder really did have in his sister an extraordinary helper, especially when it came to teaching some of the first women called to Opus Dei the arts and skills of domestic work. Her help consisted in carrying out whatever her brother asked of her, on an ad hoc basis. She never intervened in matters having to do with the foundation itself; she understood as well as anybody else that this was a mission entrusted by the Lord to the founder alone.

While the self-sacrifice of the Grandmother lasted until two years after the end of the Spanish Civil War, Carmen devoted herself to the needs of the Work for almost twenty years, going from one place to another, wherever her presence was needed.

Father, could you tell us something about the death of Aunt Carmen?

In the early months of 1957, we noticed that Carmen's health—she had always been full of vitality and energy—was deteriorating. On March 4 the doctors diagnosed cancer, and sometime around April 20 they gave her no more than two months to live.

As soon as he heard this sad news, our Father wanted me to break it to Carmen, very clearly and with the utmost charity. He wanted those two months to be for his sister an opportunity to unite herself even more closely with the Lord. On April 23, the feast of St. George, I spoke to her about her illness. I told her that it would take a miracle for her to get better, and that, in the opinion of the doctors, she had only two months to live. I added that if the therapy she received was successful, she might perhaps survive for a bit longer, but not much. She received the news with tranquillity, with serenity, without tears, like the holy person she was. Later she said, "Alvaro has already given me the sentence."

Our founder asked me to look among my friends in Rome for an experienced and holy priest who could give her some spiritual help during those two months. I spoke with Fr. Fernández, an Augustinian Recollect, a priest with a profound interior life. He accepted this holy responsibility. After talking with Carmen, he agreed to visit her on a weekly basis; we would drive him over there.

These were two months of special prayer and recollection. In May, taking advantage of a trip to France, our founder went to Lourdes to ask for the miracle of his sister's cure, while accepting the will of God, whatever it might be.

On June 18, Carmen's illness went into its final stage and she asked to be given the Anointing of the Sick. On the following day she received Viaticum, surrounded by people who loved her—the founder and all the rest of us.

On June 20, the feast of the Body and Blood of Christ, I spent a long time at Carmen's bedside. I spoke to her, and she replied with the greatest of ease, almost as if she were speaking about someone else. At one point I asked her, "Carmen, do you want to go to heaven?" And she answered, quite resolutely, "Yes, of course!" Then she said to me, "Alvaro, I want to see . . ." For a moment I thought that she might be losing her sight. I said, "But don't you see us? We're right here . . ." And she said, "Yes, I know." Then I caught on. I said to her, "But to see us doesn't really matter anymore? What you are wanting to see is the face of our Lady?" And she said, "Yes, that's it."

During her agony she could hardly speak. She repeated, stammering, the short prayers that our founder, with the help of some of us, was whispering in her ear. She responded now only to religious promptings. Just a few minutes before she passed away, when her pulse was almost imperceptible, our Father said to her, "Now, when you get to heaven you are going to pray a lot for us, aren't you?" His sister replied, "Yes!" That was one of the very last words she spoke. She died just a little after that.

Not long before Carmen's death, her confessor, Fr. Fernández, said to me, "She has a tremendous interior peace. One can see that this docility of hers to the divine will is a miracle of the Lord. I have never seen a sick person so united to God. I've been coming to her for my own edification, more than to help her."

The day after Carmen's death, our founder told a group of his sons: "The tears ended the moment she died. Now I am happy, my sons. I'm grateful to the Lord, who has taken her to heaven; I'm filled with the joy of the Holy Spirit." Reading on all their faces their sadness over the death of his sister, he added: "Yes, my sons, you really ought to be offering me congratulations; Carmen has already made it to heaven. She was thrilled at the thought that she would soon be seeing God the Father, God the Son, God the Holy Spirit, the Blessed Virgin Mary, the angels . . . Now she continues to pray for us.

"Immediately after her death, I went to the oratory to celebrate the first Mass for the repose of her soul. By all means pray for her, do commend her to the Lord, but I am sure that she is already enjoying God. *Ma proprio certo:* completely sure."

He told me himself the reason for his certainty. What he didn't tell me was that he would also leave a written account of what had happened, in an envelope marked: "To be opened when I am dead." In this account our founder tells us that when he was getting ready to celebrate holy Mass for the soul of his sister, it occurred to him to ask for a sign that Carmen was already in heaven. He immediately drove any such thought out of his mind, because it seemed to him like putting God to the test. Nevertheless, he told me, something very unusual did happen. Both in the Memento of the Living and in the Memento of the Dead, he forgot to include the Mass intention, the well-being of his sister. How could this have happened? Everything about the spiritual and psychological circumstances he was in would seem to have made that impossible: Carmen was constantly on his mind, he was grieving for her, he had never before said Mass in that chapel, etc. As soon as he realized that he had forgotten to offer the Mass for Carmen, he was filled with an absolute assurance that this humanly inexplicable forgetfulness was a response from God. He understood that this was our Lord's way of letting him know that his sister had no need of prayers.

Our Father felt, in a way that could not be described, an intervention of the Lord, penetrating into the deepest recesses of his soul. That is what convinced him that his sister had "made the leap," as she herself had wished and as she had deserved because of her life of self-surrender to the divine will.

> *Father, I would like to hear a bit more about our founder in his role as head of the family—especially in relation to his brother, when Santiago was a little boy.*

When, in 1918, our Father decided to enter the seminary at Logroño, he gained admittance as a nonresident student, never forgetting his family responsibilities. Even though his parents, with great delicacy, in order to give him the most complete freedom of decision, had not voiced the least objection, he was well aware that in entering the seminary he was shattering their hopes and dreams. This would put an end to their plans—plans that were, humanly speaking, perfectly reasonable, legitimate, and honorable—to restore, with his help, the family fortunes. He was aware that their generous acceptance of God's will meant that they would have to change all their plans and resign themselves, at least for some years, to the absence of their only male child.

And so, with a great simplicity and confidence, our Father started asking the Lord to send his parents another son. The request was not a small one: his parents were no longer young, and it was almost ten years since the birth of their youngest child, Rosario, who had died, at the age of nine months, in 1910. Several months went by, and neither Carmen nor Josemaría realized that their mother was pregnant, even when it began to show. Their joy was great, and their gratitude to the Lord even greater, when their mother finally called them in to tell them she was expecting a baby. On February 28, 1919, Santiago Escrivá de Balaguer was born.

Especially after the death of his father, our founder did everything possible to take care of Santiago, and in a special way involved himself in his education. He put all the time he could into forming him well: he taught him his catechism, introduced him to the life of prayer, and helped him with his studies. More than an older brother, he became for him also a father, a teacher, and a friend.

I remember hearing from our Father how he sometimes had to defend himself against the "collaboration" of his little brother. From an early age, Santiago tried to imitate his big brother in everything. Well, one day, having on several occasions observed how our founder would cut out newspaper articles and paste them onto special index cards, Santiago filled his brother's filing cabinet with cuttings from magazines he had found at home. Our Father promptly got hold of two skulls: one of them he jokingly called "Doña Pelade" ("Lady Bald"); the other was of a Knight Templar, so he called it "Don Alonso." He placed them on top of the filing cabinet, and the "collaboration" of little Santiago ceased.

There was another episode that our Father liked to recall. One day he and his brother had gone for a walk. The little boy was always begging him to buy him sweets, and he particularly liked a certain kind of lollipop that a little old man sold on a street corner near the house where they lived. Well, this one day, when they were approaching that street corner, a gust of wind whipped up a big cloud of dust which swirled over the lollipops. Without thinking twice, the old man took them one by one and cleaned them by licking them. From that day forward, Santiago never wanted another lollipop. Our founder, who knew how to draw out of any event a supernatural meaning, was much entertained by his brother's reaction and would often point out to him that the things of this world are really like that candy: after wanting them so much, we finally no longer are attracted by them; in fact, they end up disgusting us.

Even when Santiago came of age, our Father continued to watch out for him as a good brother should. In 1958, in his capacity as head of the family, he even went to Saragossa to ask, on behalf of his brother, for the hand of his future sister-in-law, Yoya. Nevertheless, to give his children an example of poverty and detachment, he decided to make the sacrifice of not going to his brother's wedding [he was living in Rome then, and finances were tight]. Taking advantage of a trip that I had to make to Spain at that time, he asked me to take his place. Afterwards, until the day he died, he faithfully helped his brother and his family both with prayers and with his advice, as appears clearly in the wealth of correspondence that has come down to us.

> *Our Father carried over this vivid sense of paternity, acquired and developed within his own family, to the large supernatural family of the Work.*

The Father often said that he had only one heart, and that it was with the same heart that he loved God and his sons and daughters. Nor was his an impersonal or abstract affection: like any other good father, he identified with the joys and sorrows of his children, and followed closely everything concerned with their well-being.

Two specific instances come to mind. At one time it happened that the students at the Roman College of the Holy Cross were missing some classes during the week. This had come about because they were so busy with various other duties—mostly connected with work on our central house, the construction of which was then in full swing. The students were helping to keep an eye on it, and it had been decided that the missed lessons could be made up on Sundays. Well, when our Father found out about this, he immediately put a stop to it. He had always encouraged the students to use Sundays and holy days as opportunities to visit Rome's historic and artistic places, which are a marvelous apologia for the faith. From this time forward, his exhortations to do so became even more insistent. Similarly, he once learned from a letter that in one country his sons were losing hours of sleep because of the demands of the apostolate. He intervened, and established it as one of the important duties of the directors that they make sure all the members of the Work were, as a rule, in bed for seven and a half hours every night.

His tact and consideration knew no bounds. I recall that in 1961, after having spent the summer in England, he had decided that his date of departure from London back to Rome would be September 4. We had already bought our tickets for the trip when we found out that September 4 was the name day of a numerary assistant who had been taking care of domestic needs in the house in which we were staying. Our Father felt compelled by the bonds of charity to delay our return by one day, so that he could celebrate this special day with his daughter. Not to have done so would have seemed to him most unfatherly.

He was even more attentive if one of his children was taken ill. At the time of my first journey to Rome, in 1943, an epidemic of typhus was raging in Spain; a very contagious illness, it was at that time popularly called "the green louse." In the month of March, Juan Antonio Galarraga, then director of the residence on Jenner Street, was running a high temperature. Our Father himself went over to his house and, after covering him with some blankets, took him in a taxi to the hospital for contagious diseases. There he gave him all the attention that any good father would give a child of his. During Juan Antonio's convalescence he went to see him very often, and he asked Carmen to visit him too, so that he would be looked after with great care and affection.

The death of any daughter or son of his caused him acute suffering. I often saw him break down in tears. "It's only natural that I should suffer," he would say. "The Lord has caused me to love you with the heart of a father and of a mother." When the dying one was a young person, he would make a filial protest to our Lord. Humanly speaking, he could not understand why God would decide to call to himself someone who might have served him in this world for many years more. But then he would immediately submit to God and, in the midst of his grief, make an act of acceptance of the divine will: "Fiat, adimpleatur . . ." ["Let it be done, let it be accomplished . . ."].

On December 18, 1972, our Father went to visit a young numerary of Sicilian origin, Sofía Varvaro, who was in a Roman clinic. She had cancer of the liver, and the doctors no longer held out any hope. The Father consoled and encouraged her, speaking to her of heaven. Their dialogue was profoundly moving.

"Father," Sofía confided to him, "sometimes I'm afraid that I won't hold out to the end, because I am not a strong person."

The Father promptly answered her, "My daughter, don't be afraid—Jesus is waiting for you! I am asking him to cure you, but may his will be done. Sometimes it is hard to accept that divine will when we cannot understand, but the Lord must laugh at us a little at times like this, because he loves and looks after us like a real father with a mother's heart. Do you understand? Tomorrow I will place you on the paten at Mass, with the Sacred Host, and will offer you to the Lord. And you, whether here or in heaven, must forever stay very united to the Father, to the intentions of the Father, because I need all of you to support my supplications."

Sofía told him she had prayed hard for his recent trip to Spain and Portugal to bear much fruit.

"My daughter, you have helped me so much! I never felt I was alone. Now, having seen you, I know that you will help me from heaven, or on earth if the Lord leaves you here. Pray intensely for the Church, on account of which I am suffering so much, so that this situation may end. I'm counting on all of you and do feel myself accompanied by your prayer and by your affection."

"Father, thank you for your help, and for the help of all those in the Work."

"How could we not be here for you? We are very united, and I feel deeply responsible for each one of you. I suffer when you are not well. It costs me a lot to accept it; but I love the will of the Lord. And no matter what, because we are truly a family, your affection makes me happy, and I think all of you are happy too, knowing that your Father loves you so much."

"Father, I want to make it to the very end, but sometimes the pain is so great that it wears me out."

"Yes, my daughter, I really do understand you. What you should do is call out to our Lady and say to her: 'Monstra te esse matrem' ['Show yourself to be a mother']. Or if all you can say is 'Mother!' that's good enough. She cannot abandon us. Besides, we're never cut off from each other. You support all the rest of us, and all of us are very united to you. Ask for your cure, accept the will of God, and be content with whatever he decides: the Church needs our life, either way. Pray for all the priests of the Church, and especially for those of the Work—not because we're supposed to be holier than the others, but just so we live up to our own blessed responsibility of giving ourselves totally. Pester the Lord. Tell him, 'My Jesus, it is for your Church,' and offer him everything 'for the Work, so that we may serve you more and more.' Your union with our Lord, my daughter, has to grow stronger by the day."

"Father, for a long time I have not been able to go to Mass."

"My daughter, now your whole day is a Mass: you are being consumed in very close union with our Lord. Don't worry, the Lord is inside you; just don't leave him. Pray a lot. Turn to the Blessed Virgin Mary and to St. Joseph. Go with confidence to our father and lord St. Joseph, and ask him to lead us along the road of that intimacy he had with his Son."

Leaving the sickroom, without trying to hide his grief, our Father repeated slowly the aspiration "Fiat, adimpleatur, laudetur, et in aeternum superexaltetur iustissima atque amabilissima voluntas Dei super omnia. Amen. Amen!" ["May the most righteous and lovable will of God be done, accomplished, praised, and eternally exalted above all things. Amen. Amen!"].

I have reconstructed this entire conversation, making use of the testimonials of several people who were present, because everything our Father said here shows how intimately human affection and supernatural vision were interrelated in him.

> Our founder's affection for his children was shown in the way he spent himself in giving them formation, never allowing tiredness to get the better of him.

I can certainly vouch for that. I will never forget what he did for me personally. When I asked to join the Work, in July 1935, our Father, exhausted as he was by the amount of work he already had to do, did not hesitate to start a series of classes of formation just for me. It was just one more burden that he added to the numerous demands that already filled his days.

He took very special care with the formation of the first three priests of the Work, and for this he gave five reasons, in the following order:

"Second: If our priests do not have a sound theological formation, they will be of no use to me for the specific apostolate of Opus Dei.

"Third: The members of Opus Dei do their secular studies very well, and it would be demoralizing to them if they were not expected to put the same thoroughness into their ecclesiastical studies.

"Fourth: There are many people who have a lot of affection for us, and it will be good for them to see how well the priests of the Work are trained.

"Fifth: There are also, however, some other people who regard us with less affection, and it is only right that they should grasp—they, too—the uprightness and soundness of our work.

"And first: I could die any day, and I would have to render an account to God."

> Our Father was very demanding also because the struggle for sanctity is demanding. He always affirmed that the Work is a family, but also a militia, in the sense that members of Opus Dei receive a formation tailored to their supernatural undertaking of being Christians apostolically mobilized to awaken in every baptized person an awareness of the universal call to holiness.

The Father used to set very ambitious goals, applying a principle he formulated in this way: "Normally, of the person who can give seven I ask fourteen, and they give me fifteen." And with explicit reference to apostolic work, he said, "If somebody can do ten, we must ask for twenty, so that they give eighteen." The numbers would vary, but you get the idea.

What about when he had to correct people?

In cases where he had to reprimand someone, he always bore
in mind the frequency of his dealings with that person. He corrected with immense gentleness those whom he saw only from
time to time, and, in contrast, was the most severe with those who
were nearest to him. These were just two different ways of helping
us, allowing for the difference in circumstances. I have already
spoken of how careful our Father was about choosing the most
suitable line of conduct for every occasion, how he sought to
maintain the right balance between a necessary severity and a
genuine affection. Well, in the early years, when he saw that something had been done badly, he would think, "I can't mention this
now, because I'm so annoyed. I'd better wait till I can say it in a
more detached tone of voice, so that I don't hurt anybody—that
way I'll be more effective and will not offend God. I'll talk to this
person two or three days from now, when I'm calmer." But in his
later years he decided it was better to take care of things right
away. He would now say to himself, "If I don't say it immediately,
I'll start worrying so much about how much this is going to hurt
this daughter of mine, or this son of mine, that I'll run the risk of
never saying it at all." So he would speak up at once, and he never
let anything slide, because he loved his children very much and
wanted them to be saints.

But didn't he ever make a mistake?

Not very often, but when he did, he immediately rectified
the matter and, when this was called for, apologized. I remember
this one day in January 1955, I was on my way home at noontime,
and I was passing in front of the oratory of St. Gabriel, at our
headquarters. There I happened to meet our Father; he was with
some students of the Roman College of the Holy Cross, among
whom was Fernando Acaso. After greeting the Father, I took the
opportunity to tell Fernando that he could now go get certain
pieces of furniture which we needed, because we finally had
enough money in the bank. Well, as soon as he heard that, our

founder begged pardon of that son of his. What had happened was this. Just a little before my arrival, the Father had asked about those pieces of furniture. Fernando started to explain why he had not gone to pick them up, but our Father, without letting him continue, just asked him again if he had picked them up. Then Fernando simply said no, and our founder said that he did not like for us to make excuses. But now, having heard what I said, he realized immediately what had happened, and he hastened to apologize, right there in front of us, for not having let Fernando explain. And as if that were not enough, later on, in the sitting room, in the presence of all the students of the Roman College, he once again asked Fernando's pardon and praised his humility. The quickness with which he made amends was truly remarkable, and he did not hesitate to do so in public if he felt that was called for. This was an outstanding characteristic of his behavior. And it was his desire that everyone should experience this "joy of making amends."

Father, now I would like to ask you a question that may border on the indiscreet. For forty years you almost constantly lived and worked with the founder in the closest collaboration: would you like to say something about your own filial relationship with our Father?

Yes. I am proud to consider myself—with a holy pride, realizing that I did nothing to deserve this—a spiritual son of our founder, one who is indebted and has no means of paying back what he owes. Among so many other things, I owe to him my vocation to give myself totally to God in Opus Dei. It was through him that I received my call to the priesthood, an immeasurable gift of the Lord. And he never stopped encouraging me to serve the Church in absolute solidarity with the Roman pontiff and with all the bishops in communion with the Holy See, with that spirit of obedience and adherence to the hierarchy which characterizes the spirituality of the Work.

So, yes, I am united to our Father by strong ties of filial regard—a regard that I have for him not only because he gave me an example of heroic sanctity, but also because he served as the

Lord's instrument in helping me find my vocation, my raison d'être.

Our founder was constantly showing his affection for everyone, and as for me personally, I can tell you that I was, on an ongoing basis, an object of that fatherly affection. If ever he saw that I was at all tired, he bent over backwards to watch out for me. This might seem a little thing, but it's a memory that still moves me every time I think of it—when I went to work at the Vatican, I would always wear my newer cassock; well, it would often happen that shortly before I got home, our Father would say to Fr. Javier Echevarría, "Let's take your brother Alvaro's cassock downstairs so that he can change into it, because he will be coming home tired." He also went out of his way to discover everyone's tastes, and remembered them well. For example, anytime I was sick in bed, or had to stick to a certain diet, he would get for me (within the limits of the doctor's orders) dishes he knew I specially liked.

In February 1950 some discomfort I had been suffering for several years, around the area of my liver and appendix, suddenly became a lot worse. Our founder called in Dr. Faelli, who at that time was treating him for diabetes. The doctor said I had appendicitis and needed to be operated on immediately. Until the very moment the operation was to begin, the Father stayed by my side. I was in severe pain, and he kept trying to distract me and make me laugh a bit. He even went so far as to do a sort of little dance in front of me. He later confided to me what had been going through his mind on that occasion. On the one hand, he knew that I was prepared for death and very united to our Lord, thanks to God's mercy, so there was no need to console and encourage me with spiritual considerations. On the other hand, it was clear that I was not in immediate danger of death. So, really, the only thing I needed was to forget my pain. And that's why, in front of me and in the presence of a third person, he had the great charity and humility to improvise that little dance. And he certainly did succeed in his intentions. I couldn't help laughing; I was highly amused and thought no more of my pain. After the operation he came to see me in the clinic quite often and stayed with me as long as he possibly could. In those visits, so frequent and so prolonged, I was the object of the immense charity he lavished on his children when they were sick. I will never forget it.

Are these trifling things? They might look that way to someone who doesn't understand the meaning of love. Wherever possible, he tried to alleviate his children's suffering. On March 10, 1955, a telegram arrived with the news of the death of my mother. Our Father read it, but because it was late, decided to postpone telling me this distressing news, which would surely have kept me from getting a good night's sleep. The next day he gave me the telegram and explained, "It arrived last night, but I wanted to let you sleep, so I waited till this morning. But all the prayers you would have said, I went ahead and said them for you, and I also prayed on my own behalf for your mother. Now we will, both of us, celebrate holy Mass for the soul of your mother. She was so good."

In family life he would carry out all kinds of little services with elegance and with some lighthearted remark designed to keep the recipient from feeling ill at ease. I remember how often he would clean my glasses for me, repeating with an infectious smile a saying very common in Spain: "They're so grubby you could plant spring onions on them."

But I could go on indefinitely with demonstrations of his extraordinary good-heartedness. Suffice it to say that I consider it a privilege and a great responsibility to have been witness, for forty years, to his unstinting quest for sanctity. I have often asked the Lord to grant me even a thousandth part of the love I saw in him. It is said that no man is great in the eyes of his valet. Well, I wasn't a servant of our Father, but rather a son who sought, with the help of the Lord, always to be faithful to him; but I have to say that from 1936, when I started to really get to know him, until June 26, 1975, when God called him home, my admiration for his extraordinary charity towards God and neighbor grew by the day. With regard to the Father, let me repeat, I feel myself a debtor, and a debtor with no means of paying!

7. Means and Obstacles

The aim of Opus Dei is supernatural, and therefore the only effective means of achieving it are supernatural: prayer, mortification, and work sanctified and offered to God. Looking from a purely natural point of view at what happened on October 2, 1928, one is struck by the disproportion between the huge dimensions of the apostolic task disclosed to the soul of that twenty-six-year-old priest and the scant amount of resources at his disposal.

So supernatural was the outlook of our founder that he vigorously rejected every temptation to view as impossible what the Lord was asking of him. "'Impossible!' If I'd thought that way, if I had not been absolutely confident that whenever God asks for something, he gives all the graces necessary for its fulfillment, I would still be repeating that word—'Impossible!'—like an idiot. That's what would have happened to me if I had let myself look at things from a merely natural point of view, or go along with the advice of certain people."

From the very start, with an unshakable confidence in God, he saw the Work projected into the future, and despite the fact that to many it seemed only a dream, he spoke with great assurance, as if he already saw with his own eyes all that the Lord would make a reality through the years to come.

On this subject, I recall something rather striking that happened in August 1958, during one of the times that our founder was staying in London. He was walking with some of us in the downtown area. Passing by several famous banks and other business enterprises, he was struck by the worldly power which they represented, and, in contrast, he became acutely conscious of his own weakness. At that moment, the Lord allowed our Father to see in a particularly vivid way how powerless he was to carry out, on his own, the supernatural enterprise which had been entrusted to him. At the same time, however, the Lord reassured him with an internal locution which gave new vigor to his hope: "You can't—but I can."

Our Father did not confine himself to just praying with intensity, but, with great faith, asked for prayers from everyone.

Here is one instance of this, among thousands. In Madrid, in the years that preceded the civil war, a furiously anticlerical atmosphere developed. Among other things, a newspaper called *El Sol* was published, which was notorious for its fierce attacks on the Church. It had a very large circulation because it was well produced, from a technical standpoint, and was backed by the most prestigious names of the time, including the best journalists and the most authoritative representatives of the secularist ambients of the country. Well, our founder happened to know a certain lady whom everyone called "Dumb Henrietta." Today one would say she was mentally retarded; but in any case, she had great faith and a great refinement of spirit. One day the Father asked her to pray for an intention of his: the closing down of that harmful newspaper. A few months later, *El Sol* went out of business, no explanation given, and was never published again.

Our Father asked for prayers from as many people as he possibly could, even from people he didn't know: for example, priests he met on the street, or people he saw in church who seemed to be especially recollected in their prayer. Of special significance is the way he met Fr. Casimiro Morcillo, who soon afterward became vicar general in Madrid, then archbishop of Saragossa, and finally archbishop of Madrid. For a time in the early thirties, our Father used to come across, very early each morning, a priest who always seemed very recollected. One day our Father stopped him and asked him to pray for an intention of his. Fr. Casimiro was quite surprised. Soon they got to know each other and became friends. Later, recalling the incident, our founder said to the future archbishop, "When I stopped you in the street without knowing you,

you must have taken me for a madman." Fr. Casimiro laughed and replied, "I have to admit, the thought did cross my mind, because up till then nobody had ever in my life stopped me in the middle of the street to ask for my prayers."

> *One can certainly understand, then, our Father's insistence that the members of Opus Dei have an intense prayer life involving specific times of the day being set aside for our Lord— times during which prayer ordinarily takes precedence over whatever work they have to do, no matter how important it is.*

Regarding this, there is a story which I still find very moving. In 1943, some of his daughters began to look after the domestic administration of a residence for students in Madrid's La Moncloa section. Times were hard. The Spanish Civil War had only recently ended, and World War II was raging. Besides the difficulty of getting food, there was another big problem: construction of the residence was not yet finished, and the place was full of workmen. Feeling overwhelmed by all these difficulties, two of his daughters confided to our founder, on December 23, that under these circumstances they just could not carry out their work, that they were just going from one "disaster" to another, and that, as a consequence, they were neglecting their interior life, their prayer. On hearing this, our Father could not hold back his tears. After a while, he took out a sheet of paper and wrote on it:

"1.   without tableware
2.   with workmen everywhere
3.   with no unobstructed passageways
4.   without tablecloths
5.   without pantries
6.   without personnel
7.   without experience
8.   without division of labor

"1.   with a lot of love of God

2. with full trust in God and in the Father
3. no thinking about 'disasters' till tomorrow, during the day of recollection."

A few days later, one of them asked the Father why he had wept. He replied, "I wept, my daughter, because you were not praying. And for a daughter of God in Opus Dei, the most important work, the one which must take priority over all else, is just this: prayer." Not letting the interior struggle get preempted by any obstacle—this is what has always smoothed out all the difficulties which have presented themselves along the path of Opus Dei.

Our Father often said that Opus Dei was born in the hospitals and poorer districts of Madrid, because from the very beginning of the foundation he entrusted his intentions to the prayers of the sick and the destitute.

Our Lord heeded those prayers and blessed with the cross those first steps of the Work. In the Hospital del Rey, which took in the most desperate cases and was known as "the hospital for incurables," there was a patient named María Ignacia García Escobar. One of the first women to ask for admission to Opus Dei, she was to die of tuberculosis only seventeen months later. She learned from our founder to offer up her sufferings for Opus Dei.

Referring to the Work, she wrote in a notebook: "The foundations must be laid very well. We must set them in granite, so that what happened to the house mentioned in the Gospel, the house which was built on sand, will not happen to us. The foundations must be really deep; then will come the rest."

Another of these early vocations was Luis Gordon, a young engineer with a very good spirit, a man on whom our founder could have safely relied because of his maturity and his virtue. He too died young. Our Father accepted this loss with serenity and wrote movingly about the help Luis could give to the Work from heaven.

In 1944, another dying patient, Juan Fontán, although not in the Work, offered his life for the three men about to become the first priests of Opus Dei. A vivid consciousness of the communion of saints was continually nurtured by our founder, who among other things had the habit of always applying to the souls in purgatory all the indulgences he gained.

> *The Spanish Civil War was certainly a great obstacle, a threat to the development of the fledgling Work. From various biographies of our founder we learn about many dramatic events of that period, during which our Father had to go from one hiding place to another, in constant danger of arrest and execution, until he was able to escape to the liberated zone by way of Andorra. To tell the whole story would require a book in itself, but it would be helpful if you could relate at least one or two events that illustrate in a special way our founder's supernatural stance in the face of adversity.*

Those were truly terrible times. Our founder, already well known in Madrid for his priestly zeal, was the object of a particularly virulent persecution by anticlerical groups. In fact, one man, whose name we do not know, was mistaken for our founder because of a physical resemblance to him, and was assassinated.

For a while our Father was given refuge by a man who was an old friend of the family and a companion of his in high school, Dr. Suils. This doctor was in charge of a home for the mentally ill, and he courageously took in refugees, under the pretense that they were insane. Afterwards, from March 14 to August 31, 1937, our Father lived with a small group of his sons, including me, in the Honduran consulate. There he heroically stamped a rhythm of material as well as spiritual "normality" on those days of confinement which for other refugees were only a time of anguish.

A letter which he wrote to his sons in Valencia on September 18, 1937, gives a fairly precise idea of the state of mind and spirit of our founder. I ought to point out that to evade the censors, he used code words which would be easy for the recipients to decipher. So, for instance, in the following passage, "Grandfather" or "my brother Josemaría" is himself, and "Don Manuel" is our Lord:

"My little ones, Grandfather would like very much to embrace you, but his plans always go up in smoke. Which means that it is better so. Nevertheless, who knows? I've not given up hope that my dreams will soon come true. In a word . . . , Don Manuel knows what's best.

"A bit of belated news: I've been told personally, to my face, by several people, that they found my brother Josemaría hung on a tree—at La Moncloa, according to some; on Ferraz Street, say others. Someone identified the corpse. Other reports have it that he was shot to death.

"Imagine Grandfather's face when he heard this news. But really and truly, for a madman like my brother, what could be more desirable than to come to such an end—with a common grave, to boot? What better outcome could that poor fellow have hoped for when he found himself at death's door in the luxury suite of an expensive sanatorium! I didn't say that quite right. What I mean is, this way of dying, this very ordinary way—without noise or fuss, like a filthy bourgeois—is much more in keeping with his life, his Work, and his way. To die like that—oh, Don Manuel!—crazy, yes, but crazy with Love."

Every day for the rest of his life, the Father remembered in his holy Mass that man who had been assassinated in his place.

Previously, on October 1, 1936, there occurred another episode which left a deep and lasting impression on my memory— I was only twenty-two at the time.

We were hiding in a house on Serrano Street, and my brother Ramón came to warn us that the militia men were searching other places belonging to the family that owned that house. Our Father then asked Juan Jiménez Vargas to look for another refuge. He told my brother Pepe and me, who didn't know what to do, to stay there till the next day to await news about the search for a new place. In the meantime the Father managed, after several phone calls, to speak to José María González Barredo, who said he was sure he could find us another hiding place. Then our founder went out to meet him. Later, having successfully eluded the sentry outside the adjoining building, which was a police station, he returned to the house on Serrano Street and met with us. He greeted me and started weeping.

I asked him, "Father, why are you crying?" I was very moved by the obvious suffering of our founder. He was extraordinarily spiritual, and, for this very reason, extraordinarily human; he loved his friends with all his heart. "I have learned," he said, "that they have assassinated Fr. Lino." Then he told me how, during the time he had just spent walking through the streets of Madrid, he had learned of the assassination of his priest friend Fr. Lino Vea–Murguía, as well as further details concerning the martyrdom of another good friend, Fr. Pedro Poveda, the founder of the Teresian Institute—whose cause for beatification will, I hope, soon be approved.

Then he explained to me why he had come back to us. He had met José María at the appointed place, the Paseo de la Castellana. José María, after greeting him with great joy and affection, had taken a small key out of his pocket, handed it to him, given him an address, and said, "Go to this house and stay there. It belongs to a family I'm good friends with—they're staying outside of Madrid for now. You can trust the porter."

"But how can I stay in a stranger's house?" he said. "What if someone comes or calls? What could I say?"

This son of his, without giving this much thought, said, "Don't worry. There's a maid there who is also totally trustworthy—she can give you whatever help you need."

"But how old is she?"

"Oh, I'd guess twenty-two or twenty-three."

Then our founder thought, "I can't—I wouldn't even want to—stay locked up day and night with a young woman. I have a commitment to God which is more important than anything else. I'd sooner die than take a chance on offending God by failing in this pledge of Love."

So he went over to a sewer drain and dropped the key into it.

> *External contradictions, even if very difficult and dangerous, can, in a certain sense, be relatively easy to face. More difficult to bear are misunderstandings and unjustified, prejudiced hostility, especially coming from otherwise good people who belong to the Church. Our Father experienced both sorts of trials.*

With regard to this, I would like first and foremost to emphasize that our Father always reacted in a supernatural manner, pardoning and promptly forgetting false accusations with humility, with a very great love of neighbor, with a thirst for justice, and with a silent abandonment to the will of God.

Following his example, therefore, I will refer to these incidents only in very general terms and try to avoid any sense of victimhood or any spirit of vindictiveness.

As I have already said, the misunderstandings began at the time of the birth and early development of the Work, between 1930 and 1936. The explanation I would give is the one that goes straight to the theological root of the problem. At that time, what the founder saw in his soul with such clarity (thanks to a special divine illumination), the universal call to holiness, seemed something incredibly audacious. I often heard him talk about this. On one occasion, in the late sixties, he said it in these words: "When, some forty years ago, a young priest of twenty-six started to say that holiness was not just for friars, nuns, and priests, but that it was for all Christians, because Jesus Christ our Lord said to all, 'Be holy as my heavenly Father is holy' [Mt 5:48]—whether one is single, married, or widowed makes no difference, we can all be saints—they called that priest a heretic."

Some did not accuse him of being a heretic, but declared instead that he was crazy. In fact, what today is ordinary Church teaching seemed at that time, to all the world, like sheer nonsense. The Father coined his own expression for it: "un disparatón" ["a megafolly"]. And as if the seeming novelty of the doctrine he was preaching did not cause enough problems, they were compounded by the daring of his apostolic initiatives and the great disproportion between these and the human resources available to him to accomplish them.

The difficulty of understanding theologically the spiritual message of our founder was also exacerbated by some people who were jealous, often without realizing it, and by others who had a narrow, almost monopolistic view of pastoral work. Almost inevitably, the breath of the Holy Spirit which propelled the apostolate of our founder also raised a dust cloud of misunderstanding and hostility. The history of the Church shows that the good typically finds it difficult to make headway.

Around the end of 1939 and the beginning of 1940, the animosity against Opus Dei and its founder became more bitter. At first our Father did not want to believe that he was the target of a real campaign of denigration. But finally, in the face of all the evidence, he had to admit it. The Work was accused of heresy, of clandestine plotting to get into the seats of power; accused of Freemasonry, antipatriotism . . . you name it. This was not a matter of isolated incidents; there was an organized campaign. Those involved did not hesitate to carry these falsehoods even to the highest circles of the Church hierarchy, in order to sow seeds of distrust and suspicion against the Work and our founder.

Fr. José López Ortiz, the Augustinian monk who later became archbishop of Túy–Vigo and the military archbishop of Spain, was at that time the regular confessor at our residence on Diego de León Street, in Madrid. He gave our Father a copy of a "confidential dossier" on Opus Dei and its founder. The Information Office of the Falange had had it sent to the local authorities, and Fr. López Ortiz had been lent a copy by a trusted friend of his. The document was filled with atrocious falsehoods and marked the start of another defamatory campaign against the founder. It lumped together all the previous slanders. I was at that meeting and can confirm what Fr. López Ortiz later said: "When he had finished reading it, Josemaría, seeing how upset I was, started laughing and said to me, with heroic humility, 'Don't worry, Pepe—everything they're saying here is, thank God, quite false. But if they really knew me, they'd be able to say truthfully some much worse things, for I am actually nothing but a poor sinner who is madly in love with Jesus Christ.' And instead of tearing up this pile of insults, he gave the papers back to me so that I could return them to my friend to put back in the files at the office of the Falange from which he had taken them. 'Give them back to that friend of yours,' he said, 'so he can put them back in their place—we don't want him getting persecuted too.'"

Misunderstandings also arose, in a few cases, in families of the young people who took part in the Work's apostolic activities, or even in the families of Opus Dei members themselves. Problems of this kind were almost always traceable to the involvement of certain religious who did not hesitate to promote suspicion and mistrust. They would do this in the confessional, or make visits to families to

"warn" them. More than once our Father had to intervene personally to set the record straight when some wild misconception had
made its way into the homes of his children. As he once related it,
"At the start of the Work, more than thirty years ago, some parents
came to see me. They were very angry; there was, you see, a smear
campaign being run by certain religious (whom I love very much),
and these poor families had been affected. I was then a young priest—
not even forty yet. Well, I let them speak, and when they had finished, I said to them: 'If I had been told what you've been told, I'd
be thinking the same as you. In that sense we're in agreement. But
I'll tell you something else. In that case there would be three of us
in agreement: you and me and the devil!' Then I clarified things as
well as I could, and since that time we've stayed good friends."

> *Father, you speak in a general way of "religious" and refer to*
> *our founder's use of that word or similar expressions. But we're*
> *talking about some very specific individuals. We know, for*
> *instance, that it was all started by one Jesuit—hence the talk of*
> *an enmity between Opus Dei and the Society of Jesus.*

We should be careful not to generalize. The campaign of denigration was indeed started by a Jesuit who at that time had great
influence, both inside and outside the order. However, years later,
he abandoned the religious state and ended up apostatizing alto-
gether. Our Father, right from the start, tried to help him understand the nature of our Work, he pardoned him with all his heart,
and afterwards, when this man had left the Church, he went on
trying to help him, with the aid of some members of the Work.
When speaking about this persecution and others that followed,
our Father made use of an expression of St. Teresa, "the opposition
of the good," and he applied to the persecutors the Gospel phrase
obsequium se praestare Deo ["thinking they were doing a service to
God" (Jn 16:2)]. He viewed difficulties as occasions for purification. And when he saw them coming from people belonging to
ancient and glorious institutions in the Church, he would say that
God was making use of "a scalpel of platinum."

Regarding his relations with the Jesuits, there is a reply given
by our founder himself, in an interview with the *New York Times*

(October 7, 1966). "As far as the Society of Jesus goes," he said, "I know its superior general, Fr. Arrupe, and we have good relations between us. I can assure you, our relations are of mutual esteem and affection.

"Perhaps you have come across some religious who do not understand our Work. This will be due to some mistake or ignorance of the reality of our Work, which is specifically lay and secular and never intrudes on the field proper to religious. We have great veneration and affection for all religious, and we pray to the Lord that he will make their service to the Church and all humanity daily more effective. There will never be competition between Opus Dei and religious, because it takes two to make a quarrel, and we never wish to fight anyone" (*Conversations,* 54).

This was his constant rule of conduct, and it continues to be ours.

> *Speaking of Fr. Arrupe, I remember that he was the first ecclesiastical personality to appear at the public funeral Mass for our Father at the Basilica of Sant'Eugenio, on June 28, 1975. He arrived long before the ceremony began and stayed deeply recollected in prayer for more than an hour, during which time there flowed into the church a stream of cardinals, bishops, ambassadors, civil authorities, and a very great crowd of the faithful. But to get back to the story . . .*

In 1941, the attacks became particularly intense in Barcelona. The Work had only recently become established there, in a small apartment on Balmes Street. In this residence, called El Palau, were no more than half a dozen members of Opus Dei, and they were all university students. The kind of gossip I have been speaking of was spreading quickly throughout the city—in ecclesiastical circles, among families, at the university . . . Members of the Work were accused publicly of being heretics and impostors.

Our Father, naturally, followed closely these developments in Barcelona. Above all, he wanted to minimize the damage done to the interior lives of his sons and to their apostolate. But the political and religious accusations soon reached a point where it became impossible for him to go to the capital of Catalonia without running the risk of being arrested. The nuncio himself, Msgr.

Cicognani, told him that if he had to go to Barcelona, he should travel under a false name. Our Father, however, chose not to use this tactic. When he did have to go to the Catalonian capital, he simply bought his airline ticket under the name of Josemaría E. de Balaguer, because at that time he was generally known as "Father Escrivá." On those journeys to Barcelona, he also kept his stay to a minimum. Usually he stayed for only a couple of days, at the house of a priest friend, Fr. Sebastian Cirac.

The provincial governor of Barcelona, Correa Veglisón, years later remarked, "The things that were said about him at that time were such that if I had known he was coming here, I would have sent the police to the airport to arrest him."

Our founder strove to ensure that even in those circumstances, his sons in Barcelona never lacked charity. He encouraged them to keep silent, to work, to smile, and to forgive.

The bishop of Madrid, Bishop Leopoldo Eijo y Garay, in addition to being a very great comfort, was a firm, constant supporter who time and again publicly defended the Work. In a letter to Fr. Aurelio M. Escarré, the coadjutor abbot of Montserrat (one of the most important centers of spirituality in Spain), he said: "Believe me, Reverend Father Abbot, the 'Opus' is truly 'Dei' from start to finish, in all its intents and activities." He then spoke of the extreme docility of our founder to his bishop and explicitly dismissed as false any rumor about the "secrecy" of Opus Dei. This letter was a great consolation to many families and dissipated the doubts and suspicions that had spread among the priests of that area.

But the problems did not come to an end once and for all. From 1946 onwards, when our founder resided in Rome, more difficulties and contradictions came our way.

When, for example, vocations to Opus Dei first arose among Roman university students, the Lord allowed it to happen that some families not only failed to welcome their children's vocations, but even wrote to the Holy Father to complain. They did not, however, get the results they were expecting, because our Father availed himself of supernatural resources: he consecrated these families, and the families of all the other Opus Dei members, to the Holy Family.

In the summer of 1951 our founder remained in Rome, as he had done the previous year. He began to feel a great unease, an inner turmoil, because the Lord had given him an intuition that a plot was being hatched to do something terrible to the Work. He decided, once again, to resort to the only remedy within reach: a supernatural one. He made a pilgrimage to Loreto to consecrate the Work to *Cor Mariae Dulcissimum* [the Most Sweet Heart of Mary]. That was on August 15, 1951.

Some months after this consecration of the Work to our Lady, Cardinal Schuster, the archbishop of Milan, sent word to our founder that he should think of St. Joseph Calasanz. That was his way of communicating to our Father the nature of the plot: it was to split up the Work into two separate institutions, one for men, the other for women, and then to decapitate it by expelling our founder.

On February 24, 1952, Cardinal Tedeschini took up his position as cardinal protector of the Work, in accordance with the canon law in force at that time. A little later, on March 20, our Father took him a letter—dated a few days earlier, March 12—explaining the situation. As always, I accompanied him. Well, Cardinal Tedeschini calmly read the letter, right there in front of us, and said he would see that it got to the Holy Father [Pope Pius XII]. What the founder wrote in this letter was full of charity towards those who were involved in this plot, but the Father showed that there was no cause for any action against the Work. Pope Pius, after reading the letter, said to the cardinal, "Whoever thought up such plans?" It was quite clear that all the planning had been done without the knowledge of the Holy Father.

So that attack against our founder and against the Work came to nothing. On August 15, 1951, our Father had consecrated Opus Dei to our Lady; this was her response to that act of trust.

> *The reference to St. Joseph Calasanz bears witness to how much Blessed Josemaría had in common with so many other founders: being treated so unfairly, and then becoming historically famous for their holiness, while no one remembers the names of their detractors.*

Well, in any case, for then and for always, we go by the rule of our founder, "Forgive, say nothing, pray, work, smile."

8. Outlines of Interior Life

In point No. 107 of The Forge, *our founder wrote: "The person who stops struggling causes harm to the Church, to his own supernatural undertaking, to his brothers, and to all souls.*

"Examine yourself. Could you not put a more lively love of God into your spiritual struggle? I am praying for you—and for everyone. You should do the same."

We know that our Father never gave advice that he had not first put into practice himself. So could you tell us something of his own ascetical struggle and examination of conscience?

On the last day of 1971, our Father wrote in his diary words which he would later repeat on many an occasion: "This is our destiny on earth: to go on struggling for the sake of love until the very last moment. *Deo gratias!*" He put these words into practice all the days of his life, striving constantly to root out anything that might pull him away from God. And so that we might never forget this teaching, he asked for these words to be engraved on the last stone of Cavabianca—the new home of the Roman College of the Holy Cross. We were able to carry out this wish only after his death.

He devoted himself tirelessly to becoming a more and more docile instrument for the mission God had entrusted to him. He never stopped working on his own character and training himself in the practice of the virtues.

Throughout his life, through a detailed, in-depth, and thoroughly honest examination of conscience, he kept discovering new areas in which he could improve. He set himself demanding

99

goals for the purpose of following through on the inspirations he received from God, and his main tactic was to struggle in the little things. "'Great' holiness," he said, "consists in carrying out the 'little' duties of each moment" (*The Way,* point No. 817).

We are fortunate to have some notes of his, from 1932, which provide a faithful record of his interior struggle:

"• I mustn't ask questions merely out of curiosity.

• I mustn't complain about anything to anyone, except to seek direction.

• I mustn't flatter, or criticize."

And given his naturally open and affable character, it is significant that he also noted down this resolution:

"• Be sociable at home and make a point of talking with the others."

In 1956 he told me what he considered to be the questions a contemplative soul should ask itself—for we members of Opus Dei are "contemplatives in the midst of the world." These were questions he used in his own examination of conscience:

"• Do I seek union with Jesus in the tabernacle?

• Do I transform into action my desire to win new apostles?

• Do I turn to our Lady and St. Joseph, as patrons of the Work, to learn how to keep close to our Lord?

• Do I carry out and live with love the norms and customs of the Work?

• Do I constantly greet my Mother, the Blessed Virgin Mary?

• Am I friends with my guardian angel and with the guardian angels of the others?

• Am I generous in the small and continuous mortifications of each day?

• Do I remember to select for myself—when the choice is left up to me—whatever is most disagreeable?

• Do I live in a spirit of penance?

• Do I give a supernatural tone to my conversations?

• Do I try not to argue, and do I know how to listen to the points other people make?

• Do I go in search of praise, or seek thanks for my acts of service?

• Can people entrust me with whatever job needs to be done, in the sure knowledge that I'll see it through and report back sincerely, without looking for excuses, on how I have carried it out?

• Do I act with charity, with affection, even in periods of relaxation?

• Do I mortify others by making tiresome or cutting remarks?

• Do I try to avoid treating anyone in a special way just because I like them—do I try to avoid favoritism?

• Do I forget that my holiness consists in rectifying my intention while carrying out the duties of each moment?

• Do I take due care in preparing to receive the holy sacraments?

• Do I do my midday and evening examinations of conscience with sincerity and courage?

• Do I carry out, as well as I should, my particular examination of conscience?"

As you can see, almost all these questions are aimed at maintaining or increasing intimacy with God.

> *By both word and example, our Father taught us not to trust our own judgment, but to have recourse to prudent spiritual direction, within and outside of confession. Who were his own spiritual directors and confessors?*

When, around the end of December 1917 or the beginning of January 1918, at Logroño, the young Josemaría noticed those prints left by bare feet in the snow, those footprints which awakened in his soul those "premonitions of Love"—a deep disquiet and the absolute certainty that the Lord was asking something of him—he began to seek spiritual direction from Fr. José Miguel, the Carmelite who had left those footprints.

This devout friar, noting the excellent interior dispositions of the young man and realizing that the Lord was calling him to a life dedicated to God, suggested that he become a Discalced Carmelite. This idea neither attracted nor repelled him. But after calmly praying and meditating about this, taking into account also his family duties, he realized that this was not what our Lord wanted of him. He came to understand that whatever it was that the Lord more particularly wanted of him, he could best make himself available for that mission by becoming a diocesan priest.

So he stopped going for spiritual direction to Fr. José Miguel, but retained forever a sincere gratitude to him and a very great affection for the Carmelite Order. He had a great devotion to St. Teresa of Avila, St. John of the Cross, and St. Thérèse of the Child Jesus, and was an assiduous reader of their books. In his preaching he often mentioned these great masters of spirituality and quoted their works, although he would point out, where necessary, the divergences between their approaches and his own ways of understanding and living his relationship with God.

When, in due time, he told his father of his decision to become a priest, José Escrivá put him in touch with the abbot of the collegiate church, Fr. Antolín Oñate, so that he could give him some orientation; and he also sought out another friend, Fr. Albino Pajares, a military chaplain and a very pious priest, for further help with his spiritual and intellectual preparation.

For spiritual direction in the strict sense, and for confession, Josemaría turned to Fr. Ciriaco Garrido Lázaro, capitular canon of the collegiate church and parochial vicar of the Church of Santa María de la Rotonda, the church where he usually went to pray. At that time, this good priest must have been about forty-five. He was known locally as "Don Ciriaquito," partly because of his short stature, but more because he was very much loved in Logroño—so much loved that after his death, in 1949, they named one of the city streets after him.

At the seminary in Saragossa, which did not have a designated spiritual director, Josemaría was helped mostly by the rector, Fr. José López Sierra. He received advice also from Cardinal Soldevilla himself, from Bishop Miguel de los Santos Díaz Gómara, and from Fr. Antonio Moreno. After his ordination, it was primarily Fr. José Pou de Foxá who helped him in his first steps in the priesthood; in our Father's words, he was a "good, loyal, noble friend."

In Madrid, our founder went for spiritual direction to Fr. Valentín Sánchez, S.J.; it was in the summer of 1930 that he entrusted the guidance of his soul to this priest.

This arrangement was interrupted when the republican government decreed the expulsion of the Jesuits, on January 24, 1932. In this extremely difficult situation, our Father began to go to confession regularly to Fr. Postius, a Claretian father. However, despite the decree expelling the Society of Jesus, many Jesuits remained in Spain; and as soon as it became possible, our founder took up where he had left off and returned to Fr. Sánchez for confession.

With the onset of the Spanish Civil War and the beginning of a cruel religious persecution which forced priests to go into hiding or to flee to avoid martyrdom, it became much more difficult to have a regular confessor. While he was given refuge in the Honduran consulate, the Father went to confession, usually once a week, to Fr. Recaredo Ventosa, who had been provincial of the Congregation of the Sacred Heart and who had also found refuge in that consulate. Then he went to confession for a time to Fr. Angel Sagarmínaga.

When he succeeded in crossing over to the national zone and took up residence in Burgos, our founder was able once again to have a regular confessor. At first he went to Fr. Saturnino Martínez, who was very holy, but, unfortunately, also plagued by ill health. And so, not long afterwards, he turned to Fr. Francisco de B. López Pérez, a Claretian father.

After that, when he got back to Madrid at the end of the Spanish Civil War, he went back to his old confessor, Fr. Valentín Sánchez, until 1940—when he found himself forced to leave him.

What happened? I can tell you with great accuracy, because I was present at our founder's last two meetings with his spiritual director. In 1940, our Father, at the insistence of the bishop of Madrid, prepared the documents needed for diocesan approval of the Work. And since the part which dealt with the spirit of the Work was nothing other than an exposition of the ascetical path along which the Lord was leading him—that is, his interior life—he thought it only right to show these documents to Fr. Sánchez as well. Our Father always made a distinction between matters relating to the foundation and development of Opus Dei—matters outside the jurisdiction of his spiritual directors—and what referred to his own spiritual life. So his intention was not to ask Fr. Sánchez his opinion of Opus Dei, but rather to get an assessment of his own interior life, as reflected in these documents. If I remember correctly, the meeting at which he handed over these documents took place in September.

A few weeks later, I again accompanied our founder when he went to meet with his spiritual director. This time, Fr. Sánchez—who up to that point had always encouraged our Father to remain faithful to his founding charism—declared rather curtly that the Holy See could never approve the Work, and cited as proof the numbers of several canons. Then he handed back the documents and dismissed us.

That meeting caused our Father a great deal of suffering, but he never lost his composure. By way of response he simply reiterated his confidence that since the Work had come from God, God would keep it safe and bring it to fruition. He then added, gently but firmly, that he could no longer go to confession to Fr. Sánchez, because he no longer had confidence in him.

It seems clear to me that Fr. Sánchez was under great pressure, almost coercion, from other people. What else could account for such a sudden, radical reversal? This was, indeed, a time of violent persecution of the Work.

I had jotted down the numbers of the canons that Fr. Sánchez cited. As soon as we got home, the Father and I looked them up in the Code of Canon Law and realized they had been cited at random; they had nothing to do with the issues at hand.

> *This is a very serious and very sad episode, but it should not cause scandal; even our canonized saints, many of them, suffered from misunderstandings from their confessors. Just think of how much St. Teresa had to suffer . . .*

Yes. But our Father, despite all this, forever remained extremely grateful to Fr. Sánchez for the great good he had done for his soul. And in 1963, when this Jesuit died, our Father recalled in a letter to the regional vicar of Opus Dei in Spain how Fr. Sánchez, some time later, had rejoiced when our founder went to see him to tell him that the Holy See had granted the *Decretum Laudis* to the Work.

So to whom did our Father then turn for spiritual direction?

He chose Fr. José María García Lahiguera, whom he considered a "fraternal friend" and who was at that time spiritual director at the Madrid seminary. Later he became auxiliary bishop of the Madrid diocese, and then archbishop of Valencia. His cause for beatification was opened recently.

Right from the start, our founder made it clear to his new confessor that he intended to go to confession to a priest of the Work as soon as the first ones were ordained. To Fr. García Lahiguera this made good sense. So on June 26, 1944, the day after my ordination, our Father came to the center on Villanueva Street, where I then lived. He asked me if I had heard any confessions yet, and when I answered no, he exclaimed, "Well, then, you can hear mine, because I want to make a general confession to you!" So off we went to the chapel in that center. I feel free to mention this because he himself told the story several times in public, in these same words. From then on, for thirty-one years exactly (he died on June 26, 1975), I was the regular confessor of our founder.

He told me, on that first occasion, that he was dispensing me from the sacramental seal where he himself was concerned, because he wanted to leave me absolutely free to help him spiritually at any moment of the day—not just in the confessional. For my part, I can truthfully say that, thanks be to God, I never made use of this permission. This was out of love for the sacrament, a love which our Father had inculcated in my heart with great intensity. I was always struck by the humility with which our founder, from that moment on, put himself in my hands. After all, I was a newly ordained priest, and I had received all my spiritual formation from him.

I should point out here that all the details I mention in this interview—indeed, all aspects of our founder's life to which I make reference at any time or place—are taken exclusively from the external forum. I have avoided and always will avoid any reference, however marginal or indirect, to anything covered by the sacramental seal of confession.

> *You know that as far as I am concerned, that goes without saying; I would never have had the slightest doubt about that. But I thank you for having made that clear for the sake of our readers; this should head off any scruple or doubt which might have troubled the less well-informed.*
>
> *I would be very grateful now if you could share with us some details of our Father's prayer life.*

I can testify that his union with God grew year by year, in a marvelous crescendo, until the very end of his life. As far back as 1935, when I barely knew him, it was obvious to me that he thought only of our Lord and his service. He carried out every task with full attention, but at the same time was completely immersed in God. He truly lived the counsel he gave to others: "Keep your feet on the ground and your head in heaven." By both word and example he taught us how to put all our faculties at the service of our daily tasks—in professional work, in the priestly ministry, in whatever area—but always with our thoughts turned to the Lord.

His union with God was so deep that even when he was suffering because of the lack of an adequate legal framework for Opus Dei, or, especially in the last years, because of the confusion and disobedience which seemed to be running rampant in the Church, he never lost his cheerfulness, just as he had never lost it when faced with the many difficulties of the earlier years. This union with God was nourished by specific periods of time devoted to mental prayer: as a rule, half an hour in the morning and half an hour during the afternoon. He established this practice as a norm also for all his sons and daughters.

In January 1973 he made this comment: "It is not enough to spend the whole day in prayer, as, with the help of God's grace, all of us strive to do, seeking to live in our Lord's presence at every moment. It's not enough, just as it would not be enough to have radiators in every room of the house—one also needs a furnace. For us, the furnace is those two half hours of mental prayer."

Apart from that, the most helpful thing I can tell you is that in the volume *Friends of God,* you can find two eloquent expositions of our Father's method of prayer: the homilies entitled "A Life of Prayer" and "Towards Holiness." In fact, he himself suggested that his children use these homilies as a kind of guideline for their own prayer life.

> *Precisely in the homily "Towards Holiness," our Father, after tracing out a path of prayer starting with vocal prayers and passing through meditation on the sacred humanity of Christ, affirms: "Our heart now needs to distinguish and adore each one of the divine Persons. The soul is, as it were, making a discovery in the supernatural life, like a little child opening his eyes to the world about him. The soul spends time lovingly with the Father and the Son and the Holy Spirit, and readily submits to the work of the lifegiving Paraclete, who gives himself to us with no merit on our part, bestowing his gifts and the supernatural virtues!"* (Friends of God, No. 306). *Surely he was speaking from experience?*

I have no hesitation in affirming that God granted him in abundance the gift of infused contemplation. I've already mentioned how at breakfast, very often, it would happen that while the two of us were leafing through the newspapers, our Father would stop almost as soon as he started reading, suddenly immersed in God. He would rest his forehead in the palm of his right hand and stop reading to pray. You can imagine the great emotion I felt when, after his death, I discovered among his personal papers this note, written in 1934, expressing with great simplicity his dialogue with the Lord: "Prayer—even if I do not give it to you, . . . you make me feel it outside the fixed times. Sometimes when I'm reading the paper, I have to say to you, 'Let me read!' How good my Jesus is! And I, on the other hand, . . ."

It would take forever to describe the richness of his interior life. The Holy Spirit undoubtedly led him to very high peaks of mystical union in the midst of his ordinary life. But he also experienced difficult periods of purification of the senses and of the spirit.

As happens to all souls of prayer, the Lord let our founder experience at various times in his life a sense of spiritual aridity. In 1968, for example, he confided to us: "Yesterday afternoon I was very tired when I went into the oratory to pray. I stayed there and just said to the Lord, 'Here I am, like a faithful dog at his master's feet. I don't have enough strength even to tell you I love you—but you see it!' At other times in the course of my life, I have said to our Lord, 'Here I am, like a sentry in his sentry box, keeping watch, eager to give you everything.'"

These times of aridity, whether of greater or lesser duration, were, however, the exception rather than the rule. Proof of this can be found in the many published meditations—there are others as yet unpublished—which grew out of the personal prayer of our founder.

He taught us, in any case, to do as he did: to persevere in mental prayer even when we are tired, when the Lord grants us consolations and when he denies them to us, when we receive illuminations and when we find ourselves in the most complete aridity.

On May 17, 1970, he said: "Let us struggle to be devout, to teach others with our lives to pray, to convince people that they must pray. We must lift up everything to God with unceasing prayer." This was, in essence, his life: praying constantly, bringing everything back to the Lord, reaching the fullness of contemplation in the midst of the world. He prayed right up to his last moment, that moment when the Lord called him to himself.

9. The Bread and the Word

A characteristic expression of our Father, "The Mass, center and root of the interior life," was used by the Second Vatican Council to indicate the unity of life which every priest must strive to acquire: "This [Eucharistic] sacrifice is therefore the center and root of the whole life of the priest" (Presbyterorum Ordinis, No. 14). Although this would be enough to show the intensity with which our Father applied his priestly soul to the Eucharistic celebration, I still would like to ask you for some concrete illustration.

The holy Mass was even the physical center of his day. As I've already mentioned, he divided the day into two parts: until noon he lived the presence of God by concentrating on thanksgiving for the Mass he had celebrated that morning, and after the Angelus he began to prepare himself for the next day's Mass.

He confided to me many times that ever since his ordination he had prepared himself to celebrate the Holy Sacrifice each time as if it were to be his last. The thought that the Savior might take him away immediately afterwards would stir him every day to pour out in the Mass all the faith and love that he could muster. And this is how he lived right up to June 26, 1975, when he celebrated his last Mass with an extraordinary fervor.

He used to tell the story about how, when he moved to Saragossa in 1920, he happened one day to be walking in front of a café called Gambrinus, and he saw that a famous bullfighter was there. Some neighborhood boys had managed to come up very close to that highly popular celebrity, and the Father heard one of them joyfully exclaim, "I touched him!" He was deeply moved by that scene and would often remind us of it, exhorting us to reflect on the fact that every day, in the Eucharist, we touch Jesus.

He had a custom of adoring the Eucharist by way of imagining he was entering churches which he saw in the distance or which simply came to mind; and he did not neglect to make reparation whenever he heard news of a sacrilegious theft or an act of desecration.

Once, during his trip to Peru in 1974, he was shown some photographs of the aftermath of a huge *huaico*, which is an avalanche of earth, stones, and mud. An entire village had been buried. All that stood out from the rubble was the tip of the church bell tower. In the picture you could see animals grazing there, directly above the buried church. Grieved at the realization that Jesus in the Blessed Sacrament was still buried under all that rubble, the Father spent that whole night in prayer and adoration.

It would take too long to describe how the Father lived each part of the holy Mass. So I will just mention two details which I heard him speak of many times. At the elevation of the Eucharistic Bread, and again at the elevation of the Blood of our Lord, he would repeat certain prayers—not aloud, because the rubrics do not permit it, but in his mind and heart—and he did this with a heroic perseverance which lasted for decades.

Here are the specifics. While he had the consecrated host in his hands, he would say, "My Lord and my God," the act of faith of St. Thomas the Apostle [John 20:28]. Next, again taking his inspiration from the Gospel [Luke 17:5], he would slowly repeat, "Adauge nobis fidem, spem, et caritatem" ["Increase our faith, hope, and charity"], asking the Lord to give to the whole Work the grace of growing in these virtues. Immediately after that, he would repeat a prayer addressed to the Merciful Love, a prayer which he had known and meditated upon since his youth, but which he never used in his preaching—for many years he only rarely confided to us that he recited it—"Holy Father, through the Immaculate Heart of Mary I offer to you Jesus, your beloved Son, and in him, through him, and with him I offer myself for all his intentions and in the name of all creatures." Afterwards he added the invocation "Lord, grant purity and *gaudium cum pace* [joy with peace] to me and to all," thinking especially, of course, of his sons and daughters in Opus Dei. And finally, while he was genuflecting after having elevated the Host or the Chalice, he recited the first stanza of the Eucharistic hymn "Adoro Te Devote," and he said to the Lord, "Welcome to the altar!"

All of this, I repeat, was said by him not just on this or that occasion, but every day, and never mechanically, but with all his love, with everything in him. I know about all this because he told me himself—me and Fr. Javier Echevarría. One time he confided this to us was a day in 1970, in Mexico, when he was praying aloud in the Basilica of Our Lady of Guadalupe; he had gone there, in the company of several of his sons, to make a novena to the Blessed Virgin.

> *How did our Father receive the liturgical reform decreed by the Second Vatican Council?*

As always, he obediently and wholeheartedly carried out all of the council's instructions. And so, thanks to the solicitude of its founder, Opus Dei has been an example of fidelity also in all that pertains to liturgical praxis.

He entrusted to some priests of the Work the task of examining the various possibilities provided by the reform, and of determining and explaining how they might be implemented. He personally directed this work and approved its results. So it was that all the priests of the Work began to learn the new rubrics, following the desire of the Holy Father "that the conciliar Constitution on the Sacred Liturgy be put into practice in the fullest and most faithful manner." (This is from a letter sent in the name of Pope Paul VI to all bishops and other ecclesiastical superiors: the letter sent with the booklet *Jubilate Deo*, on April 14, 1974.)

Our Father was the first to obey the new liturgical instructions; he immediately and energetically applied himself to learning the new rite of the Mass. For many years it had already been customary for another priest to serve his Mass, and from the fifties onwards, that was always either Fr. Javier Echevarría or myself. Well, when the liturgical changes were introduced, he begged us not to refrain from making any suggestions we thought fitting—to go ahead and speak up, in order to help him learn the new rite properly. But despite his good intentions, we could see that this was going to entail a great amount of effort on his part; that it would mean changing habits of liturgical devotion that he had acquired, over many years, through a persevering struggle that was full of love for God.

I tried to think of a way the Father could be spared these difficulties, and in his presence I made a passing mention of the fact that some priests, younger than he, had received permission to continue to follow the liturgical rite of St. Pius V, and go on celebrating Mass just as they had been doing before. The Father interrupted me immediately, stating that he wanted no special privileges. Well aware that I had frequent contacts with those responsible for working out the new liturgical dispositions, he prohibited me from making any such request.

Some time afterwards, I happened to run into Msgr. Annibale Bugnini, who was the one more or less in charge of this task, and who was a good friend of mine—such a good friend that we used the familiar "tu" form of address with each other. We spoke of the fact that some of the older priests, having celebrated the holy Mass for so many years according to the old rite, were experiencing considerable difficulties in adapting themselves to the new; it was a well-known phenomenon. In passing I alluded to the case of our founder, who was demonstrating an exemplary obedience, and doing so with a deep joy. Msgr. Bugnini then told me there was no need for the founder of Opus Dei to go to so much trouble, when so many other priests had already been given permission to celebrate Mass with the earlier ritual; he himself had agreed to such requests that had come to him from priests in similar circumstances. Even though I had told him that the founder wanted no privilege other than that of obeying the Holy See always, and that he had even forbidden me to request anything, Msgr. Bugnini insisted on giving me permission for our founder, and he told me I must report to our founder exactly how our conversation had gone.

> *The delicacy with which our Father safeguarded the beauty of the liturgy and of the implements of worship is expressed so well in point No. 527 of* The Way: *"That woman in the house of Simon the leper in Bethany, anointing the Master's head with precious ointment, reminds us of the duty to be generous in the worship of God.*
>
> *"All the richness, majesty, and beauty possible would still seem too little to me.*
>
> *"And against those who attack the richness of the sacred vessels, of vestments and altars, we hear the praise given by Jesus: 'Opus enim bonum operata est in me' ('She has done me a good turn')."*

I remember one time—this was in 1959 or 1960—the Father was in London, and he watched on television some kind of royal ceremony. Immediately afterwards he observed, as he had done on other occasions, that ceremonies even of this type require very careful preparation, and that when it is the Lord our God who is to be given homage, we must prepare this act of worship with a love and fervor much greater than that shown to the queen of England by her master of ceremonies.

His spirit of detachment and poverty in no way inhibited his love of beauty and artistic taste in liturgy, in divine worship. This was just one more tangible proof of his faith in, and generosity toward, the Lord.

He wanted objects for liturgical use to be of the highest possible quality; he taught that in this area, poverty should be sought in terms of quantity but not quality. For Opus Dei centers he laid down this norm: that liturgical objects ought to be beautiful and tasteful, but no more in number than is strictly necessary.

In 1940, our Father, moved by his passionate love for our Lord, and despite the financial straits we were in, began to bring pieces of jewelry (given to him by some friends) to a studio of liturgical art that was well known both in Spain and abroad. He was gathering things, little by little, because he wanted to offer our Lord a very rich monstrance, with little silver bells. The studio was called Talleres de Arte Granda; it was run by a very devout priest, Fr. Félix Granda, and his sister Cándida. As soon as he received a precious stone or a ring from which some acquaintance of his had detached himself or herself, our founder would bring it directly to the shop. Sometimes I went with him. Cándida would lay a black velvet cloth on a table and put on it everything which we had managed to collect; then our founder would say, "Now I need such and such, and this other thing is still missing . . ." For such purposes the Father went to see the Grandas frequently, and gave them all kinds of advice about the designing of tabernacles and sacred vessels. Fr. Félix and his sister were happy to receive this advice, because his suggestions were very practical and conducive to the beautifying of liturgical objects; both of them have told me that they learned a great deal from him. That is why, when they retired from the management of Talleres de Arte Granda, they entrusted it to some members of Opus Dei. The founder was constantly encouraging them to perfect their work, to make a living reality of this verse from Psalm 69: "Zelus domus tuae comedit me" ["Zeal for your house has consumed me"].

Often he was not able to offer to the Lord everything that he would have liked to. I remember that in 1935 he was unhappy about not being able to put a nicer tabernacle in the chapel of the Ferraz Street residence; the one we had was a very poor one, lent to him by Mother Muratori. It also saddened him to have to give solemn Benediction with a monstrance of little value, one made of iron—only the lunette which held the consecrated host was of silver. Since that time I heard him say that he wanted to use only precious objects for the worship of our Lord, even if he had to go hungry to do it.

Again and again, and particularly in the last years of his life, I heard him say this: "People today are so stingy toward our Lord; and I just don't understand it. Even if there were a man alive who would give to the woman of his dreams a piece of iron or concrete as a present, not even then would I give to my Lord a bit of iron or concrete, but always the very best that I could."

Throughout his life he sought to give to the service of the Lord the very best that he had. I know that shortly after 1928 he wanted to commission the making of a chalice that would have a precious stone encased in its base in such a way that nobody could admire it. It was to be a hidden sacrifice, something for our Lord's eyes only. Many years later, after he had moved to Rome, he was finally able to realize this desire of his, when a lady gave him a very large emerald.

He made sure that once a week, all the tabernacles were resupplied with freshly consecrated hosts, and he established this as a norm for all centers of the Work, urging those responsible to anticipate any problems in carrying this out. In 1940 or 1941 he was able to see realized his long-standing desire to have the hosts made in our houses. He even longed for the day, farther into the future, when his own sons and daughters would be in a position to cultivate the grain and the vines necessary for making the Eucharistic species. On January 15, 1965, he explained once again this old plan of his: "It is a way of caressing God, born in our hands; of preparing the species by means of which he descends to us." I heard him speak of this again on March 28, 1975, just a few months before he died, to a group of his daughters.

When he was the only priest of Opus Dei, he personally did the cleaning of the inside of the tabernacles in our centers. He used to do this every two weeks, making use of his trips from Madrid. As he was doing the cleaning, he would talk continually to Jesus in the Blessed Sacrament, telling him that everything being done was meant as an act of love. He used to exhort us to "take exquisite, affectionate care of your tabernacles." When he stopped doing this personally, he instructed his priest sons to fulfill this duty with the greatest care, and, while doing so, to make spiritual communions and recite many aspirations.

From the beginning he laid it down that the amices, purificators, and hand towels were to be washed and ironed after every time they were used: this is a norm that has always been lived in our centers, as a sign of love of God and of respect for the Holy

Sacrifice. A cardinal who visited our teaching hospital at the University of Navarre (an institution founded and run by members of Opus Dei) later told me what had really impressed him. While making his tour of the various departments, he happened to see in one room a pile of white cloths, very carefully stacked in baskets, and he asked what they were. The answer was that they were the sacred linens which had been used that morning, and that they were about to be washed and ironed for the next day's Masses.

His love for the Eucharist was apparent in so many particulars, even in the way he would go about setting the flowers beside the tabernacle. He told us: "When you place a flower near the tabernacle, give it a kiss and say to the Lord that you would like that kiss to be consumed along with the flower, to be used up just like the candle of the sanctuary lamp gets used up, as it shows people, with its flame, that God is here."

> In the filmed recordings of the founder's get-togethers with various groups, some of these groups numbering in the thousands—get-togethers which took place, especially in the last years of his life, in many different cities of Europe and Latin America—reference to the sacrament of Penance is never omitted. The Father's teaching on this "sacrament of joy," as he liked to call it, is especially moving.

Yes, he spoke a lot about confession, and he called it "the sacrament of joy" because it brings us back to God; it gives back to us the divine friendship lost by sin. He exhorted his priest sons to make the ministry of Penance a dominant passion of their lives, and he spurred on his lay children to bring many souls to confession. "Kill your priest brothers," he used to say, "by giving them lots of work—the work of helping many souls get reconciled with God."

He had a real passion for administering the sacrament of Penance. Right after his ordination, during his stay at Perdiguera, he succeeded in bringing to confession practically all the inhabitants of that village. When he moved to Saragossa, he continued to administer this sacrament with great assiduousness. I remember being present, in 1970, when our founder was visiting one of his friends from that city, a man who had gone on to enjoy a brilliant political career. This man said, "I went to confession to you"—as old friends, they spoke with the familiar "tu"—"before you joined my wife and me in matrimony. I recall that while I was accusing myself of my sins, you remained silent. But then, when I mentioned that I had fought in a duel, you exclaimed, 'You're out of your mind!'" He then remarked that nobody had ever reprimanded him so openly, but that at the same time he had always been grateful to him for having done it with so much charity that he did not feel offended, but instead ended up very sorry for his sin. Our founder remained silent through this whole account. He didn't add a single word, because, even though it was the penitent himself who was speaking, the Father knew that he, the priest, was bound by the seal of confession.

When he moved to Madrid, he went from one end of the city to the other to hear the confessions of as many sick people as possible, and to bring them Holy Communion. It was a mission that he carried out with a heroic generosity, a commitment into which he put all his energy. Sometimes he did not have enough money even to ride the streetcar, or to eat.

Later on, he loved to reminisce about these years when he was able to dedicate so much of his time to preparing thousands of children for first confession and Communion. He had, he said, gained many fruitful insights for his own spiritual life from the devotion of those little ones.

After October 2, 1928, he continued his priestly ministry at the Patronato de Enfermos [Foundation for the Sick], and later at the Real Patronato de Santa Isabel [Royal Foundation of St. Elizabeth]. In the church of the latter, quite a number of people went to him for confession. During these years he also gave spiritual direction to a large number of university students.

During the Spanish Civil War, he heard confessions out on the street, and going from house to house. He did not shrink from the danger of death that surrounded him: he willingly ran the risk that at any time somebody hostile to the Church might see him, identify him as a priest, and turn him in to the authorities.

In the last years of his life he was no longer able to exercise the apostolate of confession directly, because he had to devote himself entirely to governing the Work. This is not to say that he did not continue to carry out his priestly ministry intensely—certainly he did, especially through the homilies he gave to his sons and daughters, and through the care he gave to many other persons who came to him for spiritual direction. But he did not administer the sacrament of Penance to anyone but me. I would like to explain at this point that most of the people he dealt with were members of the Work. He preferred not to hear their confessions, because he did not want to find himself hamstrung by the seal of the confessional; he wanted to keep the greatest possible freedom of action. I was the one and only exception: our founder came to me for confession, and I went to him.

He preached incessantly on this sacrament. In his last years it caused him great suffering to see how the practice of frequent confession was being more and more neglected by the faithful: this inspired him to an even more insistent catechesis on the greatness of God's mercy. He energetically refuted those who said that children's first confession should be delayed because it could be a traumatic experience. He spoke of having heard the confessions of thousands of children who, far from suffering a shock, experienced with gratitude the goodness of the Lord. He gave this advice to mothers: "Mamas, take your children to confession, as my mama did me. That way, your children can easily get used to receiving the sacrament of Penance and being reconciled with God. By receiving this sacrament with all the dispositions required for a good confession, a child will acquire an ever more delicate conscience and will become happier."

He so well taught his priest sons to administer this sacrament with unstinting zeal that our Holy Father, Pope John Paul II, has affirmed that the priests of Opus Dei have "the charism of confession." I had the joy of personally hearing him say this. You can imagine my gladness at so authoritative a recognition of the efforts of members of the Work to imitate their founder.

Our Father used to say that the best way to live the virtue of penitence was to approach the sacrament of Reconciliation with true contrition. He saw a need to compensate, by his own compunction, for the many failures to love which he witnessed daily.

An eagerness to make reparation is one of the ways in which the communion of saints expresses itself. I remember one time, the sinful life of a public personality had just come to light, and one of us exclaimed, "Poor man!"—but our founder immediately replied, "Poor God!" This was not a sign of indifference or of a lack of charity towards that sinner, but rather a proof of our Father's love for God and of the degree of his hatred for sin of any kind, even the smallest sin you could imagine. "Poor God!"—because he is a father being offended by one of his children. Of course, our founder began immediately to pray for that unfortunate man.

The fear of God and the hatred of sin stirred him to repeat very often Psalm 51:17, "Cor contritum et humiliatum, Deus, non despicies" ["A contrite and humble heart, O God, you will not spurn"], and he would add, with emphasis and with a lively sorrow for his own faults, "Contritum et humiliatum valde!" ["Very contrite and humble!"]. I observed all this personally, from when I first met him to the day he died.

The familiarity of our founder with Sacred Scripture is evident in his published homilies and notably in his book Holy Rosary, *which is filled with vivid examples of his teaching about placing oneself as an eyewitness in the scenes of the Gospel. Do you have any reminiscences on this topic?*

Indeed, the Father gave constant proof of an extraordinary veneration for Sacred Scripture. The Holy Bible, together with the tradition of the Church, was the source from which he ceaselessly drew for his personal prayer and preaching.

Every day he read some pages—about a chapter—of Scripture, generally from the New Testament, and then did some additional spiritual reading, usually from the writings of the fathers and doctors of the Church. It rarely happened that he didn't pause from time to time to take note of some expression or idea which had struck him: a sign not only of the attention with which he carried out this pious practice, but also of the importance which he gave to it.

In 1944 he preached a retreat for the Augustinians of the Monastery of El Escorial, even though he was quite ill. One of the participants, Fr. Licinio González, noting that it was only after the retreat that he had realized our founder had been ill, gave this testimony: "His meditations were characterized by the continuous use of texts from the Gospel: passages which, through his voice, came newly alive and full of inspiration. . . .

"The thoughts and ideas of Msgr. Escrivá on vocation, on gratitude for vocation, on the joyful response of St. Andrew, and on the sorrowful refusal of the rich young man—these are all still alive in me. . . .

"The meditations on our Lady and on St. Joseph were also full of spiritual energy. Together with the Eucharistic meditation on the Last Supper, they left me with an impression so deep that it has not faded with the passage of the years."

The Father meditated assiduously upon the verses of the New Testament and called attention to certain aspects of them, some of which had gone unnoticed for centuries. He viewed Sacred Scripture not as an inert deposit, but rather as a living instrument which the Lord uses to infuse supernatural life into those who read it with humility and a desire to learn. My witness to all this goes back to the day I first met him, but it was especially after my ordination (in 1944) that I came to understand how deeply he meditated on the word of God.

An eloquent proof of this is the originality of his comments on the sacred texts. They are always immediate, and singularly incisive. These are not pragmatic conclusions, derived from a reflection on the Scriptures for the purpose of being introduced later into a prefabricated spirituality; nor are they simply elaborations given to buttress the concepts of a previously defined system of thought. No—our Father allows the Gospel to speak directly, with all its power. His spirituality is the life of Christ himself, his life as an individual and as manifested in the lives of the first Christians—lives which express their own perennial topicality without need of adaptations, additions, or glosses.

When our founder died, Cardinal Parente, who had read some of his homilies and other writings, remarked to me that in our Father's commentaries on Sacred Scripture he had encountered a spiritual richness of a profundity and immediacy often superior even to that found in the works of the fathers of the Church.

His preaching was always very practical; it moved souls to conversion. He had the gift of knowing how to apply passages of the Old and New Testaments to the concrete, day-to-day situations of his listeners. He never sought to be original, because he was convinced that the word of God is, of itself, always new, and that it keeps intact all its own irresistible force of attraction, provided it is proclaimed with faith. On his lips, the Gospel was never an erudite text or a mere source of quotations or platitudes. He spoke of Sacred Scripture with a tender love. An example of this is these words of his which I took down in 1954: "'There was a virgin who lived in Nazareth, and her name was Mary' [see Lk 1:26–27]. How beautiful, how divine and how human the Gospel is! It goes into the most minute particulars to show us God's predilection for his creatures. He loves her, he seeks her out, and, as a sign of affection, he calls her by name: 'Mary'!"

I was myself always impressed with the facility with which he could cite from memory exact phrases from the Holy Bible. Even during everyday conversations, he would often take a starting point from some pertinent text in order to inspire us to a more profound prayer. He lived on the word of God. One sign of his reverence for Sacred Scripture was his habit of introducing his quotations with the words "The Holy Spirit says . . ." It was not just a manner of speaking; it was a heartfelt act of faith which helped us really feel the eternal validity of, and the solid weight of truth behind, expressions which might otherwise have sounded overly familiar.

The meditative reading of Sacred Scripture is an essential practice of piety for all members of the Work. But I remember well how the Father, when he was preparing for ordination the first three of us to become priests of the Work (José María Hernández de Garnica, José Luis Múzquiz, and myself), counseled us to dedicate still more time to attentively reading and meditating on the Scriptures. He insistently entreated us to approach the Scriptures with much faith, because only in this way, only by taking our own souls to this sweet encounter with Christ, would we be able to "infect" others with a love for him and a desire for identification with him.

In the last years of his life, wanting to help make more widespread the habit of reading the Bible, and to facilitate meditation on it as much as possible, he encouraged his sons who were teaching theology at the University of Navarre to prepare an annotated edition for the general public. He wanted the notes to be straightforward, practical, and accessible to all; to have a doctrinal and ascetical slant, rather than an erudite tone; and to include abundant quotations from the Church fathers and councils. From this has emerged a work, still in progress, that will be quite valuable from a scholarly point of view, but even more so from a spiritual point of view. The specialists working on this project assure me that their inclusion of numerous quotations from texts of the founder will contribute significantly to the pastoral value of this edition.

10. Devotions

In The Forge, *our Father wrote: "Learn to praise the Father, the Son, and the Holy Spirit. Learn to have a special devotion to the Blessed Trinity: I believe in God the Father, I believe in God the Son, I believe in God the Holy Spirit; I hope in God the Father, I hope in God the Son, I hope in God the Holy Spirit; I love God the Father, I love God the Son, I love God the Holy Spirit. I believe in, I hope in, and I love the Most Holy Trinity.*

"This devotion is much needed as a supernatural exercise for the soul, expressed by the movement of the heart, although not always in words" (No. 296).

The advice given here undoubtedly originated in the interior life of the founder; perhaps it could serve as a starting point from which you could speak to us about his personal devotions.

The Father used to say, even to the first members of Opus Dei, that to grow in the interior life, "one good method is to consecrate each day of the week to a single devotion: to the Most Holy Trinity, to the Eucharist, to the Passion, to our Lady, to St. Joseph, to the holy guardian angels, to the holy souls in purgatory." This advice flowed, as always, from his personal experience; in fact, he had been living it for many years. I can vouch for the fact that these were his principal devotions: (1) the Most Holy Trinity, God One and Three (he conversed with each of the three Persons, one by one: the Father, the Son, and the Holy Spirit); (2) our Lord Jesus Christ: above all, his presence in the Eucharist, his Passion, and the years of his hidden life; (3) the Blessed Virgin Mary; (4) St. Joseph; (5) the holy angels and archangels; and (6) the saints: in particular, the twelve apostles; the saints whom he chose as intercessors for certain aspects of the apostolate of the Work (Catherine of Siena, Nicholas of Bari, Thomas More, Pope Pius X, and the Curé of Ars); such other saints as Anthony the Abbot and Teresa of Jesus; and the early Christians.

His love for the Blessed Trinity expressed itself in a myriad of details. For example, when Villa Tevere (the headquarters of Opus Dei) was being built, he wanted the oratory in which he would regularly be saying Mass to be dedicated to the Trinity. I remember also that when the Nativity crèche for the "Gallerìa del Fumo" was being prepared (this was the large room where we would gather as a family after our meals), the Father asked that another angel be added to the eight that were already there. "Then," he explained, "there will be nine of them: three for each Person of the Blessed Trinity."

The founder sought to inculcate in his children a great love for the Trinity. For this reason, in addition to beginning the daily prayers of the Work with an invocation to the Blessed Trinity, he directed that on the third Sunday of every month, the Athanasian Creed would be recited and meditated upon, and that on the three days preceding the feast of the Blessed Trinity, the Angelic Trisagium would be recited or, even better, sung.

Those of us who lived at his side knew well the depth of this devotion of his. I remember being able to figure out, simply by taking this devotion into account, how to win the "lotteries" that he occasionally set up. This is a little family memory that goes back to the first years of my vocation. From time to time the Father would bring to our get-togethers a little extra something, so we'd have an even better time—a box of candy, for example. And every now and then, if there was something special that could only be given to one person, the Father would organize a "lottery," played by guessing the number he was thinking of. I noticed rather soon that the number was always three or a multiple of three. So even in these moments of fun, his love for the Blessed Trinity showed through.

His tendency to use especially the number three or the number nine was shown in many other particulars. Perhaps most significant was the number of points he included in *The Way:* 999.

During a private audience, Pope Paul VI asked him the reason for this number. The founder replied, "It's for love of the Most Holy Trinity." I recall that for the first edition of *The Way*, he had a book jacket designed in a style that at that time was quite unusual: it featured a column of silhouetted number nines.

The commentary written by our Father on the Stations of the Cross is a touching testimony to his love for, and his devotion to, the sacred humanity of Christ.

From the time I first met him, I noticed that not only during his personal prayer, but also whenever he preached a meditation or gave a class, and all the time he spent working at his desk, he kept before him a crucifix—and always the same one. It was of a fairly good size, four or five inches in length, but (until about 1950) he constantly carried it around in his pocket. His brother, Santiago, struck by the size of it, used to say (borrowing a term used to describe pistols in the military) that it was a "regulation" crucifix. You might say that the crucifix was, in fact, the weapon of our founder.

At the end of the civil war, on his return to Madrid with the troops that liberated the city, many people approached him to kiss his hand, since for three years they hadn't seen a priest in a cassock; he gave them the crucifix to kiss instead. This happened often in those times. He also advised us always to carry a crucifix with us and to place it in front of us before beginning to study, to read, to work, and so forth, in order to remain in the presence of God and thus transform our work into prayer, uniting it to the sacrifice of the cross.

In his last years, he commissioned the Roman sculptor Sciancalepore to represent Christ on the cross, but still alive, and as he was just before his death: he wanted his eyes to be open, and looking toward those who were praying at his feet. He ordered two copies of this sculpture, one for a shrine being built at Cavabianca, the seat of the Roman College of the Holy Cross, and the other for a chapel at Torreciudad. I think this gives an insight into our founder's spirit: he wanted people to contemplate the crucified

Christ in that moment, just before his death, when he looks at each one of us and says, "I am suffering all of this for you." In other words, he was exhorting us to think about divine justice, to look at the Lord as he says to us sinners, "This is for you—my sufferings are for you; if you don't correct yourself, you will remain separated from God always, in hell"; but at the same time he was encouraging us to consider God's love, as he looks at us and pleads, "All these sufferings are for you—you must help me to redeem; do not offend me anymore."

His Eucharistic devotion was extremely intense, even in his childhood. When he was just a toddler, he learned from one of his grandmothers this simple and touching verse: "Las doce han dado, Jesús no viene, ¿quién será el dichoso que lo detiene?" ["The clock has struck twelve, Jesus hasn't come yet: who is the lucky one who is detaining him?"]. Sometimes he would use that nursery rhyme to express his desire to be near our Lord in the Blessed Sacrament.

As I already mentioned, he considered the Mass the "center and root of the interior life." He also spread the custom, mentioned in point No. 876 of *The Way*, of "storming" tabernacles.

In a letter written to his sons on September 17, 1934, from Monzón, the Father described in this way the train trip he was taking: "Ever since we got out of Madrid, I've been spending my time playing a divine game: searching the horizon for churches, so that I can say something to Jesus in the tabernacles we pass by. And this morning I recited the Breviary with more solemnity than a choir in a cathedral: I invited all the guardian angels in my compartment to sing praises to the Lord with me. Don't ever neglect the guardian angels, my sons!" I remember myself how, soon after I requested admission to Opus Dei in 1935, he taught me to get into the habit of greeting the Lord in the tabernacles I encountered when going from place to place.

You mentioned recitation of the Breviary. Can you tell us more?

He never put it off for any reason. An incident comes to mind that took place in 1942 or 1943. Our founder was ill, and yet, even though he had a very high fever, he wanted to recite the Divine Office. I told him that in his condition he was not obliged to do so, but he replied, "Listen, you're not in a position to tell me that, because you're not yet a priest. I don't want to do anything different without actual authorization. So please do me a favor and call my confessor, Fr. José María Lahiguera; explain the situation to him, and I'll do whatever he says." That's what I did, and Fr. José María answered that the Father did not have to say the Divine Office; but he gave that answer only after asking me a number of questions—about the fever, the type of illness, and so on—which surprised me, because I thought the answer was obvious right from the start. Anyway, the founder then decided to recite some vocal prayers that he knew by heart. Several years later, as a result of his diabetes, his sight became so impaired that he could hardly read; the letters were blurry, and he was seeing double. At that time he asked Fr. Javier Echevarría and myself to recite the Divine Office aloud, so that he could join in on our prayer.

> *Let's return to his Trinitarian devotion. In a famous homily, now published in the volume* Christ Is Passing By, *our Father called the Holy Spirit "the Great Unknown."*

Precisely because the Third Person of the Trinity is the least invoked, our Father had a special devotion to him. I can tell you without any exaggeration that the Father, especially in his preaching, was a great herald of the Third Person of the Blessed Trinity. I remember, for example, that in 1971 I was in Rome with him when a priest of the Work arrived, who was going to preach a retreat in L'Aquila [a city in central Italy]. Our founder made this suggestion to him: "Take with you a treatise of *De Deo Trino* [a manual on the theology of the Trinity] and pour into their hearts love for the Holy Spirit, and, thereby, love for the Father and for the Son. It's all connected because, from all eternity, the Son is begotten from the Father, and from the love of the Father and the Son proceeds the Holy Spirit. We will never understand this fully, but it doesn't cost me any effort to believe it. Every day I seek to go more deeply into the mystery of the Blessed Trinity."

The founder often told me that ever since 1926 or 1927 he
had lived an intense devotion to the Third Person of the Blessed
Trinity. Every year he made the Ten Days' Devotion to the Holy
Spirit, using the book written by Francisca Javiera del Valle. In
April of 1934 he composed a prayer to the Paraclete; he then gave
this prayer, in manuscript form, to Ricardo Fernández Vallespín, at
that time director of the first Opus Dei residence.

In the early years of his priesthood, he used holy cards instead of ribbons to mark the pages in his Breviary. One day he got
the feeling that he was becoming attached to these cards, so he
promptly got rid of them and started using strips of paper instead.
On more than one occasion he said to me, "As soon as I saw those
little blank strips, I started writing on them, 'Ure igne Sancti Spiritus!' ['Burn with the fire of the Holy Spirit!']." They served, in
short, as a most efficacious reminder to recite the Divine Office in
union with the Holy Spirit. "I used them," he said, "for many
years, and every time I read them, it was as if I were saying to the
Holy Spirit, 'Inflame me! Make me become a fire!'"

As a consequence of erroneous interpretations of the Second Vatican Council, errors put forth by certain theologians, a
tremendous confusion enveloped many ecclesiastical institutions,
to such an extent that the Holy Father Paul VI sadly referred to
this phenomenon as a "decomposition of the Church." Words cannot describe how our Father suffered on account of this situation.
His sorrow prompted him to intensify his prayer to the Paraclete—to the point where, on May 30, 1971, he consecrated Opus
Dei to the Holy Spirit. In the long formula composed by him for
the occasion, he included this invocation: "We beseech you to assist your Church always, and especially the Roman pontiff, so that
he may guide us with his word and example and may reach eternal life together with the flock which has been entrusted to him; so
that good pastors may never be lacking; and so that all your faithful, after serving you with holiness of life and integrity of faith,
may attain to the glory of heaven."

*Opus Dei was founded (in 1928) on October 2—the feast of
the Guardian Angels. The devotion of our Father to the celes-*

tial protectors and messengers, a devotion going back to his
childhood, was well founded and quite understandable.

Yes, the Father learned from his parents to have recourse to
his guardian angel. Then later on, as a seminarian, he read in a
book by one of the fathers of the Church that priests have, in addition to a guardian angel, a ministerial archangel as well; and so,
from the day of his ordination, he turned to this archangel with
great simplicity and confidence. In fact, he said he felt certain that
even if the author he had read turned out to have been mistaken,
our Lord would have given him a ministerial archangel anyway,
just because of the faith with which he always invoked him.

In any case, after the feast of the Guardian Angels in 1928,
the founder had a more intense devotion to them. He was always telling his children, "Familiarity with, and devotion to,
the holy guardian angels is at the heart of our work. It is a concrete manifestation of the supernatural mission of Opus Dei."

Convinced that God has placed an angel beside each and every
human being to help that person along the road of life, he had recourse to his own guardian angel for all his material and spiritual
needs. He would often say, quite frankly, "For years I've experienced the constant and immediate assistance of my guardian angel,
even in the smallest material particulars." In the years between 1928
and 1940, his alarm clock sometimes didn't work and he didn't have
the money to repair it, so he turned in trust to his guardian angel
and asked him to wake him up in the morning at the right time. His
angel never once failed him. And that's why our Father affectionately called him "mi relojerico" ["my dear watchmaker"].

Whenever he greeted our Lord in the tabernacle, he always
thanked the angels who were present there, for the unceasing adoration that they give to God. On more than one occasion I heard
him say, "When I go into one of our chapels, one that has a tabernacle, I tell Jesus that I love him, and I invoke the Trinity. Then I
thank the angels who guard the tabernacle and adore Christ in the
Eucharist."

With an unflagging correspondence to the grace of God, he
acquired the habit of always greeting the guardian angels of the

persons he met: he used to say that he greeted the "personage" first. One day in 1972 or 1973, the retired archbishop of Valencia, the Most Reverend Marcelino Olaechea, came to visit him, accompanied by his secretary. They were very good friends, so the Father greeted him and then asked him playfully, "Marcelino, let's see if you can guess—who did I greet first?" The archbishop replied, "First? That would be me, I'm sure." "No," the Father said, "I greeted the personage first." Archbishop Olaechea, understandably perplexed, replied, "But of the two of us, my secretary and me, I am the 'personage.'" Then our founder explained, "No, the personage is your guardian angel."

During some days of rest that we spent in a rented house in a village in Lombardy—I can't remember whether it was Caglio or Civenna—we would play bocce ball every so often, to get a little exercise. Since we didn't know the rules of the game too well, at times we would make up our own. I remember that during one of these games, the Father threw a ball unusually well and made an exceptional score. But he said immediately, "That doesn't count—I was helped by my guardian angel. I won't do that anymore . . ." I tell this little story because I consider it indicative of the constant friendly rapport he had with his guardian angel, and also of his humility; as he later told me directly, he was ashamed of having asked his angel for help in such an unimportant matter.

> Our Father liked the pictures and statues of St. Joseph in which the saint is represented as having vigorous, virile features. In one of his published homilies he said, "I don't agree with the traditional picture of St. Joseph as an old man, even though it may have been prompted by a desire to emphasize the perpetual virginity of Mary. I see him as a strong young man, perhaps a few years older than our Lady, but in the prime of his life and work" (Christ Is Passing By, No. 40). Devotion to the holy Patriarch was very deeply rooted in him.

Yes, it was—and it was well known. When Pope John XXIII decided to include St. Joseph in the canon of the Mass, Cardinal Larraona thought immediately of our founder; he phoned him to tell him the news and to congratulate him, certain that he would be thrilled.

Let me tell you about two incidents that took place during his trip to South America in 1974. In Ecuador someone showed him a painting of the Quito school, a painting which represented the child Jesus in the act of crowning the holy Patriarch, St. Joseph, with a garland of flowers. This picture filled our founder with an immense joy. "What a marvel! I am very happy," he exclaimed, "because it has taken me years to discover a good theology of St. Joseph, and here I don't have to do anything but open my eyes to see it confirmed! This is great!"

During that trip our founder began to speak of the mysterious presence—"ineffable," he called it—of Mary and Joseph beside all the tabernacles of the world. He reasoned in this way: if the Blessed Virgin Mary never in this life separated herself from her Son, then it's only logical that she should have continued to stay by his side even after he decided to remain in that "prison of love" that is the tabernacle: to adore him, to love him, to pray for us. And he applied the same reasoning to St. Joseph: he had always stood by Jesus and by his own spouse; he had had the good fortune to die accompanied by them—what a marvelous death! That is why the Father often said that he would accept death when, how, and where the Lord wanted it for him, but that he prayed that when it came to him, he would be in the company of St. Joseph: he wanted to die like he did, in the arms of Jesus and Mary. In sum, our founder truly brought St. Joseph into everything.

But there was still something of a gap in all this togetherness with St. Joseph: what to do so as not to leave him out when it came to meditating on the events of Calvary? In Brazil, while we were going somewhere by car, the Father discovered the solution, and he told it to us as soon as we got home. "I've got it!" he said. "I will put myself there in place of him—that's the answer!" The Father put himself at the foot of the cross as if he were St. Joseph, and he tried to imagine what the Patriarch would have said to Christ, if he had been nearby while the Lord was dying for us: words of reparation, of sorrow, of love.

Our Father loved traditional devotions, and he practiced many of them. Did he use any little practical devices to keep from forgetting them?

During his stay in Perdiguera (shortly after his ordination), something often happened that greatly puzzled one of the altar boys, Teodoro Murillo. From time to time, Fr. Josemaría would invite him to go on a walk with him, and would take advantage of the opportunity to explain to him some aspect of Christian doctrine. But as they were walking, Teodoro noticed, this priest would often bend down, pick up a pebble, and put it in his pocket—and never say a word in explanation.

Well, as soon as I heard this, I was able to clear up the mystery. You see, way back when I requested admission to the Work and our founder explained to me the spirit of Opus Dei, he encouraged me to say many aspirations, to make many spiritual communions, and to offer up many small mortifications during the day. And on the subject of aspirations he told me this: "There are spiritual authors who recommend counting the aspirations one says over the course of the day, using beans, chickpeas, or something similar; they suggest putting them in one pocket and moving them to the other whenever you raise your heart to God with one of these prayers. In this way you can see exactly how many prayers you have said, and whether or not progress has been made that day." Then he added, "But I don't recommend this to you, because there is also the danger of vanity or pride. It is better to let your guardian angel do the counting."

Obviously the Father, while he was in Perdiguera, was using this little device to see how well he was living the presence of God. But he afterwards abandoned this practice, presumably for the very reason he gave me.

However, he did continue to recite many aspirations. Could you tell us which ones he said most often?

There's no way I could give a complete list. Usually he drew them from Scripture or from the treasury of Christian tradition, but they were always intimately connected to his interior life, and so they varied in response to it. At times, in fact, he would change some of their words to adapt them better to the circumstances of a certain day or special period of time . . . The point I want to make is, basically, that he always put his whole heart into them; all the devotion and intensity of which he was capable. Here are some of them:

"Sweet heart of Jesus, be my love!"

"Sweet heart of Mary, be my salvation!"

"Domine, fac cum servo tuo secundum magnam misericordiam tuam" ["Lord, deal with your servant according to your great mercy"].

"Sancte Pater omnipotens, aeterne et misericors Deus: Beata Maria intercedente, gratias tibi ago pro universis beneficiis tuis, etiam ignotis" ["Holy Father almighty, eternal and merciful God, by the intercession of the Blessed Virgin Mary I thank you for all your benefits, even those unknown to me"].

"Cor Iesu sacratissimum et misericors, dona nobis pacem" ["Most sacred and merciful heart of Jesus, grant us peace"]. He began to recite this aspiration to the heart of Jesus around 1950, and in 1951 this other one to the heart of Mary: "Cor Mariae dulcissimum, iter para tutum" ["Sweetest heart of Mary, provide a safe path"].

"Benedicamus Patrem et Filium cum Sancto Spiritu" ["Let us bless the Father and the Son with the Holy Spirit"].

He often renewed a fervent prayer of his years in Logroño, "Domine, ut videam!" ["Lord, that I might see!" (Mk 10:51)], with some variations: "Domine, ut sit!" ["Lord, let it be!"]; "Domina, ut videam!" ["Lady, that I might see!"]; "Domina, ut sit!" ["Lady, let it be!"].

He used to repeat the aspiration "Domine, tu omnia nosti, tu scis quia amo te!" ["Lord, you know all things, you know that I love you!" (Jn 21:17)], not only as an act of love, but also as an act of contrition.

"I am yours, I was born for you; what is it, Jesus, that you want of me?"

"Jesus, I love you."

"Glory to the Father, glory to the Son, glory to the Holy Spirit!

Glory to holy Mary, and also to St. Joseph! Thanks be to the angels who attend you!"

"Lord, I abandon myself to you, I trust in you, I rest in you."

"I believe in God the Father, I believe in God the Son, I believe in God the Holy Spirit. I hope in God the Father, I hope in God the Son, I hope in God the Holy Spirit. I love God the Father, I love God the Son, I love God the Holy Spirit." He had this triple-triple invocation stamped upon thousands of pictures.

"Iesu, Iesu, esto mihi semper Iesus" ["Jesus, Jesus, always be Jesus to me"].

"Tu es sacerdos in aeternum" ["You are a priest forever" (Ps 110:4)].

"Quod bonum est oculis eius, faciat" ["Whatever is good in his eyes, let him do it" (1 Sm 3:18)]. He used to repeat this aspiration as an act of humble acceptance of the will of God, no matter what it was—even if it was the opposite of what he had been thinking.

"Monstra te esse matrem!" ["Show yourself to be a mother!"].

"Mother, my Mother!"

"Sancta Maria, refugium nostrum et virtus!" ["Holy Mary, our refuge and our strength!"].

"Holy Mary, hold back the day!" According to tradition, during the siege of Seville led by King St. Ferdinand III, some Christian knights invoked the Blessed Mother with this prayer, asking her to help them achieve victory over the Muslims. The sun then slowed down its progress, and they were able to defeat the enemy. Our founder advised us to use this aspiration to ask for help in finishing our daily work with order and tenacity.

"Sancta Maria, filios tuos adiuva; filias tuas adiuva" ["Holy Mary, help your sons, and help your daughters"].

"Sancta Maria, spes nostra, sedes sapientiae, ora pro nobis" ["Holy Mary, our hope, seat of wisdom, pray for us"].

"Sancta Maria, spes nostra, ancilla Domini, filias tuas adiuva" ["Holy Mary, our hope, handmaid of the Lord, help your daughters"].

"Sancta Maria, regina Operis Dei, filios tuos adiuva" ["Holy Mary, queen of Opus Dei, help your children"].

"Sancta Maria, stella orientis, filios tuos adiuva" ["Holy Mary, star of the East, help your children"]. He began to recite this prayer during his first trip to Vienna, in 1955.

"Dominus tecum" ["The Lord be with you" (2 Thes 3:16)].

"Sancti angeli custodes nostri, defendite nos" ["Our holy guardian angels, defend us"].

"St. Joseph, our father and lord, bless all the children of the holy Church of God."

"Adeamus cum fiducia ad thronum gloriae, ut misericordiam Dei consequamur" ["Let us go with confidence to the throne of glory, to attain the mercy of God" (see Heb 4:16)].

"Hail, Mary most pure, conceived without sin."

He often recited the antiphon "Sub tuum praesidium confugimus . . ." ["We fly to your protection . . ."], or simply the words "Nostras deprecationes ne despicias" ["Despise not our petitions"]; I remember his repeating these words with a special intensity during the seventies.

"Blessed be the Mother who brought you into the world" [Lk 11:27].

"Cor Mariae perdolentis, miserere nobis; miserere mei" ["Sorrowful heart of Mary, have mercy on us; have mercy on me"].

"Beata Mater et intacta Virgo, intercede pro nobis" ["Blessed Mother and inviolate Virgin, intercede for us"].

"Omnia in bonum!" ["All for the good!"]. He had copies of this, and of a number of the other prayers I've mentioned, made in many of our centers. This one he had printed on thousands of cards, as a way of encouraging people to accept always the will of God and to live in Christian hope.

"Semper ut iumentum!" ["Always like a beast of burden!"].

"Ut iumentum factus sum apud te" ["I have become like a beast of burden before you"]. At times he would add the next few words of this psalm [73]—"Et ego semper tecum; tenuisti manum dexteram meam, et in voluntate tua deduxisti me, et cum gloria suscepisti me"—and translate all this as, "Lord, I want to stand before you like a donkey; but you have taken me by the bridle and have brought me along, and will receive me into your glory."

"Fiat, adimpleatur, laudetur, et in aeternum superexaltetur iustissima atque amabilissima voluntas Dei super omnia. Amen. Amen!" ["May the most righteous and most lovable will of God be done, accomplished, praised, and eternally exalted above all things. Amen. Amen!"].

"I believe more than if I saw you with my own eyes, more than if I heard you with my own ears, more than if I touched you with my own hands."

"Ut in gratiarum semper actione maneamus!" ["May we always remain in an act of thanksgiving!"]. He often took this aspiration, and others that I have mentioned here, as nourishment for his mental prayer and the meditations which he preached.

"Montes, sicut cera, fluxerunt a facie Domini" ["The mountains dissolved like wax before the face of the Lord" (Ps 97:5)]. He used this prayer to reinforce his own hope in times of great difficulty.

"Qui tribulant me, inimici mei, ipsi infirmati sunt et ceciderunt" ["Those who trouble me—my enemies—themselves have grown weak and have fallen" (Ps 27:2)].

"Servi inutiles sumus: quod debuimus facere fecimus" ["We are useless servants: we have only done what we ought to have done" (Lk 17:10)].

"Oportet semper orare, et non deficere" ["It is well always to pray, without ceasing" (Lk 18:1)].

"Ure igne Sancti Spiritus!" ["Burn with the fire of the Holy Spirit!"].

"Veni, Sancte Spiritus, reple tuorum corda fidelium, et tui amoris in eis ignem accende" ["Come, Holy Spirit, fill the hearts of your faithful, and enkindle in them the fire of your love"].

"Oportet illum crescere, me autem minui" ["He must increase, I must decrease" (Jn 3:30)]. He used this aspiration to promote, in himself and in his children, an attitude of both personal and collective humility.

He often repeated the prayer to St. Michael the Archangel which used to be recited after Mass: "St. Michael the Archangel, defend us in battle; be our protection against the wickedness and snares of the devil. May God rebuke him, we humbly pray, and do you, O Prince of the Heavenly Host, by the power of God, thrust into hell Satan and all the other evil spirits who prowl about the world, seeking the ruin of souls. Amen."

He also frequently recited this prayer for the pope: "Oremus pro Beatissimo Papa nostro N. . . . Dominus conservet eum, et vivificet eum, et beatum faciat eum in terra, et non tradat eum in animam inimicorum eius" ["Let us pray for our Most Holy Father *N.* . . . . May the Lord preserve him, and give him life, and make him blessed on this earth, and not hand him over to the will of his enemies"].

"My God! Let me hate sin and be united to you, may I embrace your holy cross, so that I in my turn may fulfill your most lovable will . . . , stripped of all earthly affection, seeking nothing but your glory . . . , generously, not keeping anything for myself, offering myself with you as a perfect holocaust."

"Come, Holy Spirit! Enlighten my understanding so that I may know your commands; strengthen my heart against the ambushes of the enemy; inflame my will. . . . I have heard your voice, and I don't want to harden my heart by resisting, by saying 'later . . . tomorrow.' *Nunc coepi!* [I begin now!] *Now!* Let there be no 'tomorrow' for me! O Spirit of truth and wisdom, Spirit of understanding and counsel, Spirit of joy and peace, I want what you want, I want it because and as and when you want it. . . ." In our archives we keep a copy of this prayer, which was written by the Father himself, in April 1934.

With the help of these and other short vocal prayers, our Father kept himself interiorly recollected throughout the day. These favorite prayers of his have spread throughout the world; thousands and thousands of individuals have made them their own. Our founder never sought to impose them on anyone; he wanted expressions of love to come freely from the heart of each individual. Yet so great was his love, and so lively his example, that all his sons and daughters have sought to imitate it; and not only they, the members of Opus Dei, but many other friends of his as well.

> *Even though this topic has already been touched upon in the answer you just gave, I would like you to put a nice finishing touch to this chapter by speaking to us of the Marian devotion of our Father, so central to his own life and to the life of the Work.*

To respond fully to this request, one would have to write a treatise! But I'll do what I can.

It is important, first of all, to keep in mind that the founder of Opus Dei, endowed as he was with a very rich sensibility, was not inclined to sentimentality. Even his Marian devotion, therefore, was distinguished by the profundity of its theological content. By this I mean that it was based not so much on "reasons of the heart" as on faith—faith, that is, in the prerogatives given by God to our Lady and in her role in our redemption.

To give you some idea—when St. Teresa of Avila, to whom he had a great devotion, was proclaimed a doctor of the Church, the Father pointed out that "she is not the first woman doctor of the Church. The first doctor, even though she does not have the title, is our Lady, because nobody else ever has had or could have such close dealings with God our Lord as she had and will always have. She must have been given, like nobody else, light from the Holy Spirit. She it is that knows most about God. She is the one with the greatest knowledge of God."

Our founder habitually concluded his homilies and meditations with an invocation to our Lady. In his book *Holy Rosary*, he has left very moving expressions of his contemplation of the principal mysteries of the lives of Jesus and Mary; his other books as well, beginning with *The Way*, are imbued with Marian devotion. Every chapter of *Furrow* and of *The Forge* ends with a thought about Mary.

He established the custom of placing in each room of each Opus Dei center a simple and artistically tasteful image of our Lady. He taught us to direct a glance towards it, and to give our Blessed Mother an affectionate interior prayer of greeting, whenever we enter or leave a room.

He visited countless Marian shrines. His pilgrimage to the Basilica of Our Lady of Guadalupe in Mexico City is of particular historical importance. He made this pilgrimage in May 1970, for the intention of asking the Blessed Virgin Mary to be mindful of the needs of the Church and to bring to completion the canonical journey of Opus Dei.

In December 1973, referring to his travels from one Marian shrine to another, he said emphatically, "I'm doing nothing but light candles, and I'm going to keep on doing that as long as I've got matches."

His love for the Blessed Virgin Mary impelled him to keep a close eye on everything connected with devotion to her. For example, whenever he commissioned a painting or a statue of our Lady with the baby Jesus, or a picture of the holy women at the foot of the cross, he recommended that the artist try, as much as possible, to make Jesus look like his mother. Christ must, after all, have looked a lot like Mary, since his conception in her womb did not involve a man, but came about through direct intervention by the Holy Spirit; but only a soul very much in love would have placed so much importance on this detail.

Our founder suggested placing in certain areas of our centers—laundry rooms and kitchens, for example—pictures that show our Lady doing washing, cooking, or feeding the child Jesus. In this way, those of his daughters whose chosen field of service is domestic administration can have a constant reminder of this ideal: that in all that they do to tend to the needs of the household, they should strive to imitate the Blessed Virgin Mary.

Our Father used to say to his daughters that since they didn't have a foundress, they ought to consider the Blessed Virgin Mary their foundress. And to ensure that they wouldn't forget this, he established that in all the women's centers, each chapel should be furnished with an image of our Lady.

If you wanted to be poetic about it, you could say that the last stone of his Marian devotion was the shrine of Torreciudad. He gave several specifications for the construction of this shrine. It was to be large; it was to have a good-sized altarpiece (it measures about one hundred thirty square meters), made of multicolored alabaster. In keeping with an ancient Aragonese custom, he had the tabernacle placed in the center of this altarpiece—raised up high, plainly visible from the nave, and accessible from behind the altar, so that the priest never has to turn his back on the Blessed Sacrament to say a Mass facing the people. The founder also saw to it that the crypt of the shrine would contain forty confessionals, distributed in various chapels, and that all of these chapels would be dedicated to our Lady, each of them under a different title. I would like to emphasize that the very idea of building such a shrine at this time—at the end of the sixties—constituted a solid proof of extraordinary faith. This is obvious when you think about the expense involved, the unpopularity of popular devotions in those years, and the location (far removed from any tourist route, or from any city of importance), in conjunction with the building of a large crypt for lots of confessionals, at a time when the practice of confession was in decline!

On May 23, 1975, our Father returned to Torreciudad for the last time. The buildings were nearly finished. Now able to observe the complex as a whole, he admired the originality of its construction and the majestic appearance of the altar. Above all, though, he was overjoyed with the altarpiece. "It's magnificent!" he exclaimed. "What sighs will be breathed here by elderly ladies . . . and by young people! Such sighs! Good! Only we crazy people of Opus Dei would do something like this—and we're very happy to be so crazy! Congratulations! You've done a great job. You've put so much love into all this. . . . But you must finish; you must bring this to completion. Don't act in haste, though; be sure to put a lot of care into placing the statue of our Lady properly." Visibly moved, he walked around to the other side of the altar, looked back at the nave, and exclaimed, "How well people will be able to pray here!"

The Blessed Virgin has rewarded the faith of our founder. Today the shrine attracts pilgrims not only from Spain and other countries of Europe, but from other continents as well. The forty confessionals are often not enough to accommodate all the penitents. Many who come to Torreciudad at first only out of curiosity end up having a real encounter with our Lord through a good confession. I've been told that comments like this are heard all the time: "I hadn't been to confession in forty years. I feel so good now!" The Father had prayed explicitly for this, for spiritual miracles of this kind to take place at Torreciudad. In 1968 he had said, "We shall not ask Our Lady of Torreciudad for external miracles. Instead, we shall ask her for many interior miracles: changes of heart; conversions."

It was the last homage that our Father was to pay to our Lady on this earth; a month later he was to be with her in heaven. It was the homage of a heart in love. During the Spanish Civil War, when he was compelled to use a pseudonym to trick the censors, he had (at first) used his fourth baptismal name, Mariano. Later, and for the rest of his life, he signed his name as "Josemaría," running together his first two baptismal names, in order not to separate Joseph from Mary.

11. Virtues Lived to a Heroic Degree

On April 9, 1990, Pope John Paul II promulgated the decree proclaiming the virtues lived to a heroic degree by the priest Josemaría Escrivá, founder of Opus Dei. Our Father did not like catalogs of virtues, because no catalog could be comprehensive; he lived and taught what he called "unity of life," that is, the harmony of the supernatural self with the natural virtues on which it is built and which form its necessary foundation. And he liked still less the idea of reducing sanctity to a mere exercise of certain select, almost stereotypical virtues. He preferred to emphasize the interconnection of the theological virtues (faith, hope, and charity) with the moral virtues (which can be traced back to the cardinal virtues: prudence, justice, temperance, and fortitude). And so, without attempting to do this in any systematic way, I would like to ask you about some of the virtues lived by our Father.

I am firmly convinced that he practiced all the virtues in an extraordinary way, that is, in a way far closer to perfect than that attained by most other persons generally considered good and virtuous.

From the first years of his life to the moment when he gave back his soul to God, our founder practiced virtues in a crescendo of heroism: they burned ever brighter, making manifest his ever deepening union with the Lord. I consider myself, thanks to the many years I spent at his side, a privileged witness of the sincerity with which he lived the virtues. Saints are, of course, famous for having practiced what they preached. Well, in our Father, unity of life was evident and constant. He did everything with his thoughts fixed on our Lord, offering to him all his actions. Everyone who lived with him was aware of the fact that he was constantly immersed in prayer.

He acted with this steadfast heroism both in ordinary, un-complicated situations and in extraordinarily difficult ones—which certainly were not lacking in his life. He knew how to face them with serenity, decision, and energy, with an awareness of his own weakness, but counting on the strength of God. He wanted only to serve our Lord with his whole spirit, and so he used to say, like the sons of Zebedee, *"Possum!* [I can!]" (see Mt 20:22). "I can, not with my own powers, but *in eo qui me confortat* [with the strength of God]" (Phil 4:13).

He began at an early age to have this ardent desire for sanc-tity, and the Lord rewarded him with obvious fruits. When still an adolescent, he received, along with the first indications of his di-vine vocation, an imprinting on his soul of this truth: God has cho-sen all human beings *ut essemus sancti in conspectu eius* ["that we might be holy in his sight" (Eph 1:4)]. He decided to respond to this invitation from our Lord with complete generosity—to go all the way. On October 2, 1928, he was to recognize clearly what the divine plan was in his regard; from then on, he placed his entire self, without reserve, at the service of that mission, becoming a most faithful instrument.

He used to say that he had only one prescription: personal sanctity. He was, in fact, convinced that the only true evil we suf-fer is sin, and that there is no remedy for sin other than God's grace and our participation in God's holiness. He was always re-minding us, very insistently, that we were in the Work in order to become saints. "Our vocation," he would say, "requires a heroic sanctity. Heroic sanctity—it is required by the calling which we have received. We must become true saints, authentic saints; if we do not, we will have failed." And he used to add that if some son or daughter of his was not determined to become a saint, it would be much better if that person left the Work, because the Lord had called us to be canonizable saints.

His mission as founder basically consisted in clearing the path to true sanctification in secular activities; in getting Chris-tians all over the world to understand that ordinary work, done in the presence of God and with human perfection, in a solid unity of life, can become a pleasing sacrifice to the Lord; in showing that work can be transformed into prayer—into a means of cultivating an intimacy with God. Such a task required a truly unique heroism. Our Father put his whole self into it, making a sacrifice of everything he had: his health, his material possessions (and, with his family's full consent, theirs too), his reputation . . . his entire life.

The Lord bestowed on him not only countless graces for his personal sanctification, but also exceptional talents and other gifts (which, too, are treasures of the Holy Spirit) for the building up of the Church. And he blessed him also by giving him a multitude of sons and daughters all over the world—placed, as it were, within the very vitals of the world, for the purpose of sanctifying it and serving souls.

We find ourselves, then, in the presence of one of the great founders in the history of the Church, one of those instruments which the Holy Spirit uses to renew the face of the earth (see Ps 104:30) and to build up the Church in holiness.

> *Our Father always appreciated and lived the virtue of friendship; in fact, he went so far as to characterize the apostolate of the members of the Work as "an apostolate of friendship and confidence." We have already called attention to his great capacity for love, his spiritual fatherliness. Can you tell us something about the kind of friend he was?*

He heard one day, from a clergyman, an offhand remark that filled him with pain, a saying that he considered far from accurate: "A man is like a wolf toward his fellow man; a woman toward another woman is more wolfish still; but most wolfish of all is a priest toward his fellow priest." He himself had always, ever since his youth, had a profound sense of the brotherhood that should unite priests. I once heard him tell this story: "As a seminarian I was very friendly with the vice rector of San Carlos Seminary. His name was Fr. Antonio Moreno. Out of friendship and, above all, out of charity—because I didn't like the game at all—sometimes when I went down to his room I agreed to play dominoes with him. I remember how I had to let him win, because otherwise he would not be happy; he would, in fact, get quite upset. But for me that was no problem. Having made up my mind to learn from priests who had given up their whole lives for our Lord, I found those moments very pleasant, because that priest showed a very priestly spirit, had much pastoral experience, and was very human. He had a wealth of supernatural and pedagogical insight and told me many instructive anecdotes which did me a lot of good."

Between 1933 and 1936, Fr. Pedro Poveda, the founder of the Teresian Institute, had a lot of dealings with the Father. At the request of Fr. Pedro, our founder gave spiritual assistance from time to time to some Teresian vocations. Fr. Pedro himself would often go to him for spiritual counsel. A number of times I heard our Father tell of a conversation which he had with Fr. Pedro a little while before the outbreak of the Spanish Civil War, when the danger of a violent persecution against the Church was imminent. They spoke of the possibility that one or both of them might undergo martyrdom on account of their priesthood. They arrived, the Father later told me, at a firm conclusion that death would not interrupt their friendship. Even if one of the two were to be killed, in heaven he would remain a friend to the other. The first time the Father told me about this conversation was on October 2, 1936, the day that he learned, with certainty and abundant details, that Fr. Pedro had been assassinated out of hatred for the faith—simply for being a priest and an apostle. I remember how the Father wept in my presence over the death of his friend, as he told me the news and related that conversation of theirs. He maintained forever the conviction that death does not interrupt friendship: this was a clear proof of his faith and hope.

Can you recall any episodes regarding the way he practiced love of neighbor?

He was empathetic and cordial toward everyone. He could deal quite affably even with extremely annoying individuals. I'll never forget the gentleness with which he received one particular boy who had severe psychological problems, a young man whose behavior was a cause of no little suffering for himself and for others. This boy lived in a student residence, and everyone tried to avoid him. The Father, though, was there for him anytime he needed him; he spent a good deal of time with that young man. More than once he told me that the only thing that boy needed was a chance to get things off his chest, just to have someone to talk to, someone that cared about him. And so, armed with exemplary patience, the Father would let him talk for as long as he wanted. During that time, since the boy didn't care to engage in dialogue, the Father would mentally recite various parts of the rosary, praying for that boy, who invariably went away happy and grateful.

There was also a certain doctor—this man was a real genius, but a very odd individual. So odd, in fact, that he didn't have a single friend; he lived in almost complete solitude. Well, the Father went to see this man quite often and, as a sign of affection, would sometimes invite him over for lunch at our house. He was, as I say, very intelligent, but he could never tolerate any opinion that differed from his own. And the Father never contradicted him. He would always say to me, "Well, you know, nobody likes this guy, everyone shuns him, so let him get some affection from us."

In 1935 and 1936, when our founder had so little money that maintenance of the student residence in Madrid (the Ferraz Street residence) was a daily miracle, every Wednesday he invited Fr. Norberto, a friend of his, to come over for lunch, and would even send a taxi for him. Fr. Norberto was a very lonely man, because of his unusually difficult personality. The Father told me that he tried to treat this friend, to honor him, as though this man were St. Joseph. In this way he improved his own devotion to the holy Patriarch while living charity with a heroic delicacy towards Fr. Norberto, who was much older than he. Indeed, he treated the older priest as though he were his father.

Still another episode comes to mind. This one happened in 1953 or so, in Rome, in the period when he was suffering from diabetes and had to go in fairly often for blood tests. At about eleven o'clock, having fasted all morning, he had to arrive at a clinic located in the Via Nazionale. I always went with him. Well, this one morning, for some reason we couldn't go home right away, so we went into a café on the Piazza Esedra to eat breakfast. I ordered a cup of coffee and a croissant for each of us. When we had been served, a woman came up to our founder and begged him for alms. He immediately replied, "I don't have any money. All I've got, and I've only got it because it's been given to me" (he said this because I'd paid for his breakfast), "is this meal; take it, and may God bless you." I quickly offered him my breakfast, explaining that I could order another one, but he answered, "No, no, it's fine this way. I've already had breakfast." At that point the lady at the cash register said, "Go ahead and have another one— she can have hers on the house." "No, no," the Father insisted, "I'm doing fine. Don't worry, I don't need anything at all."

He exercised charity with great delicacy. In the fifties, when the retreat house of Molinoviejo was being rebuilt, one of the workers—a worker whose wife was expecting a baby—was a victim of theft. During a trip to Madrid he was robbed of everything he had saved for the hospital expenses and the new baby's clothes. When the founder heard about this, he asked Fernando Delapuente to replace the sum that had been stolen from that man, and to add a generous gift besides.

There are other touching episodes. This one happened during the Spanish Civil War, when he was on his exhausting journey across the Pyrenees to reach the liberated zone by way of Andorra. At a certain point, when the group was already high up in the mountains, the guides told the fugitives that they would not go any further without more money. Since nobody had enough to do any good, the Father offered to return to Madrid to get a loan. That way, the others could go on ahead; he would wait for another expedition. Fortunately, the problem was readily resolved and it was not necessary for him to go back to Barcelona and then to Madrid. Humanly speaking, this would have been a crazy thing to attempt—he could never have reached his destination by himself, without a guide who had a thorough knowledge of those militia-infested forests and ravines. He would certainly have been shot.

Furthermore, our founder was ill, extremely weak, and without the documentation necessary for that kind of trip. It was a truly heroic decision: to offer his own life to save the lives of the others.

He did not discriminate between persons. In the fifties he asked one of his sons to help one of the fiercest persecutors of the Work to regularize his situation with the Church and to resolve his professional problems; this man had abandoned his religious community and the priesthood, and had contracted a civil marriage. Things like this happened fairly often, and our Father always conducted himself the same way. He showed by his actions how to live a life of charity in relation to everyone, and that he was ready, not just to help everybody, but, if necessary, even to give his life.

And now, if you could add a little something about his charity and gratitude toward those who helped him . . .

Among those persons he remembered with special gratitude and affection were Fr. Angelo Malo, who baptized him, and two Piarist priests: Fr. Enrique Labrador, who prepared him for his first confession, and Fr. Manuel Laborda, who prepared him for his first Communion. I've always found it remarkable that he could remember their names; that's certainly something out of the ordinary. (I've asked quite a few people if they can remember the names of the priests who administered those sacraments to them, and I have always received a negative reply.) To me this is indicative not only of his sense of gratitude, but also of the great appreciation that he had for these sacraments even when he was very young.

I would also like to mention the never-fading gratitude he felt toward Fr. Daniel Alfaro, the military chaplain who loaned him the money for his father's funeral. He prayed for this priest, by name, every day for over fifty years.

In 1941, when the campaign against Opus Dei reached its peak and the bishop of Madrid, the Most Reverend Leopoldo Eijo y Garay, decided to give written approval of the Work, this bishop became the object of all kinds of criticism. It began to be said, even from the pulpit, that in the history of the Church many heresies had been promoted by bishops. To our founder it seemed that

Bishop Eijo y Garay was taking too big a risk, especially in light of the fact that the primatial see of Toledo had become vacant and rumors were going around that he had a good chance of being appointed to it. And so one day the Father said to him, "Your Excellency, don't defend me anymore; abandon my cause." The bishop, quite surprised, asked why he was saying this. "Because," he said, "by defending Opus Dei, you risk losing the miter of Toledo." The bishop looked at him and replied, "Josemaría, what I have at risk is my soul. I can abandon neither you nor Opus Dei."

In my view, such an initiative on the part of our founder shows a charity and self-effacement of a truly extraordinary kind. He was thinking only of the good of souls—of the immense amount of good that Bishop Eijo y Garay would have been able to bring to the Church had he been appointed to the see of Toledo.

> Our Father learned from the example of his parents how to live a life of poverty with great dignity; in Logroño, after the loss of the family fortune, the Escrivá family had to make serious cutbacks in their style of living, but this did not mean any loss of dignity or good cheer. Our founder drew instruction from this for his spiritual children.

From the time I first met him I noticed that he often referred to the virtue of poverty with an expression that was full of meaning for him: "Poverty, my great lady." That's what he called it from the time he was thirty-one or thirty-two years old to the end of his life. What he was talking about was not privation for its own sake, but rather a true treasure which leads to a real personal union with Christ, in the nakedness of Bethlehem and of Calvary: a prerequisite for the effectiveness of any apostolate. And that's why none of us was surprised at the insistence with which he encouraged us to live a life of poverty. He was always illustrating this with concrete, compelling examples: "Don't hold on to anything as if it were your own"; "Have nothing superfluous"; "Don't complain when you lack something necessary"; "When the choice is up to you, take the poorest thing, whatever is least desirable"; "Don't mistreat the objects you use"; "Make good use of time."

Even in its earliest stages the Work was accompanied by poverty, and so it always will be. One of the first to ask for admission was Luis Gordon, a young man who enjoyed an excellent position financially. Our founder told me more than once that he had thought Luis would be a good source of support, from a material as well as a spiritual standpoint, for his apostolic initiatives. But the Lord obviously had something else in mind, for Luis fell ill and died when still very young. When he spoke to me about this, the Father made this observation: "The death of Luis was providential, because it meant that Opus Dei had to continue to grow in the greatest poverty. If he hadn't died, we would have had material means, temporal means, which might have been harmful to us. It was necessary that this Work of God should have been born in poverty, just as Jesus was." This absolute detachment from all temporal sources of security highlights the premium our Father placed on the theological virtue of hope; it governed his attitude toward earthly goods.

During the Spanish Civil War, when he was in Burgos, he learned of the death of José Isasa, a member of the Work who had been studying architecture. The news was given to him by José's relatives, very good people who were, of course, fully aware of the vocation of their son. Well, not long before he died, the young man had expressed the wish that everything that he had be given to the Work. But the founder decided not to ask for anything, even though there were serious financial problems and the relatives of the deceased were very favorably disposed. He chose this course of action out of a conviction that the Lord would be better pleased with our perseverance in poverty.

It was precisely during this period of extreme poverty that the Father decided to renounce the taking of stipends for Masses. When he was still in the seminary (he told me this more than once), he had thought about not accepting any kind of stipend for his priestly services. It was a thought that constantly came back to his mind. He decided in 1938 to put it into practice. One day, after having devoted his time of mental prayer to a meditation on the words of the Holy Spirit "Iacta super Dominum curam tuam, et ipse te enutriet" ["Cast your cares upon the Lord, and he will take care of you" (Ps 55:22)], he offered to our Lord the renunciation of any kind of gratuity for his own priestly services; and from that moment on, he did not accept any more alms of this kind. (Some years later, after having meditated on this in God's presence, he decided that his sons who were numerary priests should likewise renounce every kind of gratuity for their priestly services. In 1944, when the first three priests were ordained, they too adopted this practice, and it has been our policy ever since.)

After making this personal decision, the founder wrote on January 27, 1938, to the vicar general of the diocese of Madrid, Msgr. Francisco Morán: "Next Saturday I am leaving for Bilbao, León, and perhaps even San Sebastian. After that . . . Saragossa and perhaps Seville. And all of this, Father, without a cent. I have made a resolution—is it madness? All right, call it madness—to no longer receive stipends for Masses, which up to now have been my only source of income. Now I'll be able more often to celebrate Mass for my bishop, and for my dear Francisco, for those sons of mine, . . . and for myself, a sinful priest." I think it is important to add that during this same period he took the trouble to obtain Mass stipends for needy priests, as is clear from his correspondence with the bishop of Avila.

The founder looked at financial problems from a supernatural point of view. In a letter written on January 19, 1935, to his dear friend Fr. Eliodoro Gil, he said, "Do you know that St. Nicholas of Bari is . . . nothing less than the administrator general of the Work of God? What a responsibility has fallen on his shoulders!" A few days before, having found himself in a very tight squeeze, the Father had been inspired to name that holy bishop as intercessor of Opus Dei for financial matters. At first he had thought of making the nomination contingent upon the solution of a particularly burdensome problem. But afterwards, out of a profound supernatural reaction, he corrected himself and, addressing the saint, exclaimed, "I name you as intercessor from now on, even if you don't solve this problem for me!"

The founder always appealed to the generosity of benefactors, and in the first place to the cooperators of the Work, as is done today. When preparations were being made to set up the first university residence (on Ferraz Street), the contribution made by the Countess of Humanes was decisive. The Father, realizing that it probably would be, had gone to see her after having prayed much for the meeting to have a happy outcome. The countess was a very good woman, and she immediately saw the wisdom of the reasoning set forth by our founder. Now, although she was very wealthy, and never let anyone who worked for her go without, she herself lived in the strictest poverty and did not keep much cash on hand. So this is what she did: she got up and went to her safe, took out her jewels, and gave them to our founder. This act of generosity is described in point No. 638 of *The Way:* "What holy resources poverty has! Do you remember? It was a time of financial stress in your apostolic undertaking. You had given without stint down to the last penny. Then that priest of God said to you: 'I, too, will give you all I have.' You knelt and you heard, 'May the blessing of almighty God, the Father, the Son, and the Holy Spirit, descend upon you and remain with you forever!' You are still convinced that you were well paid."

Before that, the countess had donated the first clock for the DYA Academy (on Luchana Street). After many trials and humiliations, the Father had managed three times to put aside the money needed for the clock, but each time some other, more pressing necessity had absorbed the funds. At last the countess became aware of the situation and gave him this clock. It had a square casing; it was just a simple clock, nothing fancy about it; but the Father and the young men who frequented the academy were so pleased with it that they took a photograph of it, which we still have in our archives.

Here is another episode, dating from the period at Burgos, which shows, on the one hand, the poverty in which we were living, and, on the other hand, the generosity of our founder. Every so often a professor from the Madrid School of Architecture, Dr. Francisco Navarro Borrás, who was a noted mathematician, came to see him. One day our founder was given a cigar, and since he knew that the professor liked cigars, he set it aside for him. The two members of the Work who lived with him also smoked, but they didn't have a penny to spend on tobacco; so they thought they would take just a little out of one end of this cigar. And then, of course, a few days later, they took just a bit from the other end; and so, little by little—you can guess what happened. When the professor came, the Father said to him, "I'd like to give you a cigar." He asked his sons to go get it, and they came back with what was left—a tiny stump! The professor was startled, needless to say, and as for the Father, well, he never ceased to be amused at the memory of this petty larceny.

In the first residence, notwithstanding the straitened circumstances we were in, there was no lack of good humor. The domestic staff consisted of one woman—the cook—and a young boy. The residents called the cook "Señora Cupis," because, they said, she had "concupiscence of the flesh" ["flesh" and "meat" are the same word in Spanish]—they were referring to her practice of taking home for her family some of the meat that had been purchased for the residents. The boy answered the door and served the meals. It therefore fell to the Father to clean the rooms and make the beds for the nearly twenty students who lived there. Some of us would help him in this—most often, the architect Ricardo Fernández Vallespín, who at that time was the director of the residence. The Father did these domestic chores while the residents were at the university. He was very happy to perform this service.

His generosity was boundless. In 1942 the father of one of the architecture students died; this student had lived in the DYA residence in the school year 1935–1936, and then also, along with his brother, after the civil war. The family now finding itself in a situation of financial hardship, the Father told this student and his brother that they could continue to stay at the residence, without paying, until graduation.

The Father took great care to ensure that this kind of help would always be given with the maximum discretion, so that those concerned would not suffer even the slightest amount of humiliation. So it is, for example, that by explicit instruction from our founder, whenever there are students in apostolic undertakings of Opus Dei who are there on scholarship because of financial need, they nevertheless enjoy the same rights, the same treatment, the same consideration as their companions; they are treated no differently from the others.

Another sign of his spirit of poverty was the way he took care of material things so as to avoid unnecessary expenses. The Father taught us by example to pay attention to a multitude of details, from those concerning the preservation of buildings to those concerning the proper functioning of the smallest tools. He insisted that every object be used only for the purpose for which it was made, since otherwise it could get broken and need to be replaced. He said, for example, that one should not use scissors or a knife to open a can, or use a screwdriver as a hammer. Even more: when the auditorium of Villa Tevere (our headquarters) was completed, he suggested to his sons that they make the small mortification of refraining from putting their hands on the armrests of the chairs, so as to avoid dirtying them and wearing out the fabric.

One day in 1959, the Father was visiting the construction site of Villa Tevere, as he often did, to encourage the progress of the work and to keep up with the smallest details. While we were moving from one place to the other, Jesús Alvarez Gazapo, the architect directing the construction, was turning the lights off and on. Our founder noticed that none of us was helping him. This was at least partly because we didn't know where the switches were. Nevertheless, he later reprimanded us, explaining that we ought to have helped our brother; true charity, he said, should make us reluctant to let ourselves be served. He added, "This is the spirit of the Work: not to play lord and master, not to let others work for us . . . I am almost sixty years old, but I really wished I could run along beside him and help him."

On another occasion, also during the construction of Villa Tevere, it was discovered that some antique metal decorations on the door of the entry hall were missing. The various workmen assigned to this area were the only ones who could get in there. The Father brought them together and told them in a calm tone of voice that since nobody else could go in there, everything pointed to the probability that it was one of them who had taken the decorations. He urged them not to make excuses, and to bear in mind that he too was a poor man. From the sale of those items very little could have been made, whereas he, on the other hand, would have to make a rather large expenditure to replace them, and he did not have much money. He made it clear that he had already forgiven whoever it was, and that consequently there was no need to make any restitution to him. He then added that if anyone found himself in financial difficulties, he could come to him privately, and he would try to help him as far as possible. Afterwards, to show to all of them his affection and readiness to forgive, he embraced them one by one.

In his clothing and with regard to objects of personal use, he was very sparing. He imposed on himself, as concrete practices of the spirit of poverty, these rules which I've already mentioned in passing:

"Don't have or use anything as if it were your own." For example, he didn't write his name in the books he used all the time, and he wouldn't let us call the chapel where he celebrated daily Mass "the Father's chapel."

"Have nothing that is superfluous." He was so faithful to this ideal that in his last years, he gave up the watch he was wearing, because he had *custodes* (Fr. Javier Echevarría and myself) taking care of his schedule and letting him know where he needed to be at any given time.

"Don't complain when you lack something necessary." In this his heroism was extreme. I don't remember a single complaint from his lips in the forty years I spent at his side. This was not only because of his spirit of poverty, but also because he had an aversion to speaking about himself. If anything, he complained from the opposite direction: about us being too worried about him; about us trying to make sure he wasn't lacking the bare essentials.

"When a choice can be made, choose for yourself the worst thing." He did habitually conduct himself this way, both at mealtimes and on all other occasions.

"Don't create needs for yourself." I remember how hard it was for us to talk him into using sunglasses, even though he suffered from eye troubles. Sunglasses seemed to him to be a trumped-up need, until he tried them and realized we were right. He was grateful to us ever afterwards for having insisted on this.

"Never carry money in your pocket." He lived this way for the last thirty years of his life; from the time he first arrived in Italy, he never had a cent in his pocket.

Another reflection of his spirit of poverty was his determination to get the maximum use out of everything, such as tools or objects of personal use. For example, to take notes or to make rough drafts, he always used the back sides of used sheets of paper. He liked to joke that he would "write on the edges if that were possible." A further example: as of 1940 or so he needed to get a new pair of glasses, but he managed to keep using the old ones until 1970.

These examples demonstrate that poverty was a way of life for our Father, not only materially but also in terms of interior detachment.

He truly reached a high degree of heroism. When he was a seminarian in Saragossa and was studying at the pontifical university there, he used to keep in a notebook, besides his notes on the lectures, a great many maxims he had heard from his canon law professor, Fr. Elías Ger. These maxims proved useful both for practical application in his personal life and as points of inspiration for his pastoral activity. One day in 1926, when he was in need of a special grace, he thought of offering that notebook to God. But let me tell it in his own words: "'Lord,' I said, 'if you grant me this, I will burn that notebook.' Well, that was an impulse typical of a youth. But suddenly it occurred to me that I was not being very generous, and that I had become too attached to my papers, so I immediately burned all those notes."

He was very strict as well with regard to gifts. Not only would he not accept anything that was incompatible with the lifestyle of a poor man; he rejected anything that was superfluous, even if it was a gift. He also taught us not to make concessions in this regard, but to have only what is necessary. "After all," he would say, "if someone gave us a white elephant, we certainly wouldn't keep that in the house." His policy was a clear and simple one: to sell all superfluous gifts and put the proceeds into the apostolate.

His detachment was very much a spiritual detachment. In December 1959 the Father commissioned a copy, slightly larger than the original, of a statue of the child Jesus which is still kept by the Augustinian Recollect nuns at the Foundation of St. Elizabeth, in Madrid. He had become chaplain there in 1931, and rector in 1934. That carving was associated with many dear memories of his spiritual life, with extraordinary favors and graces. The good nuns there still to this day call it "the Christ Child of Fr. Josemaría." Mother St. Joseph, who was at that time the sacristan, recalls how she often saw Fr. Josemaría speak to it at Christmastime, when it was in the sacristy; he sang songs for it, and rocked it in his arms as if it were a real baby. Well, in 1959, three days before Christmas, our founder visited the architectural studio at Villa Tevere. He sat down, tired and unusually silent, completely immersed in God. At this moment the artist, Manuel Caballero, came in. He had made a clay model of the original statue, and from that he had made a wood carving—which he had with him, wrapped up as a package. He sat down next to the Father, and slowly and deliberately began to unwrap it. As soon as the Father realized that it was that Christ Child, he took it in his arms, pressed it close to his chest, and, visibly overcome with emotion, left the room.

A little later he said to me, "Alvaro, I want to give this Christ Child to the Roman College of the Holy Cross, as a present; it will be the first stone of its definitive seat." What had happened was that the Father, as soon as he realized how much that statue affected him, how much he loved it, felt and rejected the danger of attachment. That was why he could not allow himself even this joy, a joy which in and of itself would have been entirely legitimate.

In his giving of spiritual direction, he did all he could to make sure that souls would not become attached to him. He wanted to lead them to our Lord and to help them assume their own responsibilities before God; and so he wanted to remain in the background, to disappear, so as to make it evident that the effectiveness of the priest is based *in persona Christi*. From the time I first got to know him, I was aware of his habit of sometimes telling those who came to him for direction, "Today, make your confession to someone else."

His detachment extended even to what was most truly his own, Opus Dei itself. In this connection he experienced, on two particularly important occasions, direct intervention from God. I will transcribe two documents that fill me with admiration. The first is a handwritten note recounting an event that took place on June 22, 1933:

"Last Thursday, the vigil of the feast of the Sacred Heart, for the first and only time since I have come to know the will of God, I experienced that cruel test which Fr. Postius warned me about some time ago. (When the Society of Jesus was dissolved by the present ungovernment, I lost contact with Fr. Sánchez for a while, and Fr. Juan Postius looked after me.) I was alone, in a side chapel in the Church of Our Lady of Perpetual Help, and I was trying to pray before Jesus in the Blessed Sacrament, who was exposed on the altar in a monstrance. Suddenly, for an instant and without any reason being given which could explain it—there was none— this most bitter thought came into my mind: 'And what if all of this is a lie, an illusion of yours, and you are wasting your time . . . and, still worse, you are wasting it for all these others, too?' This only lasted a few seconds, but how I suffered!

"Then I spoke to Jesus and said to him, 'Lord' (the words aren't exact), 'if the Work is not yours, demolish it; right now, at this moment, in such a way that I may know it.' Immediately I not only felt confirmed as to the truth of his will with regard to the Work, but also saw with clarity a point about the organization of it which had been baffling me; until that time, I hadn't had the slightest idea how to solve this problem."

Another time, on September 25, 1941, he had an opportunity to renew that supreme act of detachment. The Work and its founder had become subject to an incredible series of detractions and gross misrepresentations; very serious obstacles were standing in the way of the normal development of the apostolates. It was a test permitted by our Lord, but one so severe that many believed the very survival of Opus Dei was in jeopardy. That day he wrote me a letter from La Granja, in the province of Segovia—this is the second of the two documents—in which he told me what had happened:

"May Jesus protect you, Alvaro.

"It's drizzling, and we have taken refuge in the hotel. This is a life of comfort that I find truly annoying.

"Nevertheless, I am certain that some moments of it are very fruitful: yesterday I celebrated Mass for the Ordinary of the diocese, and today I offered the Holy Sacrifice and the whole day for the sovereign pontiff, for his person and intentions. By the way, after the Consecration I felt an interior impulse (though I was at the same time quite certain that the Work is to be much loved by the pope) to do something that has cost me tears: with tears that burned my eyes, I looked at Jesus in the host on the corporal, and in my heart I said to him, really and truly, 'Lord, if you want me to, I will accept the injustice.' 'The injustice'—you surely understand what I meant: the destruction of the entire Work of God.

"I know that I pleased *him*, anyway. And, really, how could I have refused to make this act of union with his will, if he was asking me for it? Already once before, in 1933 or 1934, I did the same, and he alone knows how much I suffered.

"My son, what a beautiful harvest the Lord is getting ready to give us, once our Holy Father knows us for real and not through misrepresentations; once he recognizes us for what we are—most faithful servants of his—and blesses us!

"I feel like shouting out, with not a care as to what others might say, that shout which sometimes does escape my lips when I preach the meditation for you: 'Ah, Jesus, what a field of wheat to harvest!'

"Dear Alvaro, pray a lot, and get others to pray a lot, for your Father. See how Jesus is allowing the enemy to make me aware of the exorbitant enormity of this campaign of incredible falsehoods and crazy distortions; and how the *animalis homo* ['human animal'] instinctively rebels. By the grace of God I constantly reject these natural reactions which seem to be, and perhaps are, coming from a sense of uprightness and justice. And I let pour out of me a 'fiat' which is joyous and filial ('filial' because of my divine filiation: I am a son of God!), a 'fiat' which fills me with peace, happiness, and an ability to forgive and forget."

> *The story you have already told about the key thrown into the sewer drain in Madrid, at a time when this city was being devastated by anti-Catholicism, illustrates the uncompromising in-*

*tegrity with which the founder lived the virtue of purity: he
turned down the offer of a safe hiding place, just to steer clear of
a remote occasion of sin against this virtue.*

Love for holy purity is a characteristic that accompanied him
throughout his life. He expressed it constantly in the very careful
attention he paid to the indispensable means of preserving and in-
tensifying this virtue, which he always spoke of in positive terms,
such as "Love" or "joyful affirmation." He wrote in *The Way* (point
No. 131), "Never talk of impure things or events, not even to de-
plore them. Look, it's a subject that sticks more than tar. Change
the conversation, or if that's not possible, continue, but speaking
of the need and beauty of holy purity—a virtue of the men who
know what their souls are worth."

During his time in the seminary, he practiced an ever more
constant and severe mortification of the senses, in order to keep
his body and his senses completely for our Lord. In Saragossa—
this went on for some time—some women he did not know kept
trying to attract his attention; they waited for him out on the street,
with the obvious intention of seducing him. They would brazenly
stare at him when he passed by with the other seminarians, making it clear, through unmistakably provocative words or gestures,
that he was the only one they were interested in. Never so much
as looking at them, he overcame this assault from the devil (he
had no way of avoiding it) by placing himself in the hands of our
Lady. From the outset he notified the seminary superiors and kept
them fully informed of the situation; I know he never said or did a
thing that could have offered the slightest ground for censure of
his behavior. In fact, once he saw that this trial was not going to
end anytime soon, he went out of his way to reaffirm to the rector
that he valued his priestly vocation more than life itself.

One day, Mr. Escrivá happened to be at the barber shop, in
Logroño, and he heard it said—the devil had succeeded in spreading the rumors even that far—that certain women were after his
son. He immediately went to see him, to point out to his son that it
would be better for him to become a good father of a family than a
bad priest.

Young Josemaría explained to him that as soon as he had be-come conscious of the snares laid by these women—women he didn't even know; women to whom he had never given the least encouragement—he had immediately informed the rector of the seminary. This set his father's mind at rest. He now understood that nothing had weakened his son's determination to become a priest and to live true to all that that would entail.

One of his closer friends in the seminary, Fr. Cubero, told me of a small but significant incident related to this subject. One day, in Saragossa, the two of them were on their way, as usual, to their classes at the pontifical university, and two girls that happened to cross paths with them stopped to stare at young Josemaría. Well, he paid no attention to them. But the same thing happened the next day, and again the day after that. Only this third time, when they saw him go by, they said in a challenging way, "Hey, are we so ugly that you can't even look at us?" Josemaría, without slow-ing down or looking at them, replied, "No, you're just rather shameless, that's all!" That was the end of it; those girls never bothered him again.

After his ordination to the priesthood, he further intensified his personal struggle. And as he became conscious of the respon-sibilities which the Lord was entrusting to him with regard to other souls through the foundation of Opus Dei, the urge to turn all his affections toward God became still more radical. From the time I first met him, I witnessed the heroism with which he morti-fied his sight. He imposed on himself concrete renunciations, even in matters of legitimate curiosity: he did not gaze into shop windows, and when traveling by automobile, he often decided not to look out the window, thus giving up the pleasure of enjoy-ing the scenery.

He would often explain that "seeing" and "looking" are two very different things: that the former is a neutral physiological fact, while the latter involves the application of the will in observ-ing with attention, to weigh the details. The Father did not "look." This point I would like to illustrate with an anecdote from the thir-ties, regarding a painter. At a get-together in Ecuador I asked the founder to tell the story, and this was his account:

"In the early years I had many friends. (I have even more now.) Alvaro has just reminded me of an old marchioness who died recently, at the age of about ninety; but back then she was young, and famous for her beauty. I would meet with her and her husband once a week for lunch, in the home of some mutual friends. One day an artist, a painter, approached me—he was quite a good painter, but he didn't have many clients and he was going through a very rough time financially. He asked me if I could get him some work. So during one of our lunches it occurred to me to ask the marchioness, 'How would you like to sit for a portrait? I know a young painter; he's not famous, but he's got talent. He will do a fine painting, and it won't cost you much money. I don't know what the price will be, but it won't be much.'

"'Oh, yes, I'd be delighted,' she replied. 'Just as you wish.'

"'That's great.'

"So I called the painter, and he came, and she posed for him for an hour. After that she handed him a valise with some of her dresses in it, and said, 'Go now—I don't want to pose any longer.'

"Several days later, the painter came to see me. He said to me, 'Now I need to know what color eyes she has.'

"And I had to tell him, 'Come to think of it, I really don't know. We've been friends for several years—we get together quite often and certainly like each other—but it's never occurred to me to notice what color eyes she has.'

"It quite honestly had never occurred to me.

"'But we can take care of this right away,' I said. 'Next Thursday I'll be having lunch with her family and some other people. Ask me in the evening about it.'

"That evening I could tell him only a part of the story, because this is what happened. When we sat down to eat, I casually said to her, 'Guess what, María? The painter asked me the other day what color eyes you have, and I had to tell him I don't know.'

"'Well, look at me, Father—I have marvelous green eyes!'

"'Now I'll look at them even less, silly!'"

This was a habit he kept all his life. He lived the traditional ascetical practice of "custody of the eyes" to a heroic degree; and yet his manner was so natural that this went unnoticed. There was nothing strained or affected in his personality.

Whenever our Father was asked what his favorite natural virtue was, he invariably replied, "Sincerity."

Yes, he placed a high value on this virtue, which he considered a prerequisite for perseverance in one's vocation. He said there were three phrases, "three demons," that we ought to hate: "It's just that . . . ," "I believed that . . . ," and "I thought that . . ."; in other words, we should never try to make excuses to justify or hide our errors. He himself never shirked either the weight or the consequences of his own responsibilities.

He always spoke and stood by the truth, even at the cost of suffering hostility or at least a lack of understanding from others. He refused to compromise the truth, and especially when it came to proclaiming firmly the teaching of Christ or explaining the authentic nature of Opus Dei and its apostolates.

He loved the truth so much that he would not tolerate even the smallest lie. He wouldn't let his children lie to their parents, not even when a lie could have served to get them permission to attend a formational activity. I remember one time, in the summer of 1941, he had to straighten out a member of Opus Dei for having resorted to this tactic in order to participate in a retreat the Father himself was giving. The young man's parents were opposed to his vocation, in part because they had been influenced by some propaganda against Opus Dei, so he had thought it best to tell a lie—he told them he was going to the country. As soon as our founder learned of this, he admonished the young man. In a very serious tone of voice he said, "From now on, no more lies! Love for the truth comes before all else."

He demanded from those who helped him in the government of Opus Dei clarity and precision in their presentation of information. He detested approximations, exaggerations, and any beating around the bush. Such clarity, however, was to be accompanied by a maximum of charity; objectivity was not to be confused with insensitivity toward others.

He preached to journalists that as Christians, they ought to love the truth and proclaim it courageously, and be ever ready to face the consequences. Instead of promoting a separate "religious" media, he encouraged Catholics to work, with real professional competence, within the media already in existence—to try to turn them around so that the Church's doctrine would be defended and disseminated via these media.

He did not like secrets or mysteries. On one occasion, a royal dignitary said to him, in the course of a conversation, that he wanted to tell him something "under the secrecy of the confessional." Our founder immediately replied, "Your Highness, you are speaking to a priest and a man of honor, and that ought to be enough for you. If you want to tell me something 'under the secrecy of the confessional,' let's go to one now, and I will gladly hear your sacramental confession."

> With regard to obedience, the founder used to say that what he wanted was not obedience perinde ac cadaver [like that of a corpse] but, instead, an intelligent obedience. As he put it, "I don't go anywhere with corpses; I piously bury them." Nevertheless, the obedience had to be a genuine one:
> "The enemy: 'Will you obey, even in this ridiculous little detail?' You with God's grace: 'I will obey, even in this heroic little detail!'" (The Way, point No. 618).

He loved obedience because he saw it as intimately connected with the most important Christian virtues—faith and charity, humility and simplicity . . . He set a heroic example in obeying the general laws of the Church and the specific dispositions regarding Opus Dei; with respect to its long canonical journey, for example, he never took a step without the explicit approval of the relevant ecclesiastical authority.

He exemplified obedience by being the first to put into practice whatever was established for all members of Opus Dei. He was profoundly convinced that those who exercise authority should be an example of obedience to the others. One day he said to the General Council:

"My sons, directors, don't consider yourselves exempt, and don't seek gratuitous justifications for not living up to what has been established.

"Be faithful! Remember that it is you who set the tone, who set the pace. Because the grace of God, the grace that enables us to govern well, comes to us through channels established for us by God: our norms and customs.

"Let this never be said of us, what the people of Rome laughingly say about the postures of the two statues on the steps of St. Peter's, representing the two apostles. I wouldn't dare to say this myself—indeed, I consider it a malicious insult—but for years the people have been saying that those two statues represent a reality in the life of the Church: that while Rome makes the laws that are binding on the Church, those laws are ignored in the Vatican itself. Peter, they say, has his hand pointing down in front of him as a way of telling people, 'Here's where we make the laws,' while Paul, with his arm stretched out towards the city, completes the saying: 'And that's where they keep them.'

"Whenever a directive is given, or a norm having to do with our way of living a Christian life, we directors ought to fulfill it to the letter. Even if the others don't see us, our fidelity is most important. Whether we are faithful or not is the test of whether or not we are paying attention to the grace of God, and it determines whether or not this central, vital organ of the body provides arterial blood to the rest of the body.

"In Opus Dei, therefore, the directors as well as everybody else ought to meditate upon and consider in their own examination of conscience how they are carrying out these things which come from God, which he has specifically laid down in the Work."

It should be pointed out, however, that in Opus Dei, obedience pertains only to the specific end of the Prelature, that is, the Christian life of its members and the mode of their apostolic activity. Not in the least does it interfere with their professional, social, cultural, economic, or political activities or opinions. In all temporal matters, a member of Opus Dei enjoys the same liberties as any other Catholic, and works with the same sense of responsibility that characterizes any other Christian who is faithfully united with the Church hierarchy.

The Father showed great docility even in the smallest matters. Here is an illustration of his readiness to go along with every desire of the Roman pontiff. In 1958, Prince Carlo Pacelli informed me that the Holy Father, Pope Pius XII, wanted me to become a Knight of Honor and Devotion of the Order of Malta. I didn't much like the idea; even as a layman I'd never been attracted by such a title, and now that I was a priest it seemed to me entirely inappropriate. But I talked it over with the Father, and he said, "If Prince Carlo Pacelli speaks to you about it again on behalf of the Holy Father, you ought to comply." Well, as it turned out, that's what happened. So our founder sent me to Spain to get together the necessary documentation; I left on May 25, accompanied by Fr. Javier Echevarría. Then, while the Spanish branch of the Order of Malta was looking over the papers before sending them on to Rome (to the Grand Master of the Order), Pope Pius died. But the Father did not want me to withdraw my application, and I received the nomination shortly afterwards.

This is a matter of small importance, but it is precisely in the little things that true virtue really shows. When he was a seminarian in Saragossa, the Father composed a poem in Latin, entitled "Oboedientia Tutior" ["Obedience Is the Safer Path"], for a celebration in honor of the rector of the seminary, Bishop Díaz Gómara. What was significant was not the title of the poem (which was actually the bishop's motto), but the act of obedience involved in the writing of it. By temperament our Father had no wish at all to appear on center stage; he would never have even composed that poem, much less have read it in public, had his superiors not expressly asked him to do so.

> *Our Father practiced corporal mortification intensely, and preached about the need for it. In* The Way *he wrote: "I don't believe in your interior mortification if I see that you despise mortification of the senses—that you don't practice it" (point No. 181).*

He liked to repeat, and he underscored this with his own example, that the best mortification consists in the faithful fulfillment—down to the last detail—of the ordinary duties of one's own state in life. Nevertheless, he did also undertake severe corporal penances, especially after he came to know clearly what God wanted from him. Every step of his pastoral and apostolic activity was preceded and accompanied by severe mortifications.

The Father began to use the cilice and the discipline when he was a seminarian, but I know for a fact that from 1928 on he considerably intensified his corporal mortification. His mother and brother and sister told me that during those years in Madrid, he would shut himself up in the bathroom of the apartment where they lived, and would turn on the faucets to muffle the sound of the discipline. But they were still able to hear it, and besides, even though he very carefully washed the walls and floor afterwards, his mother and sister discovered, with dismay, some drops of blood which had escaped his notice.

He carried out, in a great spirit of obedience, the plan of mortification that was approved by his confessor. Among his personal notes we have found the following:

"Since Saturday, February 17, 1934, Fr. Sánchez has advised me to follow this easier plan:

"Every day without exception, apart from Sundays: in the morning, for four hours, two cilices.

"Monday—discipline—three Misereres." (Every discipline, that is, lasted as long as it took to recite three Misereres, or three Laudates, or whatever.)

"Tuesday—three Laudates.

"Wednesday—three Benedictuses.

"Saturday—three Magnificats.

"Friday—discipline—three Te Deums, three Magnificats, and three Benedictuses."

He was always prudent enough not to endanger his health, and his advice was explicit on this point. In a letter of January 22, 1940, for example, he made this recommendation: "Don't do mortifications that might endanger your health or sour your disposition; discreet mortification and discreet penance are undoubtedly necessary, but the touchstone is Love. In your penance have this as your norm of conduct: 'Nothing without explicit permission.'"

Even more than corporal penances, however, the founder strove to practice small mortifications which helped him carry out carefully his various practices of piety, his priestly ministry, a spirit of service, fraternal charity, and so on. He maintained that such mortifications ought to be constant, like the beating of one's heart. Among his notes we have found this one, dated November 3, 1932:

"1) I mustn't ever 'look.'

"2) I mustn't ask questions simply out of curiosity.

"3) I mustn't sit down unless it is unavoidable, and must never use the back of the chair.

"4) I mustn't eat anything sweet.

"5) I mustn't drink water, except that used for the ablutions at Mass.

"6) After lunch [the main meal], I mustn't eat any more bread.

"7) I mustn't spend even five cents that a poor beggar wouldn't spend if he were in my position.

"8) I mustn't complain to anyone about anything, except to seek direction.

"9) I mustn't flatter, or criticize.

"Deo omnis gloria!"

Here is an example of how he mortified his sense of sight. When he started living in Burgos (in the early days of 1938), the city was not very large, and from all directions you could see its splendid cathedral—which is a real jewel of Gothic art. Our founder offered to the Lord the sacrifice of letting a good length of time go by before he went to visit the cathedral. And the first time he went there, it was just for prayer, not for sightseeing; it was only later that he went to see it at leisure.

He was also very strict with himself in his mortifications regarding food. When I first met him, one of the things that aroused my curiosity was a little, light-colored wooden box which he kept on his desk. I once asked him what was in it, and he opened it for me: it was aloe. He invited me to take a little on my finger and taste it. It was a mortification which he practiced now and then. I remember that when we took refuge in the Honduran consulate, that little box was one of the very few objects he brought with him.

He refused to receive any kind of special treatment when he went to visit a center of the Work; he would always respect their plans and routines. I will relate only a single incident, which took place in 1945. We had just inaugurated the Abando University residence in Bilbao, and the Father went there to celebrate the first Mass. To mark the occasion, those in charge of the center decided to prepare a meal that would be a little bit special. The founder noticed that an expensive wine was being served, and he asked if it was usual to drink that kind of wine at this center. Three or four of us were present. The person serving the table said, "No, Father, we never do." Then the Father said, "Then you shouldn't serve it to me either." And addressing those around the table, he continued: "You're giving me special treatment, as if I were a guest. I won't eat today, and that way you will learn that this is not how we do things; our poverty is something we should live all the time." A short time later, impressed by this example, the person who had served the meal asked for admission to the Work.

Nevertheless, he did arrange that in our centers, when there were liturgical solemnities or special Opus Dei celebrations, his children should prepare a more festive meal than usual. But it was precisely on those days that he ate less than usual. I remember this one time, during the Christmas season, they brought out a very fine tray of food, and our founder caught sight of someone eyeing it with a certain eagerness. He immediately got up, made some excuse, and left the table without eating.

One day in 1949 or 1950, the Marquis of Bisleti had two pheasants delivered to us, which he had shot on his land at Salto di Fondi. The Father, having never eaten pheasant, decided to offer to the Lord the mortification of not eating it even on this occasion: he gave the pheasants to his daughters in the administration.

We could speak of many other aspects of the Father's spirit of mortification and penance, such as the care he took in his use of objects, the control he exercised over his own reactions, the sacrifices involved in his keeping silence or speaking up, depending on the circumstances, and so on. In my opinion, however, the most important feature of our founder's heroic spirit of penance was his readiness to "hide and pass unnoticed," which was the motto of his life.

Our Father always said that he preferred holocaust to sacrifice. That was why, for example, he wanted the flowers that were placed on the altar, next to the tabernacle, to be placed directly on the altar, between the candles: this way, all their freshness would be used up in honor of the Lord.

Perhaps this would be a good time to discuss how he lived the virtue of humility.

I can affirm that our founder lived his whole life with the most complete self-forgetfulness. He thought very little of himself—he directed every thought, word, and deed of his to the glory and service of God. Starting in his youth, he repeated throughout his life the aspiration "Deo omnis gloria!" He explained this in a point of *Consideraciones Espirituales* which later became point No. 780 of *The Way:* "'Deo omnis gloria'—'All glory to God.' It is an emphatic confession of our nothingness. He, Jesus, is everything. We, without him, are worth nothing: Nothing. Our vainglory would be just that: vain glory; it would be sacrilegious theft; the 'I' should not appear anywhere."

On February 4, 1975, I was with the Father on board an airplane which was about ready to leave the Madrid airport for Venezuela. Suddenly, to our great surprise, a daughter of his, the Rhodesian journalist Lynden Parry, entered the cabin. She had gone to the trouble of getting there because she wanted to thank him for everything that the Work had done for her; it had led her first to a conversion to Catholicism and later to a vocation in Opus Dei. The Father replied, "We all ought to thank the Lord." When she again insisted on thanking him personally, our founder interrupted her affectionately but also decisively. "Don't thank me," he said. "God writes a letter, and then puts it into an envelope. The letter is taken from the envelope, and the envelope is thrown into the wastepaper basket."

He was, of course, conscious that the Lord wanted his cooperation for the working of marvels, and he also said this to his children: "For God to bestow graces through us, with full hands, requires humility and sanctity on our part." But he never forgot that "the monument is erected to the painter; the brush is thrown away; it has fulfilled its function by obeying the hands of the artist."

He always refused honors and dignities. The following episode is, I think, particularly significant. On February 11, 1933,
Angel Herrera, who had just been named president of Catholic
Action in Spain after having left his position as publisher of the
newspaper *El Debate* (he later became a priest, then bishop of
Málaga and a cardinal), had a meeting with Fr. Josemaría: he told
him the news of his own appointment, which was not yet official,
and offered the Father an important post. Together with the nuncio, Angel Herrera had projected the creation of a center of formation for priests who would assist Catholic Action at various levels;
he proposed that the Father accept the position of director of the
center. The founder of the Work immediately refused the offer.
President Herrera insisted, pointing out that it was a key position,
one of great responsibility, since all the best priests of Spain would
meet in that place. But the Father replied that for precisely that
reason he could not take this job—it was too important. "Besides,"
he added, "there are many others who would do it better than I."

I want to emphasize that those words were not just a polite
excuse; he was fully convinced that other priests would truly be
more capable of handling that activity than he himself would have
been. For his own part, he believed that he could be effective only
in the specific task assigned to him by our Lord, the task for which
he had a special charism, a particular grace from God.

After the Spanish Civil War, the prestige of the founder grew
still greater. In the face of the by-no-means-remote possibility of
his being named a bishop, he asked the permission of his confessor, Fr. José María García Lahiguerra, to make a vow never to accept the duty and dignity of being a bishop. Fr. José María replied
that he would not allow him to make such a vow without the consent of the bishop of Madrid. And so, in a conversation with
Bishop Leopoldo Eijo y Garay which took place on March 19, 1941,
the Father posed the question. Afterwards our founder made some
notes on the various topics they had discussed, and among them
we find this comment: "His Excellency won't give me permission.
I am really unhappy about this."

He abhorred praise; he stated quite emphatically that the
worst thing that can happen to a person is to receive nothing but

praise. The other side of this coin is that he was very thankful for the corrections that he received. Precisely for this reason, he engaged in a filial tussle with the Holy See to ensure that the president general of Opus Dei (as the Prelate was then called) would not be deprived of fraternal correction, which in Opus Dei is a fundamental means of formation. When he first presented our *ius peculiare* [particular law] to the ecclesiastical authorities (this happened also later on, in 1946 and 1949), he had to overcome misgivings concerning this aspect of it. They reminded him, for one thing, that according to centuries-old tradition, major superiors could not be corrected by their subjects. But our founder would not give in, because he did not want to be deprived of this great help. He said, "This just isn't fair. All my sons and daughters have this means of improvement that is rooted in the Gospel, namely, fraternal correction. In other words, all these others—even though it causes them pain, and both those who give and those who receive it have to overcome themselves and have to be humble and mortified—have this marvelous means of sanctification. Should I, who am a poor man, and those who will succeed me (who will be better than I am, but still only poor men) not have this means of sanctification?" Finally the role of *custodes seu admonitores* ["guardians" or "advisors"] was approved: they live at the side of the president general (today, the Prelate) and help him by means of whatever suggestions they consider appropriate.

He warded off, with great naturalness, manifestations of the gratitude, admiration, and enthusiasm felt by those who heard him, for example, on the many occasions when he preached retreats. In 1948 he preached one of these at Molinoviejo, to a group of professionals. At that time I was in Rome, but I heard about this just a little afterwards—from the principal eyewitness, Amadeo de Fuenmayor. The retreatants, it seems, had already started to voice their enthusiasm, and so the Father reminded them, several times, of the need for silence. Then just before the last meditation, to head off any onslaught of adulation, he expressly instructed Amadeo not to pronounce the customary closing aspiration—"Sancta Maria, spes nostra, sedes sapientiae"—until a while after he had left the chapel and one could hear the sound of the car that was to take him back to Madrid. So, of course, by the time the retreatants left the chapel, he was gone and there was nothing they could about it, except berate Amadeo for having let him get away. I can testify that by means of tricks of this kind, our founder was able, right up to his last day on earth, to follow the example of the hidden life that Jesus lived in Nazareth.

At the beginning of the forties, an aunt of mine and her husband invited our founder and me to a luncheon. Another guest was Manuel Aznar, a very well known intellectual; considered at that time the greatest journalist in Spain, he would later become the Spanish ambassador to the United States. Well, at a certain point this gentleman said to the Father, "How I would love to write your biography!" And the reply was, "I can give it to you right now. In the holy Gospel [Luke 2:51] the biography of the Lord's childhood is given in three words: 'Erat subditus illis' ['He was subject to them']; Jesus obeyed Mary and Joseph. And then in the Acts of the Apostles [10:38] there is another biography of Jesus, this time in just two words: 'Pertransiit benefaciendo' ['He went about, doing good']. Well, for me, one word is all that's needed: 'Sinner'! But a sinner who loves Jesus Christ very much."

Countless times—I first witnessed it in 1935, but knew he had already been doing this for many years—he would, to implore God's grace, pray prostrate on the ground; he was profoundly convinced that that was the posture best suited to him, since he possessed no merit. He told me himself that it was his habit to make his prayer prostrate on the ground because he realized the baseness of his own condition and the need he had to beg pardon from the Lord, and to implore his help, in a way befitting his own nothingness.

We could spend a long time recalling other edifying episodes, but I feel we would be trespassing against his own reserve. I will just recall one last particular. One day, in the fifties, during the construction of our central headquarters, the Father noticed that as they were taking down the scaffolding, the workmen were throwing away the large nails that had served to hold the planks together. It occurred to him that without those nails, which the workmen were throwing away with such indifference, it would not have been possible for them to put up the scaffolding. So he had the nails collected and sent many of them to the various regions of Opus Dei, as a symbol reminding us of what each of us is supposed to be: an instrument which, worthless as it is in itself, the Lord uses to accomplish his work.

12. A Reputation for Sanctity

Father, in your foreword to Friends of God, *the first of several posthumous works by the founder of Opus Dei (it came out in 1977), you wrote that our Father "never set out to be an* author, *though he figures among the leading teachers of Christian spirituality." We can see here a reflection of his humility, which explains his reluctance to publish books, even when (and perhaps because)* The Way *had already been well known for decades throughout the world. Let's talk a little about the books of the founder, which I will briefly recall here, having been gratefully involved in the preparing of their Italian editions. In order of composition, the first was* Holy Rosary, *written in 1931, though not published until 1934.* Consideraciones Espirituales, *mimeographed in 1932, was also published in 1934; in 1939 an expanded version appeared, with the definitive title* The Way. *A collection of interviews granted to the press of various countries,* Conversations with Monsignor Escrivá de Balaguer, *appeared in 1968; the first collection of homilies,* Christ Is Passing By, *appeared in 1973. Then we have the posthumous works:* Friends of God *(1977),* The Way of the Cross *(1981), and the two books of meditations which with* The Way *form a trilogy:* Furrow *(1986) and* The Forge *(1987). Finally, there is that work of scholarly research in the field of theology and canon law,* La Abadesa de las Huelgas *(1944): the founder, ever concerned to find a proper place for Opus Dei within the framework of canon law, became interested in the extraordinary case of a quasi-episcopal jurisdiction at one time exercised by the abbess of that monastery in Burgos.*

Certainly the spiritual writings of the founder have contributed substantially to his being so widely regarded as a saint.

But because he was seeking not popularity but rather the good of souls, I must emphasize that his reputation for sanctity really has arisen as a consequence of the spiritual fruits which his readers have drawn from meditating on his writings. There are countless testimonies in support of this.

I have already mentioned the high regard Pope Paul VI had for *The Way*—he used this book for his own personal meditation. His was an appreciation dating a long way back. One of the first members of the Work to come to Italy, José Luis Orlandis, gave a copy of *The Way* in 1945 to the then Msgr. Montini. In his thank-you letter (written on February 2 of that same year), the future pope said: "Its pages are a deeply felt and vibrant appeal to the generous hearts of our youth; by revealing sublime ideals to them, they lead young people to think reflectively and seriously, as a preparation for living a supernatural life to the full. . . . [This book] has already produced plentiful fruits in the Spanish university environment. I am immensely joyful that *The Way* has already had such encouraging results, and I ask the Lord to continue to bless it and to let it become more widely known, for the good of many souls."

There are innumerable testimonies, from individuals in every walk of life, of light and strength received through the founder's words. Cardinal Maurice Otunga, archbishop of Nairobi, wrote this: "I do not know Msgr. Escrivá personally, but I have read a great deal of his writings. Every time I meditate with the help of one of his books, I begin to perceive that what seems to me impossible is in fact possible: that I too can become a saint."

A Spanish nun who lives in Mexico tells an edifying story that begins in the forties. Having just been assigned to make the move from Spain to Mexico, she went to the courthouse to obtain a passport, and there she ran into various bureaucratic problems—not the least of which was the fact that the official she was dealing with was a declared atheist. What to do? The only thing she could think of was to give him a copy of *The Way*. Well, she finally did get a passport, as did another sister of the order who was going to Colombia. In 1980 she returned to Spain. One day she went to Mass at the cathedral, and on her way out she was

stopped by a man who shouted, "It's your fault! It's your fault!"
She didn't understand what the man was getting at until he
explained, "You gave me a copy of *The Way* before you left for
Mexico, and I was converted because of that book."

*The prestige which the founder of Opus Dei enjoyed among
those who met him is of a piece with his reputation for sanctity.
Can you recall some testimonies on this?*

One especially significant chapter is composed of the testimonies of many seminarians, priests, and religious who partici-
pated in some of the many retreats he preached in the years 1938
to 1945 throughout all of Spain. The origin of these testimonies is
interesting. In those years, as I have already mentioned, a very
real campaign of incredible maligning of our founder had broken
out; he was being accused of heresy and Freemasonry, of ensnar-
ing souls and exercising an evil influence over them. And yet,
despite all this, bishops of many dioceses, bishops who knew him
personally and considered him a saint, continued inviting him to
preach retreats for their clergy. Many priests were thus able to get
to know him, and they felt it was their duty to defend him
against the accusations as well as they could. The simplest way to
do that was to write to me, and so we have testimonies that are
chronologically very closely connected with the facts which are
being described. Looked at in the light of those circumstances,
these testimonies come alive with all the particular detail of
spontaneous and sincere expression.

Thus, for example, the Most Reverend Marcelino Olaechea,
the bishop of Pamplona, wrote to me on November 22, 1941: "My
dear Alvaro: My dearest friend Fr. José María, that very good
father that God has given you, preached the spiritual exercises for
all the new parish priests of this blessed diocese of Pamplona, the
clergy of which is truly exemplary. I say 'all,' because even though
we have not yet had the last retreat, I hope that he will also be able
to preach that one. . . . May God keep him with us for many, many
years, for the great glory of his holy Church. I beg you to take
good care of this treasure."

And the present Cardinal Angel Suquía, the archbishop of Madrid, wrote in 1942, in reference to a course of spiritual exercises he had taken as a seminarian towards the end of 1938: "I remember to this day the love of Christ that breathed through all his phrases. I have an indelible memory of these words of his: 'Love Christ to madness, with the passion of those who are in love: like a miser loves his gold; like a businessman loves his business; like a lover loves his lady; like a poor wretch loves his sensual pleasures.'"

From October 3 to 11, 1944, the founder preached (as I have already mentioned) a retreat for the Augustinian monks of the Monastery of El Escorial, at a time when he was in very poor health. He had a virulent boil on his neck and a very high fever; it was also during this time that he was diagnosed as diabetic. Even so, he kept his promise of preaching to them. The Augustinian provincial, Fr. Carlos Vicuña, wrote to me on October 26: "I would like to convey to you a brief impression of the spiritual exercises preached by Fr. José María Escrivá to the Augustinian religious of the Royal Monastery of El Escorial, in this month of October. Everyone agrees that he has surpassed all expectations; he has completely satisfied the desires of the superiors . . . We are now waiting on God, expecting that the fruits will be very abundant. Everyone without exception—every one of our fathers, theologians, philosophers, brothers, and young men in formation—was hanging on his words and, as the expression goes, holding their breath. Every one of those half-hour conferences seemed to them to last only ten minutes, overpowered as they were by that torrent of fervor, enthusiasm, sincerity, and outpouring of the heart. 'It comes from within—he speaks that way because he has an inner fire and life'; 'he is a saint, an apostle—if we outlive him, many of us will see him raised to the altars' . . . These are some of the statements I have heard from the participants. The unanimity of the praises is highly unusual and remarkable, especially when you consider that the audience was composed mostly of intellectuals and scholars. Not a word was heard that was less than approving. It is true that he came preceded by a reputation for sanctity, but it is no less true that, far from gainsaying that reputation, he has completely confirmed it."

Many priests who spoke with our founder—whether in Rome or various other European localities, starting in 1946, or later during his trips to Latin America in 1970, 1974, and 1975—have made similar statements.

I have already spoken of how much Popes Pius XII, John XXIII, and Paul VI appreciated him. I would like to add now that Pope Paul, during an audience granted to me on March 5, 1976, affirmed that he considered the founder of Opus Dei "one of the individuals in the history of the Church who received the most charisms and who responded to the gifts given by God with the most generosity." He repeated these ideas to me in another audience, on June 19, 1978, adding that he had realized the extraordinariness of this figure in the history of the Church from the day he had first met him, in 1946.

I would like to mention also that Cardinal Ildefonso Schuster, the archbishop of Milan, told the members of the Work who were beginning apostolic activities in Milan—and did so in a tone of profound conviction—that our founder was one of those saints that Providence raises up every so often, as the centuries pass, to renew the Church. He compared him to the great founders: St. Bernard, St. Francis, . . . And the cardinal went on to express to me, in similar terms, his personal admiration for the Father.

The famous historian Msgr. Hubert Jedin put it this way: "As a Church historian I can state that an effect so profound and universal in the Church of God can be produced only by a person who has placed himself or herself fully at God's disposal, thus converting their whole being into an instrument for the sanctification of others and for the realization of the Kingdom of God on earth. The results produced by the founder of Opus Dei would not have been possible had he not been a saint."

One more episode, from the many I could tell: During our Father's brief stay in Guatemala, on the occasion of his second trip to Latin America (in 1975), Cardinal Mario Casariego, the archbishop of Guatemala City, expressed a number of times his desire to receive our founder's blessing. The evening the Father arrived in the country they had dinner together, and when they were finished, the cardinal went down on his knees and asked for a blessing. At that, our founder also knelt down, and he replied, "I don't give blessings to cardinals." When, in the face of the cardinal's insistence, he did give in just so far as to trace the sign of the cross on his forehead, he got this amiable protest: "Today you have not given me a blessing, but I won't let you leave Guatemala without giving me one." On the day of the Father's departure, Cardinal Casariego came to meet him at the Opus Dei center where we were staying. They entered the chapel together and spent a few moments in prayer. Then, when the Father was getting ready to leave, the cardinal blocked his way and exclaimed, "In the presence of Jesus in the Blessed Sacrament, and before these sons of yours, I tell you I will not budge from here until you give me your blessing!" "Mario, you are making me do what nobody else has ever been able to make me do!" the Father replied, seeing himself forced to give in. Afterwards the cardinal explained, "I was not about to miss out on receiving the blessing of a saint!"

During that trip to Guatemala the Father was, unfortunately, quite unwell, and he had to cancel some get-togethers where he could have reached many people with his preaching. Even so, the day we left, thousands and thousands of people came to the airport just to see him, even from a distance, and receive his blessing.

> *In our hearts, all of us in Opus Dei have always considered the founder a saint, though when he was alive we had to keep this from showing, so as not to incur his displeasure. We were always wanting to have a photograph of him, and anyone lucky enough to have received something written with his own hand has preserved it as a precious souvenir, something destined to become a relic. You, who got to be at his side for over forty years, will certainly have personal memories in this regard.*

From 1950 on, the Father had to go to the dentist with a certain regularity; he went to a good friend of mine, Dr. Hruska. I asked the doctor to unobtrusively give me, after each visit, any pieces of tooth that he might have extracted, because I wanted to keep them. We tried to do this without the Father's knowledge, but eventually he did catch on. Somehow he found out what was going on. So one day, in 1961, while I was in a hospital in Rome awaiting surgery, the Father asked Fr. Javier Echevarría to help him find the fragments. He was bound and determined to throw them all away, because he did not want us to have any souvenir of his person. "Let's go find those nasty things," he said.

> In the life of our Father, there were some extraordinary events, supernatural interventions, especially in connection with the founding of the Work. May I ask you to say something about this aspect of the life of a saint?

Well, of course, this is a question that can't be answered in a full or detailed way. The humility and prudence of our founder led him to keep such things to himself, though he did not deny that on more than one occasion, extraordinary interventions of God had taken place. Following explicit instructions from the Holy See, he spoke about these matters only for the good of our souls, and even then he told only the minimum necessary.

I am also convinced that just as our founder burned the first of his spiritual notebooks because they contained many accounts of supernatural experiences, it is very probable that there were many other experiences which he never revealed at all, which are known only to God. He wanted at all costs to make sure no one would get the idea, from reading his notebooks, that he was a saint.

Moreover, we ought not to forget that the nucleus of the spirituality entrusted by the Lord to the founder of Opus Dei consists precisely in striving to find God in ordinary life and in one's ordinary occupations: nothing would be more opposed to this, therefore, than to draw attention to extraordinary phenomena. Our founder often said, "The miracles in the Gospel are enough for me," and indeed, his conduct and his preaching were distinguished by an exaltation of the value of the most common situations, and by his effort to imitate the hidden life of Jesus.

I remember that on October 2, 1968, the Father celebrated this day, the fortieth anniversary of the founding of the Work, in our retreat house of Pozoalbero, in Jerez de la Frontera [in Spain];

I was there with him. During a get-together he expressed his appreciation for the fact that none of us had asked him any questions about the founding of Opus Dei [as we usually did on October 2]; he added that if we had, it was likely that some intimate, confidential detail would have escaped his lips. We then began to ask him earnestly about how the Lord had intervened in the birth of the Work, but he skillfully avoided answering our questions. Once the clamor died down, he said, in a very serious tone of voice, "My sons: I have deliberately refrained from telling you anything. I would be lying if I told you that the Lord has not made extraordinary interventions in my case. He has done so, whenever it was necessary for the progress of the Work. . . . Yet, and especially on a day like today, I have not wanted to tell you anything about all that, so that it will remain impressed on you, and you can repeat it in the future to your brothers, that our path is one of ordinary things: it is to sanctify the common, ordinary actions of every day; to transform the prose of daily life into the heroic verse of epic poetry."

All of that notwithstanding, I would like to mention a few extraordinary episodes I do know something about. I've already made passing reference to the interior locutions that constituted one of the means chosen by the Lord to form the soul of the Father. These locutions, he used to explain, were "intellectual, without the noise of words, but they remained as if branded by fire on my soul." Some particularly important ones have been recorded in biographies of the Father which have already been published; I will speak of other ones.

Often this kind of inspiration would consist of an unusually profound understanding of a scriptural text. This is what would happen: suddenly a psalm verse or some other scriptural text, a passage which up until that time he had never dwelt upon with special attention, would come irresistibly to his lips. Afterwards, in the same sudden and irresistible way, without his seeking it, there would come to him a completely new spiritual interpretation, one which raised the level of his contemplation still higher: the Holy Spirit was taking him by surprise and showing him, beyond the shadow of a doubt, that all this was the work of the Lord. In his personal notes we find records of many such instances.

The Father told me himself that in the midst of the great difficulties at the beginning, the Lord had made him see how utterly powerless he was, but at the same time did not fail to keep alive in him the serene certainty of divine assistance. Thus, for example, on December 12, 1931, the Lord impressed upon his soul, with unusual force, the words "Inter medium montium pertransibunt aquae" ["The waters will pass between the mountains" (Ps 104:10); see *The Way*, point No. 12]—indicating that despite all difficulties, the Work would spread everywhere.

Leaping over a long span of years, I'd like now to call attention to some locutions of the Lord that took place in more recent times. If our founder's whole existence was stamped with the sign of the cross, the last years of his earthly life appear as perhaps the most sorrowful. The cause of the Father's profound suffering was the insults cast at the Church by precisely those who should most have loved and defended her. Doctrinal errors, moral and disciplinary disorders, flagrant disobedience in liturgical matters, a seemingly unstoppable loss of priestly and religious vocations—all these, together with the confusion that spread everywhere among the People of God, made our founder suffer a prolonged and very acute Calvary. Then, in the midst of such turmoil, the Lord intervened. On May 8, 1970, he made these words resound in his soul, thus enriching it with new light: "Si Deus nobiscum, quis contra nos?" ["If God is with us, who can be against us?" (Rom 8:31)]. This, of course, strengthened him in his faith; the Father now had a clear confirmation that the Divine Spouse had not abandoned his Church, that he would without fail bring her safely through the storm. At the same time, it gave him a firmer understanding of his own responsibility, and that of Opus Dei as a whole, to work hard at the task of confirming and propagating correct doctrine.

But his hope did not lessen the intensity of his sorrow. Grateful as he was to God for his having spared Opus Dei such tribulations, his soul was still in grief over the terribly hard times the Church was going through. On August 6, 1970, the Lord made these words of Isaiah echo with an unexpected force in his mind—

"Clama, ne cesses!" ["Cry aloud, do not hold back!" (Is 58:1)]—
and he understood that God was asking him not only to intensify
his own prayer and penance, but also, by means of energetic and
insistent preaching, to reach the most distant regions with an
exhortation to firm loyalty to the Church. This, among other
things, was why he left Rome on October 4, 1972, to go to the
Iberian peninsula and traverse all of Spain and Portugal before
returning on November 30. These were two months of exhausting catechesis, during which his burning message of fidelity
reached hundreds of thousands of souls. Later on, from May 22
to August 31, 1974, and again in February 1975 (yes, just a few
months before his death), he journeyed to Latin America: he
traveled through seven countries, carrying out a vast and intense
catechesis in meetings with thousands of persons who came to
hear him. I would like to add that the interior locutions I have
been describing not only brought a new stimulus to the
founder's heroic self-denial in spending his energies in the service of the Church, but also gave sustenance to his certainty that
a definitive solution would be found with respect to the juridical
configuration of Opus Dei.

> *In the life of our Father, then, extraordinary gifts were not
> lacking.*

I can personally attest to the fact that he could give precise
answers to problems which no one had mentioned to him, and
could "see" events which were taking place in distant regions or
which would take place in the future. Let me tell you of an event
that took place in 1939, in which I myself was involved. As soon as
the war ended, our founder returned to Madrid. For some months
it was not possible for me to join him, because the army had put
me in command of the first company of a battalion which was
assigned to Olot (in Gerona), near the French border. There I
became acquainted with a very fine lieutenant by the name of Fernando Delapuente, and began to do some apostolate with him. One
day I received a letter from our founder which said something to
this effect: "Tell your friend Delapuente that what happened to him

today is because of such and such." I was amazed—I had said absolutely nothing to our founder about that friend. Furthermore, in that period just after the war, communications were in such a terrible state that it took several days just to go from Olot to Madrid; and Fernando had not been to Madrid. Nor did he know the founder. I decided to invite my friend to go horseback riding with me outside the city, where we could have some peace and quiet. I was able to tell him the whole story calmly—and yet his surprise was so great that he fell out of his saddle. He told me that he was going through a very hard time over something, and he told me all about it, adding that until then he had not spoken of it to a soul. Needless to say, he happily followed the advice of the Father.

Around that same time, it also happened that some girls were making an attempt to seduce a member of the Work. We later found out that on the very day they were going to try to put him in a compromising situation, our founder was with some of his sons and suddenly exclaimed, "At this moment one of your brothers is in great need of help! Let's say a Memorare for him." I should add that the brother in question had not had time to inform the Father about what was going on. Well, the danger instantly vanished. And thus arose the custom we have of saying this prayer at least once a day. The Father called the Memorare the "oratio saxum" [the "rock prayer"], because he thought of it as a secure support for the member of the Work most in need of help at any given moment.

In 1948, during a trip to Sicily, the founder met Fr. Francesco Ricceri, a priest working in Catania, and he described for him the spirit and apostolate of Opus Dei. I was present at the meeting, but I prefer to use the words of Fr. Ricceri himself. This is how he related it on February 21, 1978, by which time he was bishop of Trapani: "Attracted by the beauty of this institution, I asked the Father, with some insistence, to set up an Opus Dei residence in Catania; and I said that I could help him in every way, since I was pastor of a prominent parish and served as the counselor for the Italian Catholic University Federation. The Father tried his best to keep from giving me an answer, but I kept insisting, until finally he said,

'If you were going to stay in Catania, I'd love for you to help me set up a residence. But you're not going to be around, so how can you help me?' I replied that I had no intention whatsoever of leaving Catania. Then the Father gave me a steady look, fixing on me those penetrating eyes of his, and said, 'You can be sure of this: in a few years they will make you a bishop, and you will have to leave Catania.' I thought he was just joking with me, but in 1957, reality confirmed the prophetic nature of those words." In the note Fr. Ricceri sent to our founder on April 24, 1957, to announce his imminent episcopal consecration, he said it was impossible for him to "have any doubt about the prophetic spirit" of the Father.

In Burgos, in 1938, a high-ranking government official was taking steps to initiate a completely unjustified indictment of a member of the Work, Pedro Casciaro. To begin with, he had it in for Pedro's father, who had collaborated with the republican government; this official accused Mr. Casciaro of being a Freemason and a communist, and of being responsible for numerous assassinations of right-wing people in Albacete. He further maintained that Pedro himself was a communist and that he had propagated that ideology in Albacete on the occasion of the elections in February 1936, which had resulted in a victory for the Popular Front. He inferred from all this that Pedro had infiltrated the national zone for the purpose of spying on Franco's army—more precisely, at the headquarters of General Orgaz.

The accusation was utterly false, although based on a partial truth. Under the circumstances, an accusation of this sort was a very serious matter; Pedro was in real danger of being condemned to death. Military trials in those days were often quite summary, and without the legal guarantees needed to get at the truth.

Our founder tried to dissuade the accuser from committing such a terrible injustice. He went to speak with him, in the company of Professor José María Albareda. It was a very difficult conversation. The man's attitude was cold and haughty; nevertheless, the founder managed to stay calm, defending Pedro with all the paternal affection he could muster. At first gently, and then with great energy, he tried to make it clear to this man that he was committing a monstrous injustice. At one blow, he would be bereaving Pedro's mother of a son and a husband. He asked him to think of his own wife.

But the man replied that since it was not possible at that time to capture and punish the father, the son ought to pay the penalty in his place, even if he was innocent. Furthermore, he observed, many innocent persons were dying at the front or in the prisons of the Red zone. With a vehemence that startled José María Albareda, our founder declared that such an attitude was inconceivable in a Christian—didn't this man realize that he would have to render to God an account of his actions? He added that he would certainly not like to be in his position and risk having to stand before God's judgment seat with such unjust rancor in his soul. He exhorted him to realize that the Lord could call him to account that very day to answer for his intentions, or even punish the deed in his children. But neither these charity-filled supplications nor the dynamism of the Father succeeded in softening the heart of that unfortunate man. He obstinately kept repeating, "Either the father or the son has got to pay the price!"

Our founder walked out of the man's office dejectedly and in silence. José María Albareda was amazed both by the manner of the Father's defense of Pedro and by the degree of hostility displayed by the other to the very end. The Father descended the stairs with his eyes cast down, and said, as though thinking aloud, "Tomorrow or the next day, a funeral."

The afternoon of that same day, the founder went out in the company of another of his sons to get some things done. He told him also what had happened, and in a sad tone of voice repeated what he had said, in reference to the family of Pedro's accuser: "Tomorrow or the next day, a funeral." A little later, the young man who was accompanying him suddenly stopped and went pale: he had just seen an announcement of the sudden death of that official. (It was the custom in Burgos to post death notices on store windows and on the walls of buildings.) Our founder recited the responsorial prayer for the dead, and said he had "interpreted" wrongly. When he had interiorly heard the words "Tomorrow or the next day, a funeral," he had thought they referred to a son of that man—a son who was the same age as Pedro Casciaro, and who at that moment was at the front.

Poor Pedro, when he heard the news, was so upset that he got sick and had to go to bed. Our founder tried to calm him down; he encouraged him to be thankful to the Lord for having protected him and his father. He also told him that he should not worry about the fate of that unfortunate official, for even though the event was in itself very sad, he had the moral certainty that our Lord had had compassion on that man and had given him the grace of final repentance. He confided to him that ever since he'd left the man's office, he had not ceased praying for him and his children.

These are truly impressive episodes which testify to the level of his intimacy with God. I have also heard tell of something in connection with "Our Lady of the Kisses," a statue of our Lady that the Father used to always kiss before leaving the house.

We have access to some of his personal notebooks, and if we turn to the fifth of these, we find an entry which reflects at the same time the divine favor our founder received, his humility, and his obedience:

"Octave of the patronal feast of St. Joseph, April 20, 1932: Later on, if I have time, I'll catch up on some other notes I need to write up. For now I just want to jot down something that—once again!—makes clear the goodness of my Immaculate Mother, and my own wretchedness. Late yesterday, as usual, I humbled myself: I put my forehead on the floor, before going to bed, and I asked my father and lord St. Joseph, and the souls in purgatory, to wake me up at the right time. . . . As always happens when I humbly beg for this (no matter what time I've gone to bed), I came out of a deep sleep, just as if someone was calling out to me, certain that it was the right time to get up. . . . So I did get up, and, filled with humble gratitude, I prostrated myself on the ground . . . and began my meditation. Well, sometime between six-thirty and a quarter to seven, I saw for quite some time that the face of my Lady of the Kisses was bright with happiness, with joy. I looked very carefully:

I thought she was smiling, because it had this effect on me, even though her lips never moved. I was very calm, and I spoke many affectionate words to my Mother.

"This same thing has happened to me on other occasions too—this which I have just related in such detail. I've tried not to give it any importance, almost not daring to believe it. I even came to the point of improvising a little test, to see if it was just my imagination, because I don't easily believe in extraordinary events. It didn't work: when I positively wished that she would smile, trying to make it happen by my own imagination, the face of my Lady of the Kisses kept the hieratic seriousness which the poor little sculpture has. In other words, my Lady, holy Mary, on the octave of St. Joseph, has given a little caress to her child. Blessed be her most pure heart!

"Feast of St. Mark, April 25, 1932: This morning I was with my Father Sánchez. I decided to tell him what happened on the twentieth, though I felt a kind of reluctance or shame. It was difficult, but I told him."

Were there also extraordinary interventions through other people?

An odd question! However, an event of 1935 comes to mind—the founder was setting up the first chapel of a center of the Work, at the residence on Ferraz Street. It was a time of serious financial difficulty, and the Father had worked hard to get together the necessary (simple but dignified) liturgical vessels, vestments, etc. For the tabernacle, as I have already mentioned, the Father had gone to Mother Muratori, a Reparation nun who was very supportive of him; this good nun had loaned him a wooden tabernacle. But there were still some other things he needed, and it seemed impossible for him to find them, or the money with which to buy them. Then the Father remembered that phrase of Sacred Scripture, "Ite ad Ioseph" ["Go to Joseph" (Gn 41:55)], the phrase used by the pharaoh to tell the Egyptians how they could obtain food during the famine. And he began to invoke the holy Patriarch, St. Joseph, and to ask him for whatever was needed in order for the Blessed

Sacrament to be reserved in that house. One fine day—he told me this himself—a man showed up in the porter's lodging of the building where the residence was, and left a package. When the Father opened it, he found precisely the things he needed to initiate liturgical worship in that chapel.

Were there any favors obtained through his intercession while he was still alive?

In our postulation archives, we have some testimonies about healings obtained through his intercession while he was still with us; healings attributed to the merits of his holy life. There are some accounts of really substantial favors; others have to do with little graces obtained suddenly and in a scientifically inexplicable manner.

Such episodes demonstrate that even during the life of our founder, people attributed to him a special power of intercession with God; people who knew him were so convinced of his extraordinary closeness to our Lord that they felt themselves inspired to confide their pains and sorrows to him. But that's not all. I even know of cases in which, already in the early forties, the people concerned would invoke the founder in their prayers and present the merits of his life to our Lord, for the purpose of moving the Divine Mercy to grant the graces they were seeking. With great naturalness they were anticipating what tens of thousands of faithful throughout the world would one day be doing: invoking the founder of Opus Dei, and thus entrusting him with their own needs.

In other words, more significant than the particular miraculous interventions worked through the founder during his life (and these were not lacking)—what seems to me even more revealing, as a proof of his sanctity, was this custom of invoking him privately that started when he was still alive, as well as the great confidence with which people entrusted their gravest necessities to his prayers. Our founder, even on this earth, had a reputation for obtaining heavenly favors.

Working constantly at his side, I had the privilege of getting to read with him lots of letters in which people confided to him their sufferings and entrusted them to his prayers; I am a witness of how he took to heart all these problems, and of the intensity with which he recommended them to the Lord, almost as though he felt it his duty to wrest these graces out of God's hands. I remember particularly the impression he made on me in those frequent instances when, after reading a letter, he would become recollected for a few moments, and then make a gesture of complete tranquillity, which seemed to denote his certainty that the matter had already been resolved. In this connection I was especially struck by the case of young Octavio Sitjar de Togores, who had suffered an accident in which his mouth, including his upper palate, was severely burned and deformed. When Octavio's father told him of the sufferings of his child, our founder told him he was sure that the boy would get better—as if he were quite certain that the Lord had heard his supplication—which is indeed what happened. I recall a similar trust he showed in the case of a worker who, during the construction of Cavabianca, was involved in an accident and had his right hand and part of his forearm cut off. For several days the Father prayed intensely for his cure, and then he stopped being concerned; suddenly he was convinced that that man would recover and return to work. And that is what happened.

13. June 26, 1975

*The founder taught us to fear neither life nor death, because
"God is the Lord of life and death." And in* The Way *he wrote:
"You talk of dying 'heroically.' Don't you think that it is more
heroic to die unnoticed, in a good bed, like a bourgeois, . . . but
to die of Love?" (point No. 743). Was our Father, before 1975,
ever in danger of death?*

Yes. As a matter of fact, the cure of his diabetes, which was
diagnosed in 1944 but probably began much earlier than that, was
connected with an event in which he nearly lost his life.

This illness, which was very serious and had side effects that
were particularly painful, ran its course until April 27, 1954, the
feast of Our Lady of Montserrat. Two or three days earlier, the
Father's physician, Dr. Faelli, had prescribed a new brand of long-
acting insulin, and had told us we should give him 110 units per
injection. As usual, I made this my responsibility. Well, when I
went to give him his first injection, I took care to read the leaflet of
directions that came with the insulin, and it said that each dose of
this new type of insulin was equivalent to a little over twice the
normal dose. So it seemed to me that 110 units would be excessive,
and because I knew that the higher dose of insulin would increase
the Father's migraines, I reduced the dosage, going against the
doctor's directions. Even so, it provoked an allergic reaction of a
kind I had never come across before. I spoke of this to Dr. Faelli,
but he told me to keep using that insulin.

On April 27, then, I gave the Father his injection of insulin, five
or ten minutes before lunch, and afterwards we went together to the
dining room. (Since the Father had to keep to a very strict diet at
that time, he and I ate by ourselves, so that none of the others would

feel inhibited or obliged to eat less; that way they could be served things he could not eat, such as pasta, potatoes, and so forth.) Shortly after having said grace, he said to me in a very labored voice: "Alvaro, absolution!" At first I did not understand him; I just couldn't understand him. God permitted that I should not understand his words. Then he said it again: "Absolution!" And then, after a few seconds, "Absolution: '*Ego te absolvo . . .*'"; and just at that moment he lost consciousness. I remember that he went bright red, and then an ashen yellow. He looked as if he had shrunk.

I gave him absolution immediately and did whatever else I could. After calling the most readily available doctor, I put some sugar in the Father's mouth, and then a little water to help him swallow; he did not react, and his pulse was imperceptible. The doctor, Miguel Angel Madurga (he's a member of the Work), arrived thirteen minutes later, when the Father was beginning to regain consciousness. He checked his pulse, measured his blood pressure, and told us what needed to be done. Our founder had the courtesy to ask him if he had eaten yet. When the doctor replied that he had not, the Father insisted that he eat then and there, and he conversed with him quite tranquilly, answering all his questions. When the doctor left, the Father said to me, "My son, I have gone blind; I can't see a thing." I asked him, "Father, why didn't you tell the doctor?" And he replied, "I didn't want to cause him unnecessary worry; this might be just something temporary."

He had to stay in the dining room for several hours, because he could not move and he did not want to cause anyone anxiety. Eventually he began to regain his sight, and I accompanied him back to his room. When he looked in the mirror, he said, "Now I know what I will look like when I'm dead." I told him that actually he was looking much better by then, and that he should have seen himself a few hours before, when he really looked like a corpse. I then found out that he had, indeed, experienced something that people say happens when one is at the brink of death. He told me that the Lord had allowed him to see his whole life in the twinkling of an eye, like a film in super-fast motion; he'd had time to ask pardon for all the failings he'd been guilty of, and also for something else: an apparent misinterpretation. What had happened was that the Lord had at one time given him to understand, or so he had thought, that he would not die until quite a few years later. But now here he was, already looking death in the face, so obviously (he thought) he must have gotten that wrong; he therefore asked God's pardon for not having understood him correctly.

Well, Dr. Faelli came to visit him right away, and was amazed to discover that all the symptoms of diabetes had vanished, even though, as everyone knows, it is an incurable illness. That something extraordinary had happened was so clear that the doctor immediately stopped treatment and declared him cured. Our founder made the simple observation that the same Lord who had sent him that disease had now taken it away on a feast day of our Lady, and a very special one at that: it was the feast of Our Lady of Montserrat, to whom he was particularly devoted.

Another episode illustrates his calm, supernatural attitude in the face of death. This happened in 1963.

During the Second Vatican Council, in my capacity as secretary for the conciliar commission for the clergy, I had to travel to Venice to talk over some questions with the Patriarch of Venice, Cardinal Urbani, who was on the central coordinating commission of the council. The Father wished to accompany me, and so on February 4 we left Rome by car, together with Fr. Javier Echevarría and Javier Cotelo, who was driving. We were still traveling the next day, and after a while we noticed that the road had become icy in some places and that driving was becoming hazardous. We had just passed Rovigo, we were about four kilometers from Monselice, when the car skidded on the ice, spun around several times (without, thank God, turning over), and then started off at high speed backwards, down the road we had come. There was no way to control the car, and next thing we knew, we were heading toward a precipice. We stopped right on the edge of it—we ran sideways into a stone road-marker. It was on the side where the founder was sitting, and that door was completely bashed in; only with difficulty were we able to get out of the car, which was still teetering on the brink. Our founder reacted in an exemplary way: he did not let himself panic; he immediately invoked the protection of our Lord and our guardian angels. Fr. Javier Echevarría and Javier Cotelo did feel a bit queasy, though. So once we reached Venice, I quickly took care of the matters that were the reason for the trip, and we then returned to Rome.

> *Father, we come now to that twenty-sixth day of June 1975, the day when our Father reached his true homeland. Could you please reconstruct for us, in detail, the events of that morning?*

On June 26, 1975, the last day of his earthly life, the Father arose at his usual hour. Assisted by Fr. Javier Echevarría, he celebrated holy Mass, a votive Mass in honor of our Lady, shortly before 8:00, in the oratory of the Most Holy Trinity. I celebrated Mass at the same time, in the main sacristy, because that morning our founder wanted to go with Fr. Javier and me to Castel Gandolfo, to take leave of his daughters at Villa delle Rose—we were getting ready to leave Rome [for the summer]. He seemed to be in as good health as usual; there was no sign at all of what was about to happen.

At about 9:25, just before leaving the house, he went to the committee room, where he had called in two of his sons who were on the General Council, a priest and a layman, to ask them to do something for him: to go on his behalf to visit an Italian professional, Dr. Ugo Piazza, a man who was very dear to the Holy Father, and who was gravely ill. This man had expressed a desire to speak with our Father. It did not, he said, have anything to do with spiritual direction—he was already well taken care of in that regard—he just had some news that he wanted to convey.

The Father asked them to tell this man that since he would be leaving Rome in two days' time, a visit would not be possible; however, if he wished, he could convey his news to a member of the Work, either a priest or a layman. He added, with great forcefulness, that they should "tell him this: that for years I have been offering the holy Mass every day for the Church and particularly for the Holy Father. You can assure him—you know how often you have heard me say this—that I have offered my life to our Lord for the pope, whoever he might be. We keep quiet and we try to work very hard and serenely, even if there are some in the Church who don't think kindly of us."

About 9:35 the Father left by car for Castel Gandolfo, accompanied by Fr. Javier Echevarría, Javier Cotelo (who was driving), and myself. As soon as we were out of the garage, we began to say the rosary, the joyful mysteries. We finished before we got to the beltway, and then just carried on a regular conversation. The Father said, among other things, that that afternoon we could go to Cavabianca, the new location of our international center of formation; he wanted to check on some details concerning the oratory of Our Lady of the Angels—details which he himself had suggested in order to make the decor more balanced and the general atmosphere more conducive to recollection and devotion.

The trip lasted longer than usual, because of a traffic jam on the beltway. It was very hot. Javier Cotelo spoke to our Father about some of his nephews, who had been in Rome some time before, and about other things related to his family. The Father listened attentively and took an affectionate interest in all these things.

At about 10:30 we arrived at Villa delle Rose. Some of his daughters were waiting for us in the garage. As usual, he brought them some gifts: this time, a box of candy and a duck carved out of crystal. (The Father had a habit of distributing to others the gifts that he received.)

While we walked down the corridor he remarked that these were his last hours before leaving Rome, and that although officially he was not available for anyone, he was available for his daughters. He went to greet our Lord, remained on his knees before the tabernacle for a few moments, and then, after kissing the wooden cross, went to the "Room of the Fans" (a room decorated with fans from around the world), where the gathering was to be held.

Upon entering, he turned his glance toward a very special picture in that room. This is an oil painting in which the child Jesus appears very well groomed, and very charming. He has plump, rosy cheeks, and has his arms around his mother's neck, while she is offering him a tea rose. This painting came from the Escrivá household, and had been in the room of the Diego de León Street center where the founder's mother died. Divine Providence willed that this same *Virgen del Niño Peinadico* ["Our Lady of the Well-Groomed Child"] should also receive one of the founder's last glances.

His daughters replied with lilting voices to the Father's greeting, telling him how happy they were to see him. He commented with a smile, "What fine voices you have!" Then he sat down, but leaving for me the armchair they had brought in for him. He said again that he was about to leave Rome, and then he said, "I very much wanted to come here. We've got to use our last hours of being in Rome to take care of some unfinished business, so as far as everybody else is concerned, I'm already gone; I'm just here for you."

After that, he talked about how every Christian ought to have a priestly soul, and about how important it is to love the pope and the whole Church. He also spoke of the first three priests of the Work, and of the fifty-four sons of his who would receive priestly ordination a few days later. "Yesterday," he said, "you celebrated, I'm sure, the anniversary of the ordination of the first three priests, and surely you are praying as well for the fifty-four who are about to be ordained. Fifty-four—that seems like a lot, an almost unbelievable number for these days, if you think about what's going on around us. Yet really they are very few; they disappear so soon. As I'm forever telling you, this water of God which is the priesthood always gets quickly absorbed by the soil of the Work. These drops of water, our priests, they disappear at once.

"You, my daughters, have priestly souls. You know I tell you this every time I come here. And your brothers who are laymen have priestly souls also. Each of you can and should help, with that priestly soul of yours; and in this way, with the grace of God and with the ministerial priesthood of us, the priests of the Work, we will all be able to do an effective job."

Then they told him some apostolate-related anecdotes, and he took the opportunity to encourage them to be faithful in the small things of everyday life and in the fulfillment of the devotional practices of Opus Dei.

He also remarked, "I suppose you're using your time well? And making sure that includes some rest and relaxation—some kind of sports activity, perhaps, or an occasional excursion?

"I hope, above all, that you are carrying out well your norms" —that is, our practices of piety—"and that you are using everything as a springboard for seeking out intimacy with God and with his Blessed Mother, with our father and lord St. Joseph, and with your guardian angels, to help the holy Church, our Mother, who is at this time in such great need, who is going through such a rough time in the world. We have to love the Church and in particular the pope, whoever he may be, very much. Beg the Lord that our service to the Church as a whole, and to the Holy Father in particular, will be effective."

He didn't cease for an instant to enliven the conversation in a way that was both pleasant and edifying. When one of the young ladies told of the fruits of a catechetical apostolate carried out in South America, the Father gave them all a gentle reminder: "Just don't forget that that was not your fruit—it was the fruit of our Lord's Passion, of his suffering, of the labors and pains borne with so much love by the Mother of God; the fruit of the prayers of all your brothers and sisters, and of the holiness of the Church. From the outside it may have looked like the fruit of your work, but don't ever let yourself fall into the pride of actually thinking of it as such."

The get-together was short; it lasted less than twenty minutes, because our Father began to feel tired. But before he finished, he did renew the act of love for the Church, and for the pope in particular, which he had made on so many occasions. A few minutes later he began to feel worse. Fr. Javier and I accompanied him to the priest's room, where he rested for a while. Together with the directors of the center, we encouraged him to rest a little longer, but he turned down the offer, perhaps to remind us one more time that the priests of the Work are to spend no more time in the women's centers than is necessary for carrying out their priestly ministry [and so avoid even the impression of attempting to interfere with the way they run their activities]. As soon as he seemed to have recovered a bit, we left for Rome, by car. On our way out, we passed by the oratory, where he stopped in again for a few moments to say good-bye to our Lord. As we walked to the garage, he listened with interest to the daughters he met on the way, and he jokingly said to them, cheerful as always, "Please excuse me, my daughters, for the trouble I've caused you." And then he said, "Pax, my daughters." Finally, from the car, he bade an affectionate farewell to the ones who opened the garage door for us: "Good-bye, my daughters." It was about 11:20 by then.

When the Father left Villa delle Rose, he was tired, certainly, but also happy and serene. Attributing his indisposition to the heat, he asked Javier Cotelo to take him to Rome "per breviorem," that is, by the shortest route. In the meantime, he went on talking with the three of us, but it was a somewhat disconnected conversation, to tell the truth, because we were impatient to get to Villa Tevere, to have him get some more rest. Javier drove quickly, but also very carefully, so that the Father wouldn't get carsick. We got home in just a little over half an hour.

It was almost noon when we drove into the garage of Villa Tevere. A member of the Work was waiting for us at the door. The Father stepped quickly from the car, with a cheerful expression on his face; he moved with agility, even turning back to close the car door himself. He thanked his son who had given him a hand, and then he went into the house.

He greeted our Lord in the oratory of the Most Holy Trinity, making (as he always did) a slow, devout genuflection accompanied by an act of love. We then went up to my office—that's where he liked to do most of his work—and a few seconds after crossing the threshold, he exclaimed, "Javi!" Fr. Javier had stayed behind to close the door of the elevator. Our founder repeated more loudly, "Javi!" Then, in a weaker voice, "I don't feel well." At that point he suddenly fell to the floor.

We did everything we could to help him, both spiritually and physically. As soon as I realized the seriousness of the situation, I gave him absolution and the Anointing of the Sick, which he had so ardently desired to receive. (He was still breathing.) Many times he had begged us earnestly not to deprive him of that great gift.

Then came an hour and a half of struggle, full of filial devotion—the giving of artificial respiration, oxygen, injections, cardiac massage. Meanwhile I repeated the words of absolution several times. Under the medical direction of Fr. José Luis Soria, Fr. Javier and I took turns with other members of the General Council—Fr. Dan Cummings, Fernando Valenciano, Umberto Farri, Giuseppe Molteni, and Dr. Juan Manuel Verdaguer—in helping him. We could not believe that the hour of our greatest sorrow had arrived.

We went on hoping against all hope. I telephoned the head of the Central Advisory [the women's equivalent of the General Council] and asked her to get all the women who were living in Villa Sacchetti to assemble in the chapels, and to have them pray for at least ten minutes, with great intensity, for a very urgent intention.

In the meantime we kept on trying to do the impossible; we just could not believe that he had died. Nevertheless, despite all our efforts, the Father was not to recover from his heart failure. We resigned ourselves to this when we saw that the electrocardiogram was flat.

At 1:30 I left the room and invited the other members of the General Council, who were waiting in the old meeting room, quietly praying and weeping, to come and pray beside the remains of our beloved founder.

We all knelt around his body. With tears in our eyes, we kissed his hands and forehead with immense affection. Some still could not believe it, and thought there must be some mistake— that perhaps our founder would recover, or that God might be wanting us to ask with great faith for the miracle of his return to life. We recited the responsorial prayer for the dead and afterwards continued to pray, broken by sorrow, without being able to restrain our tears, nor wishing to.

The body of our founder was still lying on the floor of my office, near the wall on which hangs a large crucifix. Underneath his body we had placed my bedspread, covered by a clean sheet. On the wall opposite was the picture of Our Lady of Guadalupe which had received his last loving glance.

For us, of course, it was an unexpected death. For our founder, however, it was something that had been maturing, I would dare to say, more in his soul than in his body, because each day he was more frequently offering his life for the Church and in particular for the pope.

I'm convinced that the Father had a premonition of his death. In his last few years, he often remarked that his presence on earth was superfluous, and that he could be much more helpful to us from heaven. It really grieved us to hear him speak that way, in that tone of voice of his that was so strong and sincere and humble, for while he considered himself a burden, for us he was an irreplaceable treasure.

He never worried about his own health, even when, in the last few years, his kidney and heart troubles increased. We knew very well that he was not afraid of death, and that he was not attached to life. Assiduous meditation on the Last Things had, since his youth, prepared his heart a little more every day for the loving contemplation of the Blessed Trinity.

For many years he had been offering his life to God, and would have offered "a thousand lives, if I had them," for the Church and in particular the pope. This was an intention of every Mass he celebrated, and his Mass of June 26, 1975, was no exception; on that day, however, the Lord definitively accepted his offering.

I would also like to add that our founder confided to us, several times, that he was asking our Lord for the grace to die without being a nuisance to anyone. Out of love for his children, he wanted to spare them the troubles of a long illness. God granted this request. Our Father died, in accord with the spirit which he had been encouraging in his preaching since 1928, working for the Lord "ut iumentum" ["as a beast of burden"].

In the room where he died, we put together a kind of board, covered it with a white sheet, and placed our founder's body on it, in order to carry him to the chapel of Our Lady of Peace.

Our Father was wearing around his neck a reliquary, in the shape of a cross, which contained a fragment of the True Cross. I took this reliquary, reverently kissed it, and put it on, saying aloud that I would wear it until the election of his successor. We then removed the scapular medal of Our Lady of Mount Carmel that he was wearing, and replaced it with a new cloth scapular.

We placed the body of our founder, still dressed in his black cassock, in the nave of the chapel of Our Lady of Peace, at the foot of the altar. We had already laid on the floor the black cloth used to cover the casket in Masses for the dead. It was about 2:15 P.M.

We turned the cross on the altar toward the nave. For the Masses to be celebrated *de corpore insepulto* [before the burial], which would be said continuously, one right after the other, we put a small crucifix on the altar, facing the celebrant.

Before clothing him in his priestly vestments, Fr. Javier Echevarría, weeping disconsolately, took from the Father's pockets the things he was carrying: his notebook, crucifix, rosary . . . and a whistle that had been given him a few weeks before by some members of a girl's club who wanted to join the Work.

Afterwards, although he had shaved that morning, I shaved him again, and took off his shoes. Earlier, I had suggested that we recite another responsorial prayer for the dead, with the special ending prayer for priests. This prayer was led by Fr. Dan Cummings. Immediately after that, I asked the architect Jesús Alvarez Gazapo to purchase a coffin, to call in a sculptor who could make plaster casts of the founder's face and hands, and to prepare the tomb. In the meantime, Fr. Ernesto Juliá brought over the priestly vestments. Fathers Javier Echevarría, Carlos Cardona, José Luis Soria, and Julián Herranz clothed the body of our founder: over his cassock they put an amice, an alb, a stole, and a chasuble. The alb was of cambric, with lace; the chasuble was of a semi-Gothic style, and had the seal of the Work both in front and on the back.

We placed a velvet cushion under the Father's head, and in his crossed hands we placed the crucifix which St. Pius X had held at the moment of his own death. Later, not long before the burial, we replaced this crucifix with another, and we've also kept that second one as a relic.

Once everything was prepared, access was allowed to the chapel of Our Lady of Peace, where his body was lying. From that moment until the burial, there was an uninterrupted flow of mourners: sons and daughters of our founder, and many other people as well, from Rome and other places. I had the door to 75 Viale Bruno Buozzi left open to provide direct access to the chapel. In the vestibule we had a table set up, covered with a black cloth, and on it we placed the book for signatures. By now it was around 3:30 P.M.

In the center of the nave two prie-dieus were placed, in front of the founder's body and in line with the pews which run lengthwise down the nave, in order to allow free passage. We put there also some holy water, a sprinkler, a black stole, and the text of the prayer for the dead. Around the body, four candles were burning.

A little before 4:00, the sculptor came to make the plaster casts of the face and hands of the founder, and so the chapel was cleared. The artist carried out his work with great delicacy, moved by the sorrow and the peace which reigned in the house. Present were Jesús Alvarez Gazapo, Fr. Carlos Cardona, Fr. José Luis Soria, and a few others. They took every precaution necessary to keep the vestments and the chapel floor from getting stained; they covered everything that might be at risk, as the Father himself had taught us to do. When the work was finished, Fr. Carlos and Fr. José Luis knelt down and tearfully cleaned our founder's face and hands and combed his hair again.

I then asked his daughters to clean his face, hands, and clothing, and to comb his hair once again, so as to make sure all the little white specks left from the sculptor's casts were removed. This filial task was carried out by Carmen Ramos, Marlies Kücking, Marisa Vaquero, Blanca Fontán, María Dolores Mazuecos, and Conchita Areta. I knew that it would be a consolation for them, albeit a very sad one. They did everything with immense affection. Following the suggestion of Fr. Javier Echevarría, they cut some locks of hair from the back of the founder's head, in such a way that it could not be noticed; then they cleaned the floor and placed red gladioli and roses all around.

They also had the delicacy to cover one side of the white cotton border around the collar area of the chasuble with another piece, a clean one, since the casting had left a little smudge.

It was now a little past 5:30 P.M. Not wanting to let any more time go by before this, I celebrated the first Mass *de corpore insepulto,* in tears. Members of the Central Advisory and of the [domestic] administration were present. It seemed especially right to me on this occasion to put into practice this teaching we had received from the Father: "In the first place, my daughters." Fathers Javier Echevarría and Joaquín Alonso served the Mass. I used the best vestments and the richest sacred vessels that we had. Before Communion I spoke some words to those present, the words the Lord put on my lips. Once holy Mass was over, I knelt at the right of the presider's seat, took my crucifix from my pocket, recited the prayer "En Ego" (also called "To Jesus Crucified"), and continued my thanksgiving.

Afterwards Fr. Javier celebrated Mass, and he too was visibly moved. Members of the men's centers that are directly connected with our headquarters were present at this Mass. At the end, just before returning to the sacristy, Fr. Javier stopped before the mortal remains of our founder and made a deep bow. All the other priests who celebrated after him did the same.

Masses for the repose of his soul were said one after another, without interruption, for the rest of the evening, all night, and the next day as well, until the funeral Mass. The celebrants were all numerary priests of the Work, with one exception: Msgr. Pedro Altabella, a canon of St. Peter's Basilica who dearly loved the founder; he spent hours and hours before his body, praying and weeping. In all, fifty Masses were celebrated, not counting the one sung Mass and the funeral Mass.

One or two hours after his death, I had the sad news communicated to the Central Advisory and to all the centers directly connected with the General Council and with the Advisory, respectively, and then to all the regional governing bodies of Opus Dei throughout the world. I asked everyone to offer to the Lord many prayers for the founder, as filial piety required us to do, but at the same time also to begin to have recourse to his intercession. Since the Father had never liked grand solemnities, I thought it best that everyone remain at home, in their own region. The only exception I allowed myself was one I considered quite reasonable. I asked the regional vicar of Spain to come, along with some members of the regional commission, and I also invited the head of the women's branch in Spain, along with some members of the regional advisory. This was a justifiable exception, since the region of Spain was the "firstborn." I also called, as it was just as natural to do, the regional vicar of Italy. (The regional vicar and the delegate from Peru also came, but that's because they were already on the plane when the message came that everyone should stay at home.)

At 3:00 that same day, I telephoned the cardinal secretary of state to inform him of the death of our founder. Cardinal Villot was very moved. With great affection he gave me his condolences and assured me that he would immediately tell the pope, who was at that time resting. This was the first official announcement of the founder's death; from that moment on it was public news, and spread quickly in Rome and throughout the world.

In all countries the media spread the news with respect and veneration: it was a reflection of the impression received directly by the journalists who came to Villa Tevere. Within the next several days there appeared a succession of newspaper articles and radio and television reports which explained in detail the importance of the work of the founder in the life of the Church. His reputation for sanctity became more obvious than ever from the events following upon his death.

Beginning in the evening of June 26, people from all walks of life came to express their sorrow and to pray. We collected moving testimonies of their profound love for our founder, and statements showing a unanimous certainty that they were in the presence of the body of a saint. Great personalities of the Church and of civil life, office workers, blue-collar workers, young people and old, mothers with babies in their arms—they all wanted to "see the Father."

The chapel of Our Lady of Peace was filled with an atmosphere of intense prayer, and of serene sorrow, that is difficult to render in words. Even very small children, holding their parents' hands, looked at the Father's peaceful face without the slightest fear.

While the Masses went on, a steady stream of visitors flowed through the place of mourning. Among the first was Archbishop Benelli, undersecretary of the Vatican Secretariat of State, representing the pope. He remained a long time, recollected in prayer, kneeling in front of the body of our founder. Cardinals also arrived, and bishops and priests, ambassadors, persons of high social status and ordinary folk, and innumerable members, cooperators, and friends of the Work. Many of them showed their own sorrow and affection by spending long periods in prayer before the remains of the founder.

I can say without exaggeration that even just those first few hours after his death constituted an extraordinary catechesis. "How much good he will do the Church from heaven!" exclaimed Cardinal Wright, who was very fond of him. Cardinal Ottaviani, prefect emeritus of the Sacred Congregation for the Doctrine of the Faith, said to me, "Not only for Opus Dei, but for the whole Church, this is a day of mourning." Bishop Deskur, a Polish bishop who would later be raised to the cardinalate by Pope John Paul II, embraced me and said to me, "Today I celebrated Mass for his glorification. I hope to be one of the first bishops to request his beatification. I want to show my gratitude to the Father (and to Opus Dei) for what he has done for the Church in the field of social communications and for what he has done for my own soul." Archbishop Antonio Travia embraced me and exclaimed, "I too have been left an orphan!" The prefect of one of the congregations suggested to all his colleagues that they should go to pray before the body of the founder, because then they would see the serenity of a saint's face.

In midafternoon three workers arrived who had for a long time worked on construction projects in our headquarters and who were personally acquainted with our founder; they had come to remove the marble slab covering the tomb. They stopped to pray for a few minutes, and then, with reverent emotion, went down to the crypt [of the chapel of Our Lady of Peace] and respectfully accomplished their work.

With each passing hour, the flow of visitors increased. And through the whole night, our Father's sons and daughters took turns keeping vigil. The Masses continued, one after the other.

Shortly after midnight Santiago Escrivá de Balaguer, the brother of our founder, arrived with his wife. A sister of mine and her husband came with them. They all spent a long time in prayer beside the Father. Santiago was especially stricken and made no attempt to hide his immense sorrow. They attended holy Mass and received Communion. At about 1:30 we suggested that they go get some rest.

At dawn on Friday morning, June 27, we were all awake. At 8:00 the priest secretary of the General Council celebrated a solemn Mass for the women of Opus Dei, in the chapel of Our Lady of Peace.

Fr. Javier and I remained a long time that morning beside the Father, together with cardinals, bishops, priests, and other friends who had come to pray and to say a last farewell to our founder. At midmorning I got up from one of the side pews and knelt beside the head of our founder. I placed my own forehead on his for a few seconds; then I took three red roses from one of the bunches of flowers there and placed them at his feet. These words from St. Paul came to my lips: "Quam speciosi pedes evangelizantium pacem, evangelizantium bona" ["How lovely are the feet of those who bring the gospel of peace, the gospel of good things" (Rom 10:15)].

Santiago and his wife also remained almost the whole morning, keeping watch beside the remains of their brother.

In the early afternoon, several countries' ambassadors to the Holy See came to Villa Tevere, including the dean of the diplomatic corps. Among the dignitaries who came were Cardinals Rossi, Wright, Seper, Baggio, Garrone, Philippe, Oddi, Guerri, Ottaviani, Palazzini, Traglia, and Violardo; the ambassadors of Spain to Italy and the Holy See, as well as diplomatic officials from other lands; Msgr. Carboni, the papal nuncio in Italy and dean of the diplomatic corps to the Republic of Italy; the tailor who had made the Father's vestments, and the tailor's wife and daughter; workers who had helped build Villa Tevere; the cardinal archbishop of Guatemala, who a few days later would confer priestly ordination on fifty-four members of the Work; the assistant chief of police; the maid of the grandnieces and grandnephews of St. Pius X (they had given us many relics of our holy intercessor); numerous nuns (many of whom had relatives in the Work) and also many men religious, among whom was the superior general of the Society of Jesus; Italian intellectuals; a delegation from the City of Barbastro . . . a continuous procession of people who felt a debt of gratitude toward our founder—too many to list.

In those moments I was greatly consoled by the affectionate response of the Holy Father, Pope Paul VI, to the news I had sent him in my capacity as secretary general of the Work. Through Archbishop Benelli, the Holy Father expressed the sorrow he felt, and said that he too was praying, in spirit, beside the body of "so faithful a son" of Holy Mother Church and of the Vicar of Christ. Before the public funeral a telegram arrived at Villa Tevere from the Holy See. In it Pope Paul expressed again his own grief, assured us that he would be offering up prayers for the soul of the founder, and reiterated his own view that the founder was a soul chosen and favored by God; he concluded with an apostolic blessing for the whole Work. As is customary, the telegram bore the signature of the cardinal secretary of state: he said he united himself wholeheartedly, on his own behalf, with our sorrow and with the sentiments of Pope Paul, who wanted this message to reach us as soon as possible.

A little later we received another proof of affection on the part of the Holy Father: a letter which showed even more fully the intensity of his sorrow and of his affection for our founder and for Opus Dei. The cardinal secretary of state wrote to say that His Holiness had celebrated Mass on June 27 for the Father, and that the passing of the days had not diminished the intensity of his prayer, nor that of his sorrow over the loss suffered by the Church with our founder's departure for heaven. He would, he assured us, continue to pray that the Lord would give us the grace to remain faithful to the spirit which the founder, by God's will, had transmitted to us.

Thousands of telegrams and letters began arriving at our headquarters from all over the world. They all expressed, along with deeply felt grief, the conviction that this person who had died was a saint, that he was one of the great founders raised up in the Church by the Holy Spirit.

But let us return to Friday, June 27. Around 2:00 that afternoon, the casket was brought in, and we very carefully put the founder's body into it. The casket was of red mahogany, and had inside of it a zinc case, lined with violet silk. The Father's head rested on a small pillow, also violet; we kept as a relic the little pillow upon which his head had been resting before.

Shortly afterward, there arrived the official responsible for verifying compliance with the Italian laws for the burial of a body outside of a cemetery. He was, of course, accustomed to being in the presence of people grieving for a lost loved one. Nevertheless, he was quite surprised by the extraordinary affection he found—and so impressed that he refused to accept payment for his services.

As soon as that most sad and pious duty was performed, the numerary women of the Central Advisory and the related centers prepared the chapel for the last Mass *de corpore insepulto*, the solemn funeral Mass. They brought in some trays filled with crucifixes and rosaries and knelt down to touch the hands of the founder with them; these now became very precious relics for all. They also kissed the Father on his forehead.

Beside the casket were Santiago Escrivá, his wife, and the relatives of mine who had accompanied them. The Mass was sung, in Gregorian chant, by the choir of the Roman College of the Holy Cross. In the sanctuary and in the gallery there were also many numerary priests, all in surplices. I used the chalice which we had given the Father on the previous March 28, on the occasion of the fiftieth anniversary of his ordination.

The Mass began at 6:00 P.M. I was the celebrant, and was assisted by Fathers Javier Echevarría and Dan Cummings. I gave a brief homily, imploring all those present to make a very firm resolution to be more faithful than ever to him whom the Lord had given us as a father, and to be very united and very humble.

At the end of the Mass, I went down (preceded by the acolytes and by the cross-bearer) into the nave to recite a responsorial prayer for the dead, while the choir sang the "Libera Me, Domine." It was the last one we recited for him before his burial. The time for that had come.

The casket was closed at about 7:30. Fr. José Luis Soria and Jesús Alvarez Gazapo were present. Just before the casket was closed, we took the crucifix the Father was holding, and replaced it with another one. Then he was buried in the crypt.

The General Council and the Central Advisory of Opus Dei set the public funeral Mass for 11:00 A.M. the next day, June 28, in the Basilica of Sant'Eugenio, in Valle Giulia. This church had been constructed at the request of Pope Pius XII, with the offerings of the faithful of the entire world; the founder himself had helped (this was in the early forties) with a contribution that was very generous, considering our financial circumstances at that time.

A thousand chairs were brought in; the pews had a seating capacity of only four hundred or so. The majority of those present had been informed of the time and location only by word of mouth—an unexpected strike on the part of newspaper distributors had kept the printed information out of circulation. The church began to fill at around 10:00. Some directors and other members of the Work ushered in the civil and ecclesiastical authorities. Fr. Francisco Vives was the celebrant; he was assisted by the regional vicar of Italy and several other priests. Thousands of persons of every age and social position thronged the basilica. Numerous cardinals and other dignitaries of the Holy See were present. Members of the diplomatic corps to the Holy See and to the Italian government were led by their respective deans: the papal nuncio in Italy and the ambassador of

Guatemala. There were also representatives of the most diverse areas of civil life, as well as many other faithful, arriving from the areas around Rome, from many other Italian cities, and from abroad.

Representing the pope was Archbishop Benelli, who sat beside me in the sanctuary. Also present were Cardinals Violardo, Ottaviani, Fürstenberg, Baggio, Palazzini, Oddi, Aponte, and Casariego, together with many other bishops, priests, and superiors of religious orders and congregations.

The cardinals and other members of the clergy were seated in the sanctuary; afterwards they told me how vividly and deeply impressed they were at the sight of such a heterogeneous multitude praying together with such great faith, and thereby giving open testimony to the resonance in their lives of the example and teaching of the founder of Opus Dei. The distribution of Communion required many priests and lasted over thirty minutes, in an atmosphere of profound recollection and fervent prayer.

Some time later, Cardinal Oddi described his own impressions of that funeral. "I will never forget," he said, "all those edifying manifestations of devotion and piety—they moved me so profoundly—both on the occasion of the funeral and on the first anniversary of the return to God of the soul of his faithful servant. The great church of Sant'Eugenio was literally filled with members and sympathizers of Opus Dei who attended the Sacrifice at the Altar with exemplary recollection, and who approached the Sacred Table with a spirit of conviction and faith which it is not easy to meet with in celebrations of this kind."

On the very same day [the day of the public funeral], I sent a second telegram to all the regions, asking for the celebration of a funeral Mass in a public church in every city where there was a center of the Work. We could not disappoint the expectations of the many people all over the world who wished to express their own affection for the founder, and, of course, it was only right to offer everyone that kind of opportunity to pray for his soul. These Masses of suffrage constituted an impressive testimony of filial piety and sincere gratitude: in numerous cities all over the world, thousands and thousands of persons came together *cor unum et anima una* [with one heart and one soul] to pray for the soul of the founder, filling churches and cathedrals which had perhaps not seen for centuries such a massive gathering of the faithful.

Everywhere there reigned the same climate of serene sorrow and piety, of prayers and tears, which had characterized the solemn funeral Mass on June 28 in the Roman church of Sant'Eugenio. It was truly another of the Father's catecheses, and from it came forth the same supernatural fruits as from his apostolic forays: a great number of confessions and Communions, personal commitments to greater faith and generosity, conversions great and small; the only difference was that now, after his death, the dimensions of the phenomenon began to take on really universal proportions.

These effects have been amply documented in the press and in some unpublished eyewitness accounts. The reports of these Masses emphasize not only the exceptional number of those who were present, but also the variety of their social situations: there were personages of the highest ranks in public life, mothers of families, rural people, professors, students, employees, professionals . . . To participate in the ceremonies, many had to overcome considerable difficulties having to do with their work schedules, the long distances they had to travel, and so on. In many cases the local ecclesiastical hierarchy joined in our mourning by taking part in these Masses.

I was particularly pleased by a phenomenon that took place everywhere: the conversion of so many souls who had been away from the sacraments for years, who now felt themselves impelled to go to confession and receive Communion. There were also a number of non-Catholics who decided to prepare themselves for reception into the Church.

The new shrine of Torreciudad was dedicated on July 7, 1975—just ten days after the Mass at the Basilica of Sant'Eugenio—with a Mass for the repose of the soul of the founder of the Work. In the church itself, in the atrium, and on the esplanade there were, in all, about seven thousand persons. Among those present were the vicar general of the diocese of Barbastro, the provincial and local authorities, many of the workers who had helped to build the sanctuary, the families of these workers, and many people from other localities. Hundreds of confessions took place.

A few kilometers away, in Barbastro, the hometown of the founder, the city council organized a funeral Mass that was celebrated in the cathedral, by the bishop of the diocese. All the local authorities were present, and a huge number of the faithful. There was a general sense of personal loss, for it was hardly more than a month since the founder had been among his fellow citizens, receiving from them the Gold Medal of Barbastro.

The founder was, as I have said, buried in the crypt of the chapel of Our Lady of Peace on June 27, 1975, the day after his death. On October 4, 1957, he had given to Jesús Alvarez Gazapo the words he wanted inscribed on his tomb—though he did say afterwards that this was only a suggestion, and that we were free to decide otherwise. This was what he wanted:

IOSEPHMARIA ESCRIVA DE BALAGUER Y ALBAS

PECCATOR

ORATE PRO EO

GENUIT FILIOS ET FILIAS

[Josémaria Escrivá de Balaguer y Albas / Sinner / Pray for him / He begot sons and daughters]

Regarding that last phrase, he said, with a smile, "You can add that, if you like."

I decided, in the presence of God, that we could not go along with the first part—especially since our founder had left the decision up to us. For a long time he had liked to sign his name as "Josemaría, Pecador" or "El pecador Josemaría." He had defined himself as "a sinner who loves Jesus Christ." That was truly a great lesson in humility for us all; but it seemed to me that we would not be good sons and daughters if we inscribed on his tomb an expression of that kind.

In accordance with the desires of all, I decided that on the marble covering of his tomb there should be written, in letters of gilded bronze, just these words:

EL PADRE

Above them would be the seal of the Work (a circle with a cross in it), and below them, the dates of his birth and death.

There then began a continuous pilgrimage to the tomb of the founder, to whom Catholics of every nationality and state of life have entrusted their prayers and their resolutions of spiritual renewal. Later, on February 19, 1981, Cardinal Poletti, vicar general of the diocese of Rome, promulgated the decree that introduced the cause for canonization of the founder of Opus Dei. On April 9, 1990, Pope John Paul II declared heroic the degree to which the Christian virtues were lived by the Venerable Servant of God. On July 6, 1991, in the presence of the Holy Father, the decree was read which pronounced miraculous the character of a certain cure brought about through the intercession of the Venerable Josemaría Escrivá. And on May 17, 1992, Pope John Paul II proclaimed him Blessed.

A Chronology of the Life of
Blessed Josemaría Escrivá de Balaguer

BARBASTRO—Birth, infancy, boyhood

1902   Josemaría Escrivá is born in Barbastro, in Aragón, on January 9. He is the second child of José Escrivá y Corzán and Dolores Albás y Blanc, both fervent Christians, who were married in the cathedral of the same city on September 19, 1898. (His sister Carmen was born on June 16, 1899.) His father, who was part owner of a textile business and of a small chocolate shop, was a native of Fonz, and his family originated in Balaguer. His mother was born in Barbastro, of a family that came from Aragón.

On January 13 he is baptized by Fr. Angel Malo, in the cathedral of Barbastro, with the names José, María, Julián, and Mariano. Later in life he will bring his first two names together, as a way of expressing his love for our Lady and St. Joseph.

In accord with local custom, he is confirmed shortly after his baptism: on April 23, 1902, by the Most Reverend Juan Antonio Ruano, bishop of Barbastro.

1904   When he is two years old he falls ill, so ill that the doctor feels certain he will not live. His parents have recourse to our Lady and promise her that if he lives, they will take him on a pilgrimage to the ancient shrine of Torreciudad, which is dedicated to her. His healing is immediate, and his parents carry out their promise.

1904–1910   In the bosom of his family he receives a deeply Christian upbringing and an example of genuine piety. From his third to his seventh year he attends a school run by the Daughters of Charity; he is the only student from that school proposed as a contender for the "Prize for Virtue," one of the festivities set up by the diocese in 1908 to celebrate Pope Pius X's golden jubilee as a priest. After this he begins his first studies at the school of the Piarist Fathers.

At the age of six or seven, he receives the sacrament of Penance for the first time, accompanied by his mother. For the rest of his life he will remember the joy he feels on this occasion.

1912   On April 23 he receives his first Communion. During his preparation for this he memorizes the formula for the making of a spiritual communion, and from that day forward he recites it often, with devotion.

1910–1915   His three younger sisters, whom he dearly loves, all die. Rosario dies at the age of nine months (October 2, 1909 – July 11, 1910), María Dolores at the age of five years (February 10, 1907 – July 10, 1912), and María Asunción (called "Chon" for short) at the age of eight (August 15, 1905 – October 6, 1913).

In 1912 he begins middle school, still with the Piarists. For the next three years, while his family is still in Barbastro, he has to take his exams in the neighboring cities of Huesca and Lérida.

LOGRONO—Adolescence

1915–1917   His father's business fails; the family leaves Barbastro and moves to Logroño. In this city, the capital of Rioja, Mr. Escrivá finds work in another clothing business. Josemaría finishes middle school at the institute of Logroño; he also attends St. Anthony School.

1917–1918   Sometime around the end of December 1917 or the beginning of January 1918, a decisive event takes place for the future Blessed: the sight of some footprints in the snow, prints made by the bare feet of a Discalced Carmelite friar, stirs up in him a strong desire to dedicate himself generously to God. It is his first presentiment of being called to a mission, but what that mission will be is still unknown to him. In order to put himself most completely at God's disposal, he decides to become a priest. After obtaining his father's permission, and with the definite encouragement of two pious priests whom he consults (Fathers Antolín Oñate and Albino Pajares), he begins his ecclesiastical studies at the seminary of Logroño, to which he is admitted (according to local custom) as a nonresident student. Josemaría's interior life grows on the sure foundation of prayer and penance.

1919   On February 28 is born Josemaría's brother, Santiago. Josemaría realizes that this is God's answer to the prayer he made ten months before, when he asked God to make up for the gap in the family line which his total consecration to God's service would cause. Josemaría and his only living sister, Carmen, are Santiago's godparents.

SARAGOSSA—Seminary and priestly ordination

1920   He completes his preliminary studies in philosophy and the other humanities, and passes the examination for the first year of theology. After spending a year at the seminary of Logroño, he requests and receives permission of the respective Ordinaries to transfer to the seminary of Saragossa, in order to complete his studies at the pontifical university in that archdiocese. He will remain in Saragossa, the capital of Aragón, until 1927.

1922   At St. Francis of Paola Seminary, the conduct of Josemaría offers an example of zeal in a life of piety and diligent application. Cardinal Soldevilla, archbishop of Saragossa, appoints him a seminarian-superior. Since superiors must be clerics, and Josemaría is still just a seminarian, the archbishop confers the tonsure on him privately, in a chapel of the archiepiscopal palace; a little later, he receives minor orders (those of porter and lector on December 17; those of exorcist and acolyte on December 21).

1923   With the permission of his superiors, Josemaría enrolls in the law school of the University of Saragossa as a nonresident student, which means he is exempt from the obligation of attending lectures. This enables him, from now until June 1924, when he concludes his ecclesiastical studies, to pursue both kinds of study: the ecclesiastical, during the regular school year (from October to June), and the secular, during summer vacation (from June to September).

1924   On June 14, Bishop Miguel de los Santos Díaz Gómara—titular bishop of Tagora, former auxiliary of Cardinal

Soldevilla (who was assassinated the year before by anar-
chists), and now director of San Carlos Seminary—confers
the subdiaconate on Josemaría in the seminary church.
On November 27, Josemaría's father dies. Josemaría will
always treasure the memory of his father's exemplary
Christian virtue. From this time forward he will have to
be directly involved in the support of his mother and
brother and sister, who now move to Saragossa. On December 20, Bishop Díaz Gómara ordains him deacon, in
the church of San Carlos Seminary.

1925–1927   On March 28, 1925, he receives priestly ordination from
Bishop Díaz Gómara, again in the seminary church—a
church in which he has spent much time in prayer, including many nights all by himself, during his years as a seminarian. He celebrates his first Solemn Mass on March 30,
in the "Holy Chapel" of the Basilica of Our Lady of the
Pillar; the ceremony is a quiet one, because the family is
still mourning the recent death of Josemaría's father. On
the same day, Josemaría is given his first pastoral assign-
ment: he is to be administrator of the parish of Perdiguera, a hamlet of 870 inhabitants on the slopes of the Al-
cubierre mountains, in the province of Saragossa. He
arrives there the following day. Despite the shortness of
his stay, he carries out his duties with such zeal that he ac-
quires a reputation for holiness among the inhabitants of
the district. (Inquiries made after his death reveal that this
reputation persists there to this day.)

On his return to Saragossa on May 18, he assumes a chaplaincy in the Jesuit church of St. Peter Nolasco, and seeks
involvement in other pastoral activities as well. At the same
time, he continues his legal studies and carries out an intense and highly effective apostolate among the university
professors and students. In addition, he organizes catechism classes in the suburbs of Saragossa. To support his
family, he also gives private lessons and teaches law at the
Amado Academy.

During these years, his spiritual life reaches ever higher
levels of contemplation and penance as he prepares himself
to discover God's will. "Domine, ut videam!" ("Lord, that I
might see!"); "Domine, ut sit!" ("Lord, let it be!"); "Domina,
ut videam!" ("My Lady, that I might see!"); "Domina, ut

sit!" ("My Lady, let it be!")—these supplications have been a part of his prayer since the first days in Logroño, from the first presentiments of his vocation, and are becoming more insistent with each passing day. Meanwhile, he is receiving from the Lord numerous graces which he calls "operative" graces, because of the power with which they move his will and actions.

MADRID—Father Josemaría moves to the Spanish capital

1927   In January, he obtains his licentiate—the first degree in the Spanish university system—in civil law. On April 19, he moves to Madrid (with the permission of the archbishop) to obtain his doctorate, which at that time could only be done there, at the central university. Before this, he works for a while in the rural parish of Fombuena. On April 28, he registers for his first examination.

In Madrid he is appointed chaplain of the Foundation for the Sick, a charitable institution founded by a women's congregation called the Apostolic Ladies. Here he carries out an enormous priestly apostolate. He prepares thousands of children for first confession and Communion, he assists the sick and the needy, he administers the sacraments to the dying, he brings the light of the Gospel and the comforting love of Christ to the most wretched suburbs of the capital. The nuns entrust to him the most difficult cases, and every one of them gets resolved: the zeal of Fr. Josemaría brings many estranged souls back to Christ. These are tasks that go beyond his duties as chaplain, but he gladly offers to do them. Here, too, a widely spread and long-lasting reputation for sanctity arises, as his priestly activity puts him in contact with all levels of society in Madrid.

The work is exhausting: in order to support his family, who have in the meantime come to Madrid, he continues his private tutoring and teaches Roman and canon law at the Cicuéndez Academy.

Fr. Josemaría keeps in regular contact with the ecclesiastical authorities both in Saragossa and in Madrid.

218 IMMERSED IN GOD

The founding and the first steps of Opus Dei

1928   On October 2, Fr. Josemaría is in Madrid, making a retreat at the central house of the Vincentian Fathers, when suddenly the Lord shows him the whole mission of which he has been having presentiments for the last eleven years. It is exactly at this moment that he perceives and accepts the divine will in this regard and Opus Dei is born in his soul. This day is the date of the foundation. A new path is now opened in the Church. People of all social classes are explicitly encouraged and helped to pursue personal sanctity and the realization of the apostolate precisely by fulfilling their ordinary Christian duties—in particular, by sanctifying their own work—in the midst of the world and without changing their state in life.

Fr. Josemaría lays the foundations on which the Work of God will grow: with a heroic spirit of prayer and mortification, he intensifies his pastoral activity and begins to seek out persons who are able to understand and live the ideal he has received in trust from our Lord.

1930   On February 14, while Fr. Josemaría is celebrating holy Mass, our Lord makes him understand that women are also called to become part of Opus Dei.

Little by little, the first vocations to Opus Dei appear. Among them a special mention should be made of Isidoro Zorzano, an old school companion of Fr. Josemaría's, who requests admission on August 24, 1930; he will die on July 15, 1943, with a reputation for sanctity, and the cause for his beatification will be opened on October 11, 1948, in the diocese of Madrid–Alcalá. These beginnings take place against the background of Fr. Josemaría's utter poverty of human means for carrying out this apostolic enterprise, the many difficulties he experiences in opening up the way for a message so new, and, finally, the loneliness of the founder himself. So many souls come near to him, attracted by the sanctity of his life and the vigor of his preaching, but soon abandon him, intimidated by the radical nature of the Christian commitment he puts before them.

1931   The Lord sustains the founder and guides him in these first steps: there are numerous extraordinary graces, and interior locutions come to strengthen him and give him an ever more profound understanding of the founding charism, of its principal theological and ascetical implications, and of the institutional format into which, in due time, it will need to be translated.

On April 14, a new political regime, a republican one, takes over in Spain, replacing the monarchy. The country begins to experience a mounting of hostility against religion. The burning of churches and convents in May is followed by many other violent episodes; there are serious confrontations with the religious orders, and the Society of Jesus is suppressed. Fr. Josemaría increases his personal acts of penance in expiation for all this sectarianism and for the sins committed in ignorance by the masses who are the victims of secularist propaganda. He sees with ever greater urgency the need to promote in all levels of society an adequate understanding of the faith.

It is still 1931 when Fr. Josemaría gives up the chaplaincy of the Foundation for the Sick and becomes chaplain of the Foundation of St. Elizabeth. Just three years later, on December 11, 1934, the government will name him rector of the Foundation: a nomination which, with the permission of the bishop of Madrid and of the archbishop of Saragossa, he will accept.

From 1931 to 1936, periods of relative calm alternate with periods of intense violence. Despite the danger involved, Fr. Josemaría continues to wear his cassock and intensifies his pastoral ministry, especially his care of the sick (which he carries on without worrying about the increased danger of infection) and his teaching of the catechism to children in the outskirts of the city. He manages to get other souls involved in this apostolate as well: priests and lay persons who are attracted by his zeal. The range of his activities is so extensive that some of his students can scarcely believe the reports that circulate: they follow him secretly and are amazed at what they see with their own eyes. And besides all that, he spends many hours in the confessional, reaching in this way a great number of persons from every walk of life. It is during these years that God calls to Opus Dei its first women members.

Meanwhile, our Lord sends trials to the founder by calling to himself some of the first members of Opus Dei—individuals he's had great hopes for, in connection with the initial launching of this apostolate. On July 16, 1932, Fr. José María Somoano dies; he is a young priest with whom the founder became acquainted through his hospital ministry. On November 5, 1932, Luis Gordon, a promising young engineer, passes away. And the next year, on September 13, 1933, María Ignacia Escobar dies; this young lady, whom the founder came to know during her long stay in the hospital, literally offered her life for Opus Dei.

1933   On January 21, Fr. Josemaría initiates a formational activity for university students, aimed at leading them to a solid spiritual life and apostolic witness in their professions. It is the first germ of an apostolate which will have an ongoing fruitfulness. He does not yet have a definite place where he can hold these meetings; he has to make do with ad hoc solutions.

He opens the DYA Academy, on Luchana Street—the first established apostolic activity of Opus Dei.

1934   In Cuenca he publishes *Consideraciones Espirituales*, a book that will later be expanded and come out in 1939 with the title of *Camino* (*The Way*). Also making a first appearance in 1934 is *Santo Rosario* (*Holy Rosary*). Both works will eventually be published, in many languages, throughout the world. (More than three and a half million copies of *The Way* have been sold. It has been called "the *Imitation of Christ* of modern times.")

In September, the DYA Academy is expanded. It is moved to 50 Ferraz Street, where it will work in conjunction with the first student residence. This gives further impetus to Fr. Josemaría's already extensive apostolate among people at the university. The bishop of Madrid, through his vicar general, gives his approval and his blessing to these apostolic initiatives. With his permission, the Blessed Sacrament will, as of March 31, 1935, be reserved in the chapel of the DYA residence.

1935–1936   The Lord blesses the zeal of the founder with numerous vocations.

On May 2, 1935, Fr. Josemaría, in the company of two of his sons, completes a penitential pilgrimage to the shrine of Our Lady of Sonsoles, in Avila. This is the start of a custom: it will become one of the pious practices of the members of Opus Dei for the month of May, and thus one of the ways in which they will contribute to the increase of Marian devotion.

Fr. Josemaría plans to relocate the DYA residence to 16 Ferraz Street and to expand it. He also prepares to start the work of Opus Dei in Valencia (he travels there on April 20, 1936, and is received quite favorably by the diocesan authorities) and in Paris.

The Spanish Civil War

1936–1937   The war breaks out on July 18, 1936. During its early months, Fr. Josemaría is in Madrid, where antireligious violence is raging. Practicing Catholics, priests and religious especially, are exposed to mortal danger: many are assassinated for no reason other than their service to the Church or the simple fact that they are known to practice their faith. And so Fr. Josemaría is compelled to go from one place of refuge to another. One of these places is a psychiatric clinic. Another is the Honduran consulate. Despite all the risks, he never gives up his priestly activity. And while the city is gripped by famine, Fr. Josemaría still insists on fasting and doing other penances as well. He encourages and calms those who are at his side, urging them to forgive and helping them to live a life of contemplation and courageous apostolate.

In September 1937, the Honduran consul obtains for him some documents which will allow him a certain liberty of movement. With the encouragement of his sons, he prepares to depart from the Red-controlled part of Spain. On December 2, 1937, after a strenuous and extremely dangerous crossing of the Pyrenees in the company of a few of his sons, he reaches Andorra and then France, where he stops at Lourdes to thank our Lady. He reenters Spain on December 11, at the Hendayan border crossing, and is received by an old friend, Bishop Marcelino Olaechea, who invites him to stay for a while at his residence. Here, in thanksgiving to the Lord and in preparation for the enormous tasks ahead, he makes a spiritual retreat in solitude.

1938   For this whole year, starting in January, he is settled in Burgos. Still in precarious health as a result of those many months of privation, he nevertheless sets out immediately on travels to the various war fronts and to all the places in Spain where the Church is no longer being persecuted, to renew contact with friends and acquaintances who have been scattered all over the country by the war. While his apostolate has not been interrupted, it has been seriously hindered, first by the persecution against the Church and then by the vicissitudes of the war. Now it can be normalized and extended, so far as the continuing state of war permits. His vast correspondence at this time testifies to the range and energy of his priestly activity.

Various bishops grant him generous faculties to exercise his ministry in their dioceses. In this way, Fr. Josemaría is enabled to give himself generously to the spiritual support of many diocesan priests, religious communities, and associations of the laity. At this juncture, when he sometimes doesn't have enough money even to eat, he decides to refuse to accept any stipends for the celebration of Mass, for preaching, or for any other liturgical function—a decision to which he will remain faithful till the day he dies.

During these very difficult months at Burgos there is also the suffering caused by the deaths in combat of some of his sons, and by different kinds of discouraging news regarding others.

Return to Madrid and expansion of the apostolate in Spain

1939

Fr. Josemaría returns to Madrid on March 28, with the first convoy of liberating troops that enters the city. The residence at 16 Ferraz Street has been destroyed by shellfire, but this does not prevent him from reactivating immediately his apostolate. Within a few months he opens a new university residence on Jenner Street. In the meantime he has given the house which he occupied as rector of the Foundation of St. Elizabeth to the local community of Augustinian Recollect sisters, whose convent has been seriously damaged by the war.

In such difficult material circumstances, he makes many trips to various Spanish provincial capitals, where he makes contact with numerous individuals and promotes the setting up of stable apostolic activities. The Lord blesses his faith and very soon sends him new vocations.

In December he fulfills an old promise made to his father, by completing his doctorate in law at the University of Madrid.

1940–1942   Harsh misunderstandings arise regarding the founder: he is accused of preaching heresy, of having founded a secret sect, of wanting to supplant the religious orders; he is denounced to the "Tribunal for the Repression of Freemasonry." He totally forgives those who seek to impede his apostolate: he prays for them; he counts them among his benefactors; he is convinced that they are acting in good faith. He continues to work with serenity. But he does suffer, because these false rumors offend God and cause damage to individual souls and to the Church as a whole. He asks his sons and daughters to remain silent, to forgive, and to keep smiling; he exhorts them not to respond to the attacks made on them, and not to lose charity, even in their thoughts. He accepts the cross as a divine blessing and a purification.

The bishop of Madrid, wishing to put an end to this painful situation, decides to give Opus Dei its first canonical approval in writing. Fr. Josemaría has never even wanted to ask him for anything like this, there being no configuration in the canon law currently in force that adequately corresponds to the foundational charism. Nevertheless, he acquiesces and presents Bishop Eijo y Garay with the required application and the regulations of Opus Dei. On March 19, 1941, the Work is approved as a pious union.

At the same time as misrepresentations of Fr. Josemaría are being circulated, his reputation for holiness is also growing: many bishops invite him to give retreats for their clergy, for seminarians, and for lay people in Catholic organizations. He travels throughout the country, diligently performing, in a most self-denying manner, this service for the Church. In this way thousands of priests hear his preaching and receive, on an individual basis, the light of his counsel.

While Fr. Josemaría is preaching a retreat in Lérida for the bishop and the priests of the diocese, his mother dies unexpectedly, in Madrid. It is April 22, 1941. Dolores Escrivá, with the help of her daughter, Carmen, has taken care of the domestic administration of the first centers of Opus Dei, and has spent the last years of her life generously supporting the apostolic projects of her son.

In July 1942, Fr. Josemaría opens the first center of Opus Dei for women, on Jorge Manrique Street in Madrid.

Fr. Josemaría is also thinking about the future development of the Work. He wants it always to have the stamp of *romanitas*, which has been one of its essential characteristics from the moment of its founding. He sends two of his sons to Rome to study for an ecclesiastical degree at the Pontifical Athenaeum of the Lateran.

1943   On February 14, while celebrating holy Mass in the center on Jorge Manrique Street in Madrid, he receives, by a special grace, the solution to the juridical problem, until then seemingly insoluble, of how to ordain as priests men who have joined Opus Dei as laymen: individuals who would make themselves available to give spiritual assistance to the other members of the Work, and to the apostolic activities fostered by the Work. Fr. Josemaría thereupon founds the Priestly Society of the Holy Cross, which is inseparably united to Opus Dei. He directs that, as a rule, his sons are to be ordained only after having practiced a secular profession for a number of years, and after having completed their theological studies with the earning of an ecclesiastical doctorate.

On the advice of the bishop of Madrid and other ecclesiastics, Fr. Josemaría decides to expedite this part of the Work's juridical journey by sending Alvaro del Portillo (a young engineer) to Rome, to work on the canonical establishment of the new foundation. On October 11 the Holy See gives its approval, and on December 8 the Priestly Society of the Holy Cross is canonically established by the bishop of Madrid.

1944   On June 25, Bishop Eijo y Garay ordains the first three priests of Opus Dei: Alvaro del Portillo, José María Hernández de Garnica, and José Luis Múzquiz. All three are engineers and have been working on their ecclesiastical studies for years; their spiritual and pastoral formation has been taken care of by the founder himself. Until this time, he has been the only priest of the Work, and the spiritual formation of its members has fallen completely upon his shoulders. Now, thanks to the ministry of the new priests, he is able to broaden the apostolic and formational initiatives of the Work.

In the same year, he publishes a historical study in canon law and theology, entitled *La Abadesa de las Huelgas.*

At the beginning of October, he preaches a retreat for the Augustinian community in the Monastery of El Escorial. It is at about this time that he is diagnosed as having an acute form of diabetes mellitus. But despite the seriousness of the illness, he does not slow down his incessant pastoral activity.

1945 Fr. Josemaría sets up three university residences in different provincial capitals of Spain; he also undertakes three trips to Portugal, to prepare for the imminent beginning there of organized apostolic activities.

Fr. Josemaría settles in Rome

1946 Fr. Josemaría believes that the moment has arrived for giving the Work the juridical stability that it now requires in virtue of the stage of development reached by its apostolates. The universal character which it has had from the beginning needs to be expressed in a canonical framework which not only respects the essential characteristics of its specific charism, but also guarantees them through an interdiocesan and centralized structure of government. He prepares the documents to be submitted for pontifical approval and sends Fr. Alvaro del Portillo to Rome once again, entrusting to him the negotiations with the Holy See. From the first contacts it is evident that the theological, juridical, and pastoral novelty of Opus Dei raises problems that will not be easily solved in the absence of the founder. Fr. Alvaro informs him of this, and he, after consulting with the other members of the General Council of the Work, and in spite of the serious condition of his health, undertakes a journey to Rome.

On June 23 he reaches the Eternal City, where he is to take up permanent residence. He enters into contact with several personalities in the Roman Curia. Among them is

Msgr. Giovanni Battista Montini (the future Pope Paul VI), who receives him with great cordiality and expresses repeatedly his own esteem for the founder. He is received in private audience by Pope Pius XII on July 16 and on December 8.

On August 13, 1946, the Holy See issues a document of *Lode dei Fini* ("Praise of the Objectives") of Opus Dei.

1947   On February 2, Pope Pius XII promulgates the apostolic constitution *Provida Mater Ecclesia,* which creates a new canonical structure, the secular institute. On February 24, Opus Dei obtains the *Decretum Laudis* ("Decree of Praise"), in accordance with the norms of the new constitution.

This is to be a temporary solution, just one more stage in the long institutional journey of Opus Dei. Indeed, even from the start, the new canonical formula does not appear to be fully adequate to the charism willed by God for his Work; the founder is conscious of certain fundamental problems which that formula entails.

On the advice of Msgr. Montini and Msgr. Tardini, the founder establishes the central headquarters of Opus Dei in Rome. Despite the lack of economic resources, he succeeds, with the help of Divine Providence, in acquiring a building suitable for this purpose. He names it Villa Tevere.

On April 22, the Holy Father confers on him the title of prelate of honor (monsignor).

1948   On January 3, Msgr. Escrivá makes his first pilgrimage to Loreto. This is a shrine to which he will return many times to make supplications to our Lady.

On June 29, Msgr. Escrivá sets up the Roman College of the Holy Cross: an international center for the training of members of Opus Dei who will become priests or who will otherwise be involved in tasks of spiritual and doctrinal formation. From now on, to this college will come thousands of persons, of various professions and from many countries of the world, in order to improve their ascetic and apostolic formation, and to complete their ecclesiastical studies *sub umbra Petri* ["under the shadow of Peter"].

The founder lavishes the best possible care on them: for him, to "Romanize" the Work means to assure for it a permanent unity of spirit.

Msgr. Escrivá promotes worldwide diffusion of the apostolate

1949

From Rome, the founder continues to promote and guide the expansion of the apostolate all over the world. By the end of the year, some members of Opus Dei are living in the United States and Mexico. Others have already gone to Italy, France, England, and Ireland. Every year new nations are added to the list.

On November 22, Msgr. Escrivá undertakes his first trip to central Europe. He goes to various countries, where he meets the bishops of many dioceses, consolidates some of the existing apostolates, and studies at first hand the immediate prospects for new foundations.

1950

Pope Pius XII has proclaimed this as a Holy Year, and so the founder goes immediately—on the very first day, January 1—to St. Peter's Basilica to gain the Holy Year indulgence. He also encourages all the members of Opus Dei to strive, through their prayer and apostolic endeavor, to bring the greatest possible number of souls to the sacraments.

March 28 is the twenty-fifth anniversary of the priestly ordination of Msgr. Escrivá, and he celebrates it quietly, with no special solemnity or festivity. Such anniversaries, and also those connected to significant dates in the history of the Work, are for him nothing more or less than occasions on which to thank the Lord for gifts received and to humble himself before God and before his own sons and daughters.

On June 16, the feast of the Sacred Heart of Jesus, Pope Pius XII grants the definitive approval of Opus Dei. Given the inadequacy of the juridical form it has provisionally assumed, the founder has to concede some nonessential points, but he does this "without giving in, and with the intention of later recovering" what has been conceded.

From the very beginnings of the foundation, Msgr. Escrivá has promoted the sanctification of daily life and has explicitly affirmed that marriage is a way to holiness. Thanks to his pastoral activity, many married persons have already been living the spirit of Opus Dei for years. Now, in virtue of the definitive pontifical approval, he at last has the opportunity to admit married people into the Work, in a way that involves a fullness of vocation, and of interior and apostolic commitment: these are the first supernumerary members. Thousands and thousands of souls will follow this path, bringing the leaven of the Gospel—first of all, through Christianization of the family—into all the environments of society.

The new juridical step makes possible the fulfillment of another long-standing desire of Msgr. Escrivá: to promote the desire for sanctity and a specific spirit of priestly fraternity among the secular clergy. Perceiving the urgency of expanding this apostolate, and considering the Work to be by now sufficiently well established (both spiritually and institutionally), he has for some months been planning to initiate an entirely new foundation for this very purpose. He has communicated his intention to the Holy See and has received the fullest encouragement. Just before the approval of the Work, however, a new divine illumination makes him understand that this sacrifice will not be necessary. He is suddenly provided with a juridical solution enabling him to satisfy two distinct needs: (1) for diocesan priests to have the opportunity to realize, according to the spirit of Opus Dei, their vocation to seek holiness in and through the exercise of their ministry; and (2) for this to not involve any compromise of their commitment to their own respective dioceses. The solution, which is readily approved by the Holy See, is simple: diocesan priests who become members of the Priestly Society of the Holy Cross will not be subject, in any way, to the jurisdiction of the directors of the Work. They will keep intact their canonical dependence on their respective Ordinaries, and will receive from the Priestly Society only whatever help they may need in order to pursue sanctity in the fulfillment of the duties entrusted to them by their bishop; for these duties as such, they must answer to him alone. In this way an essential characteristic of Opus Dei is reaffirmed: its role of service to the needs of the local church.

At the same time, Msgr. Escrivá obtains permission from the Holy See to accept non-Catholics and even non-Christians as cooperators of Opus Dei—a completely unprecedented ecumenical innovation.

In this same year, stable apostolic activity in Argentina and Chile is begun.

1951   In connection with the development of the apostolate in Italy, new misunderstandings arise, which reach the point of threatening the institutional integrity of the Work as guaranteed by the recent pontifical approvals. Msgr. Escrivá seeks the protection of heaven and consecrates, first of all, the families of the members of Opus Dei to the Holy Family (on May 14, 1951); then (on August 15, 1951) the entire Work to *Cor Mariae Dulcissimum* [the Most Sweet Heart of Mary]; and a little later, in the following year (on October 26, 1952), to the Sacred Heart of Jesus. The dangers dissipate, and the founder directs that these consecrations be renewed every year in each center of the Work.

Msgr. Escrivá draws up for the members of Opus Dei, focusing for now on the men's branch, a detailed curriculum providing for a systematic study of philosophy and theology, a program tailored to the professional needs of these members; it allows them to follow a schedule of studies that is wholly equivalent (in subject matter and scholarship, as well as in the quantity of time allocated to each topic) to that of the pontifical universities. The Holy See praises the depth and quality of the formation planned by the founder for his sons.

Msgr. Escrivá then further consolidates apostolic endeavors, in countries where groups of his sons and daughters are already established, by encouraging the opening of centers in new cities; he also encourages expansion to countries (Colombia and Venezuela, for example) where stable initiatives are still lacking.

1952   After years of preparation through prayer, Msgr. Escrivá promotes the creation, at Pamplona, of the first nucleus of what will later become the University of Navarre. The Studium Generale of Navarre, which he conceives as a center that will foster a commitment to promote science and culture in the light of faith, is set up in October. In 1960 this institution will become, in accordance with the express desire of Pope John XXIII, a formally Catholic university.

At the same time, Msgr. Escrivá gives the first impulse to the establishment of a school in the region of Bilbao; this school, called Gaztelueta, comprises elementary, intermediate, and high school levels. The founder also specifies what are to be the principal characteristics of this institution: a harmonizing of natural with supernatural formation, by means of an individualized education in the virtues; equal access to this kind of education, facilitated by a system of financial assistance for those who need it; full freedom for the students with regard to participation in religious activities; and, finally, a harmonizing of the values set forth in the school with those lived in the family, achieved by means of constant apostolic contacts between the faculty and parents.

1953   At Molinoviejo (near Segovia) he celebrates quietly the twenty-fifth anniversary of the founding of Opus Dei. He returns to Rome by way of Paris, where he exhorts his sons and daughters to continued hope and daring in the apostolate.

On December 12, 1953, Msgr. Escrivá establishes the Roman College of Holy Mary, an international center for the ascetical, doctrinal, and apostolic formation of women. This center is particularly intended to prepare the women of Opus Dei in the sacred sciences and to develop professional skills in the areas of spiritual formation and direction.

After having initiated work in Germany in 1952, the founder, in response to the pressing demands of the respective nuncios and local hierarchies, sends small groups of members for the first time to Peru and Guatemala; the next year, it will be Ecuador's turn.

1954   On April 27, the feast of Our Lady of Montserrat, Msgr. Escrivá suffers a sudden anaphylactic coma in Rome; it brings him close to death, but ends with an extraordinary, permanent healing of the severe diabetes which has afflicted him for ten years.

Every year, there are priestly ordinations of numerary members. They have been increasing in numbers over the years, and constitute a phenomenon of undoubted importance in the life of the Church. More and more professionals, already mature in experience and formation, receive Holy Orders and are sent to places all over the world; wherever they are, they give themselves generously, with self-denial, to the service of souls.

1955   February 14 marks the twenty-fifth anniversary of the establishment of the women's branch of Opus Dei; once again, however, the founder does not call for any solemn celebration.

During this year, Msgr. Escrivá prepares for the women a plan of study parallel to that for the men, which has already received the approbation of the Holy See.

His apostolic journeys in Europe continue. In April and May, he goes to northern Italy and then travels to Switzerland, Germany, and Austria. In the last two months of the year, he journeys to France, Belgium, and Holland, and then once again to Germany, Switzerland, and Austria. On December 4, while in Vienna, he for the first time invokes our Lady with the aspiration "Sancta Maria, stella orientis, filios tuos adiuva!" ("Holy Mary, star of the East, help your children!")—entrusting to her the apostolate of the nations of eastern Europe.

He obtains a doctorate in theology at the Pontifical Lateran University.

1956   When the founder moved to Rome, the Holy See gave its approval for the General Council of Opus Dei to remain in Madrid. He has, however, continued to govern, from Rome, and this has required frequent trips to Madrid for him or for Fr. Alvaro Portillo, his closest collaborator. Bearing in mind the growth of the apostolate, the Second General Congress of Opus Dei, held in August at Einsiedeln, Switzerland (near the famous Marian shrine), decides to transfer the Work's central organ of government to Rome. (This move has already taken place earlier, in 1953, in the case of the Central Advisory, the central organ of government for the women of Opus Dei.)

From this time forward, among the principal concerns of the founder are the consolidation of the government of Opus Dei and the formation of directors. He devotes his energies generously to these concerns: he prepares documents which lay down fundamental criteria, and frequently holds meetings in Rome with those who direct different aspects of the apostolate in the various countries of the world. He emphasizes the preeminently supernatural outlook which should inspire the entire activity of Opus Dei: that priority is to be given not to organizational matters, but rather to the care of the interior life of the members. Two important aspects of the government of the Work are collegiality and decentralization. Organization is reduced to a minimum; this flexibility facilitates a maximum of personal responsibility.

It is also during this year that Opus Dei becomes established in Uruguay and in Switzerland.

1957   On June 20, Carmen Escrivá, who has helped her brother in so many ways, dies in Rome. A few days later, a particular grace from God gives him to understand that she is already in heaven.

In August and September, Msgr. Escrivá travels to Switzerland, Germany, Belgium, the Netherlands, Luxembourg, and France. Everywhere he goes, his presence gives new impetus to the souls who come to see him.

There are new foundations in Brazil, Austria, and Canada. Also, the Holy See entrusts the prelature nullius of Yauyos (in Peru) to priests of Opus Dei. It is the desire of the Holy Father, and the founder responds with his accustomed ready submission.

Msgr. Escrivá is named consultor of the Congregation for Seminaries and Universities, and becomes a member of the Pontifical Roman Theological Academy.

1958   Pope Pius XII dies. During the Holy Father's last days, Msgr. Escrivá prayed intensely, and asked for prayers throughout the world, for his recovery. He now asks for prayers of suffrage and supplication for the new Roman pontiff. He receives with deep joy the news of the election of Pope John XXIII.

The founder travels for the first time to England, where he prepares apostolic initiatives aimed toward expansion into the nations of the Commonwealth. One day, when he is feeling overwhelmed by the contrast between his own limited capabilities and the vastness of the apostolic horizons before him, he is comforted by a divine locution. For five consecutive years (from 1958 to 1962), he will visit Great Britain every summer, to stimulate the activity of his sons and daughters there.

In September, he makes another trip to northern and central Europe (the Netherlands, Germany, and Switzerland).

In December, the work of Opus Dei takes root for the first time in a country of the Far East and in a country of Africa: Japan and Kenya. Work is also initiated in El Salvador. Within the next few years, it will begin in Costa Rica, the Netherlands, and Paraguay as well.

1959   In Barcelona, Montserrat Grases, a numerary only seventeen years old, dies, with a reputation for sanctity. The process of inquiry for her beatification will begin, also in Barcelona, in 1962.

1960   On January 9, the founder gives visible form to one of his characteristic ascetical teachings, his teaching on the sanctification of work, by blessing and inserting the last stone of the building housing the headquarters of Opus Dei.

On March 5, he is for the first time received in audience by Pope John XXIII.

On April 19, Msgr. Escrivá approves the beginning of construction work on the new seat of the Roman College of Holy Mary: Villa delle Rose, a building in Castel Gandolfo. This move will make possible an increase in the number of students.

On October 21, he receives an honorary degree from the University of Saragossa; on October 25, he presides at the inauguration (as a pontifical university) of the University of Navarre and receives the title of "Adopted Son of Pamplona." During this trip, in every city where he stops, large crowds gather to hear his priestly words; his reputation for sanctity has by now spread far and wide.

1961   Msgr. Escrivá is named consultor to the Papal Committee for the Authentic Interpretation of the Code of Canon Law.

The Second Vatican Council and the postconciliar period

1962   On October 11, the Second Vatican Council begins. From the moment of its being announced, Msgr. Escrivá exhorts all his sons and daughters to pray and to offer mortifications so that the Lord will grant the fruits expected by the Church from this council.

He makes available for the work of the council some of his closest helpers, including Fr. Alvaro del Portillo. They have already worked on some preconciliar commissions. Now they will work on some of the conciliar commissions, and later they will work also on some postconciliar ones.

Msgr. Escrivá meets numerous council fathers and *periti* who wish to speak with him: in these conversations he expresses his faith, hope, and love regarding the Church. Those who speak with him will, years later, testify to his exemplary fidelity to the magisterium, his supernatural prudence, and his transparent sanctity.

His constant preaching and numerous writings in these years demonstrate that Msgr. Escrivá has not fallen into a facile optimism. While fully trusting in the renewal which the Holy Spirit will bring about through the council, he is also well aware of the pressures that will be brought to bear by means of the mass media, and the resultant danger that dubious theological positions will be widely and uncritically embraced. His words are a testimony to his faithfulness to the Church, and an urgent invitation to sanctity.

1963   Msgr. Escrivá approves the start of apostolic activity in Australia; other foundations follow soon after in Nigeria, Belgium, Puerto Rico, and the Philippines.

On a trip to Spain, during a brief stay near Reparacea, he fosters an initiative that is destined to have great repercussions. The idea is to make parents aware that they are the

ones primarily responsible not only for the Christian upbringing of their children, but also for the foundation—
along with all the sacrifices and effort that this requires—of
educational institutions, such as elementary and secondary
schools, that will provide people in all levels of society with
a solid Christian formation and a sound cultural and professional preparation. Msgr. Escrivá sets out the principles
that are to inspire the activity of such educational institutions. Under his direct influence they begin to appear, first
in Spain, and soon thereafter in many other nations all over
the world.

Pope John XXIII dies, and on June 21 Cardinal Montini—
the man who in 1946 welcomed Msgr. Escrivá to Rome,
with unforgettable expressions of esteem and encouragement—is elected to the throne of St. Peter as Pope Paul VI.
Half a year later, on January 24, 1964, the first private audience takes place. The founder places himself and Opus Dei
entirely at the service of the pontiff, as he recalls with emotion so many occasions when he experienced in the presence of the then Msgr. Montini a strong sense of priestly
solidarity.

1965   On November 21, in Rome, Pope Paul inaugurates the Centro ELIS, a trade school for disadvantaged youth which the
Holy See has entrusted, for both its planning and realization, to Opus Dei. Msgr. Escrivá extends words of greeting
which show his love for the one whom he calls, using the
expression of St. Catherine of Siena, "the sweet Christ on
earth," and which show as well the depth of emotion he always feels in the presence of the pope. Many council fathers are in attendance.

The council closes on December 8. Msgr. Escrivá has the
joy of seeing solemnly confirmed some of the basic fo-
cuses of the spirit of Opus Dei which have been a part of
his preaching since 1928: the universal vocation to sanctity, the mission of the laity to give life to temporal structures (and the consequences that flow from this on the
ecclesial plane), the centrality of the holy Mass in the life
of the Christian, an active participation of the faithful in
the liturgy, a legitimate and healthy pluralism among the
People of God, and so forth.

The founder sets an example of obedience and care by way of his own diligent application of the conciliar decrees.

1966–1967   A number of study conferences take place in Rome, promoted by the founder, for the directors of various apostolic activities of the Work. He personally guides them, giving a decisive impulse to all the initiatives. He sees Opus Dei becoming, in line with its own nature, ever more consolidated.

On October 7, 1966, the title of "Adopted Son of Barcelona" is conferred on him.

1968   February 14 is the twenty-fifth anniversary of the founding of the Priestly Society of the Holy Cross. As usual, Msgr. Escrivá does not wish any external celebrations; he simply invites all his daughters and sons to thank the Lord for the countless gifts which he has given to the Work. He sees the passing years as a history of God's mercy.

He promotes the establishment of the University of Piura, in Peru.

The founder endorses a new apostolic initiative: a gathering in Rome, during Holy Week, of students from all over the world, coming together to compare their apostolic experiences in the hundreds of universities which they attend, and, above all, to express their resolve to remain faithful to the pope. Such meetings will take place every year, providing thousands of young people a special opportunity for strengthening their commitment to Christ.

1969   Already in previous years (1960, 1962, and 1964), Msgr. Escrivá has made it clear to the Holy See that the problem of the canonical classification of Opus Dei is as yet unsolved, and that he feels in conscience, before God, the obligation of seeking a definitive solution that will be in full accord with the foundational charism; and Rome has responded to such concerns. The conciliar decree *Presbyterorum Ordinis* (1965) envisions the institution of prelatures for the realization of special pastoral goals, and Pope Paul's *motu proprio* to implement it (*Ecclesiae Sanctae*, 1966) specifies in greater detail the characteristics of this new juridical figure.

On June 25, with the authorization of the Holy See, the founder convokes a special General Congress of Opus Dei for the purpose of discerning what adaptations will need to be made to the particular code of laws of Opus Dei in the event of its being transformed into a prelature. The first phase of this meeting begins on September 15. The work is preceded by extensive consultations: all the members who want to express their thoughts on the matter are asked to send their communications to Rome. The congress receives all these communications and finds itself able to express to the founder a unanimous desire of the members of the Work to arrive at a definitive juridical solution.

Conversations with Monsignor Escrivá de Balaguer, a collection of interviews he had with journalists of various countries, is published. The text contains important explanations of the true theological nature of the vocation to Opus Dei, the ramifications of such a vocation on an institutional level, Opus Dei's apostolic methods, and its organizational structure. In particular, he emphasizes the complete freedom of its members with regard to those temporal choices which the magisterium of the Church leaves to the discretion of the individual believer; he states unequivocally that Opus Dei never imposes on its members or even suggests any ideological, political, or economic policy whatsoever. Because its purpose is exclusively supernatural, he says, Opus Dei rigorously abstains from the exercise of any worldly influence; in fact, it actively encourages its members to make, as faithful and intelligent Christians, their own choices in such matters. The founder's absolute fidelity to these principles has provoked more than a few misunderstandings. He always responds to them with charity and reiterates the truth with a heroic patience.

On November 13, a new instrument of service to the Church is inaugurated at the University of Navarre: the theology department. It is warmly supported by the Spanish episcopate, and especially by the bishops of the local ecclesiastical province.

New apostolic journeys, and the death of Msgr. Escrivá

1970   The last years of the founder's life are characterized by
              prolonged and intense suffering, caused by crises that are
              overtaking large sectors of the Church: wholesale defec-
              tions of priests and religious, the sharp decline in the num-
              ber of new vocations to the priesthood, liturgical and dis-
              ciplinary abuses, the diffusion of erroneous doctrines, and
              a general dropping off of devotional practices and even of
              the fulfillment of basic religious obligations. The repeated,
              heartfelt admonitions of Pope Paul VI find prompt and
              fully concordant echoes in Msgr. Escrivá's teachings. These
              are years of sorrowful prayer, of generous expiation, and
              of an even more extensive and insistent apostolate. The
              founder does, however, receive divine locutions that com-
              fort him. And despite his advancing age and uncertain
              health, he decides to undertake long catechetical journeys
              to preach the faith in many countries.

              From May 14 to June 22, he is in Mexico, mainly for the pur-
              pose of making a penitential pilgrimage to the Basilica of
              Our Lady of Guadalupe. This pilgrimage represents a con-
              tinuation of the supplication which he has already been
              making to the Blessed Virgin in many shrines of Europe:
              Lourdes, Fatima, Our Lady of the Pillar (in Saragossa), Ein-
              siedeln, Loreto, Our Lady of Ransom (in Barcelona), Maria
              Laach, Maria Pötsch, Maria Zell . . . ; in all of these places he
              has prayed for the Church as a whole, and for the Roman
              pontiff in particular. But this journey is also an occasion for
              a widespread catechesis to persons of all social conditions.

              From August 30 to September 14, the second part of the
              special General Congress takes place. This too has been
              preceded by extensive consultations, which have brought
              more than fifty-four thousand communications to Rome.
              Msgr. Escrivá contemplates with thankfulness the unity of
              spirit of Opus Dei, the perseverance of its members, their
              proven fidelity to the magisterium, the continuing expan-
              sion of the apostolates, and the common desire of the mem-
              bers to join together in reaching a favorable solution to the
              institutional problem.

1971   On January 9, construction of the new buildings of the
              Roman College of the Holy Cross is begun, in the Grot-

tarossa district; until this time the college has been located at the headquarters of Opus Dei. The new buildings will allow for an increased enrollment and better facilities.

Msgr. Escrivá, good shepherd that he is, directs his vigilance principally toward the flock which the Lord has entrusted to his care: he frequently reminds the members of their call to sanctity, and by word and example inspires in them an ascetic zeal and an uncompromising loyalty to the faith. On May 30, he consecrates Opus Dei to the Holy Spirit.

1972   He dedicates the months of October and November to a long and tiring apostolic journey to numerous cities of Spain and Portugal; now, as before in Mexico, thousands of persons come to hear him. He speaks with vigor and simplicity, in a colloquial and persuasive way, of the fundamental truths of the Christian faith. With the forceful magnetism of his living faith and with a love of God which penetrates every fiber of his person, he exhorts them to love the Church, to be faithful to the pope, and to pursue sanctity in the ordinary activities of life by means of prayer and a frequent reception of the sacraments. He exalts the sanctity of the family and of human love in general; he strongly emphasizes the need of a constant recourse to confession. Many conversions take place.

1973   *Christ Is Passing By,* a collection of his homilies, is published and soon becomes a best-seller.

1974   The founder undertakes another long trip, which lasts from May 22 until August 31. This time he goes to South America: to Brazil, Argentina, Chile, Peru, Ecuador, and Venezuela. He is spurred on by the desire to reach people everywhere, to lead them to a joyous Christian witness. Huge crowds gather to hear his preaching, which is stamped by a heroic firmness of faith. Once again, it is a demonstration of the widespread recognition of his sanctity.

On October 1, Msgr. Escrivá sends to the printers the revised "code of particular law" for Opus Dei, having made the necessary modifications. He himself, in other words, has sketched out the definitive juridical configuration of Opus Dei. It will, after extensive studies, become a reality in 1982, when Pope John Paul II (with the apostolic constitution *Ut Sit*) establishes Opus Dei as a personal prelature.

In the month of February, the founder undertakes a second journey of catechesis to Venezuela and Guatemala, and this too is blessed by the Lord with abundant spiritual fruits.

On March 28, which falls on Good Friday this year, Msgr. Escrivá celebrates the fiftieth anniversary of his ordination to the priesthood, in a way that, once again, is consistent with this motto which has inspired his whole life: "To hide and disappear, so that Jesus alone shines out."

In the last days of May, he makes what is to be his last trip: he goes to pray at the new shrine of Our Lady of Torreciudad, a construction which he initiated and which is about to be dedicated. Torreciudad could be called a monument to his love for the Blessed Virgin.

A few days after his return to Rome, at noon on June 26, Msgr. Escrivá dies in his place of work, as simply as he has lived. His body falls to the floor in front of a picture of Our Lady of Guadalupe—the object of his last glance. He is already unconscious when, in fulfillment of a desire which he has often expressed, he receives absolution and the Anointing of the Sick. Just a few hours ago, in his morning Mass, he has renewed the offering of his own life for the Church in general and for the pope in particular. After Mass he has gone to Castel Gandolfo, where he has spoken to his daughters at the Roman College of Holy Mary, in words that they will never forget: his words are a final witness to his love for the pope and to his zeal for souls.

The next day he is buried in the crypt of the oratory of Our Lady of Peace, at the central headquarters of Opus Dei, while prayers of suffrage for his soul are being said all over the world.

Masses for the repose of his soul are celebrated in every city where there is an Opus Dei center. Everywhere, large groups gather to express their sorrow and their thankfulness. Many people who have been a bit distant from the Church are converted or return to the practice of their faith.

Testimonies to Msgr. Escrivá's reputation for sanctity are numerous and immediately forthcoming. Thousands of persons, including cardinals, bishops from all over the

world, civil authorities, and ordinary faithful of every social category, send in requests for the Holy Father to initiate the cause for his canonization. News soon begins to arrive in Rome, through various channels, of vast numbers
of graces attributed to the founder's intercession. Within
the next two and a half years, the Office of Postulation will
receive about ten thousand reports of large and small favors obtained, including some miraculous healings.

At the time of the founder's death, Opus Dei is present in
countries all over the globe; it has more than sixty thousand
members, representing eighty different nationalities. Apostolic activities are in place in thirty-one countries. The number of centers is over seven hundred, and comprises student
residences, schools of every type and level, youth clubs,
retreat houses, medical clinics and dispensaries, etc. Msgr.
Escrivá's concern for justice has, from the very start, given
a strong social dimension to these initiatives. They are endowed, as he wished, with financial aid programs that
make them accessible to people of all social levels. At the
same time, they are a response to the needs of the local
community or of particular professional sectors; there are,
for example, hotel schools, family agriculture schools, and
various types of professional training schools. But above
all, the founder has conceived and realized these institutions as having an apostolic purpose: they are to be instruments for an integrated formation (both religious and secular) which will flow out from the person and benefit the
surrounding environment.

In the course of his life, Msgr. Escrivá has brought hundreds of members of Opus Dei, of various professions, to
the priesthood, and has promoted countless vocations for
the diocesan priesthood and for religious orders.

Stages of continuity and the path to beatification

1975   On September 15, an elective congress of members of Opus
        Dei unanimously elects Fr. Alvaro del Portillo as successor
        to the founder.

1977   The first posthumous work of the founder is published:
        Friends of God, a second collection of homilies.

1981   On February 19, Cardinal Poletti, the cardinal vicar of Rome, promulgates the decree which introduces the cause for Msgr. Escrivá's canonization. He does this at the request of sixty-nine cardinals, thirteen hundred bishops (over a third of the world episcopate), forty-one superior generals of religious congregations, and numerous lay people, including many political and cultural leaders.

The Way of the Cross is published.

On May 12, the first step in the canonical process leading to Msgr. Escrivá's beatification, an intensive study of his life and writings, begins in Rome.

1982   On November 28, with the apostolic constitution Ut Sit, Pope John Paul II establishes Opus Dei as a personal prelature. This is the founder's dream come true: a canonical framework for Opus Dei that is congruent with its foundational charism. Msgr. Alvaro del Portillo is appointed as its first Prelate.

1984   On January 15, Pope John Paul visits the Centro ELIS and the adjacent parish of San Giovanni Battista al Collatino (in the Tiburtino district of Rome), a parish entrusted to the priests of the Prelature.

1985   The Congregation for Catholic Education, with the decree Dei Servus of January 9, canonically establishes the Roman branches of the University of Navarre's theology and canon law departments. There commences thus the Roman Academic Center of the Holy Cross (Centro Accadèmico Romano della Santa Croce).

1986   In October, the book Furrow is published.

On November 8, Cardinal Poletti, as cardinal vicar of Rome and therefore head of its diocesan tribunal, declares that the process of inquiry into the life and virtues of the Servant of God Josemaría Escrivá de Balaguer has been concluded. (A parallel process undertaken by the curia of the archdiocese of Madrid was concluded on June 26, 1984.)

1987   The Forge is published. With The Way and Furrow it forms a trilogy of books of points for meditation.

1990   On January 9, the Congregation for Catholic Education, taking into account the development of the Roman Academic Center of the Holy Cross, canonically establishes its philosophy and theology departments as the Roman Athenaeum of the Holy Cross. The canon law department of the University of Navarre continues its work at the Athenaeum, although not yet in a fully integrated way.

On April 9, Pope John Paul II declares heroic the degree to which the Venerable Servant of God Josemaría Escrivá de Balaguer lived the Christian virtues.

1991   On January 6, in St. Peter's Basilica, Pope John Paul confers episcopal ordination on the Prelate of Opus Dei, Msgr. Alvaro del Portillo.

On July 6, in the presence of the Holy Father, the decree is read which recognizes as miraculous the character of a certain cure that has taken place through the intercession of Venerable Josemaría Escrivá. The preliminaries to the beatification are thus concluded.

1992   On May 17, in St. Peter's Square, Pope John Paul II beatifies the founder of Opus Dei.

Bibliographical Note

The works of Blessed Josemaría Escrivá de Balaguer

Msgr. Escrivá's published writings, apart from the study in theology and canon law entitled *La Abadesa de las Huelgas* (1944), are works of spirituality that have been translated into many languages. In the following list, the date of publication of the original Spanish edition is followed by the date of the first English translation.

The Way (1939; 1953). Appearing originally in 1934 under the title *Consideraciones Espirituales*, this book was revised, expanded, and given its definitive form and title (*Camino*) in 1939. It is a best-seller of ascetic literature: it has seen some two hundred fifty printings in thirty-nine languages; close to four million copies have been sold. The book consists of 999 points of meditation for the Christian life, which the author derived, for the most part, from his experience as a priest.

Furrow (1986; 1987) and *The Forge* (1987; 1988). These two posthumous works are written in the same style as *The Way*; they form with it a trilogy that sets forth an orderly path of spiritual progress.

Holy Rosary (1934; 1954). Written at about the same time as *The Way*, this is a booklet of meditations on the fifteen mysteries of the rosary. Fr. Josemaría wrote it at one go, during his after-Mass thanksgiving one day in 1931. It has seen ninety-three printings in eighteen languages.

Christ Is Passing By (1973; 1974). A collection of eighteen homilies (or, rather, preached meditations) by the founder of Opus Dei, on various themes pertaining to the ascetic Christian life, and following the cycle of the liturgical year.

Friends of God (1977; 1981). Another collection of eighteen homilies, centered on the Christian virtues.

The Way of the Cross (1981; 1982). A meditation on the scenes of the Passion.

In Love with the Church (1986; 1989). A collection of four of Blessed Josemaría's homilies on the Church.

Conversations with Monsignor Escrivá de Balaguer (1968; 1968). A series of interviews with the founder of Opus Dei, conducted between 1966 and 1968 by members of the international press, this book concludes with the homily "Passionately Loving the World" (given in 1967), in which Msgr. Escrivá describes the most important features of the spirituality of Opus Dei.

Works about Blessed Josemaría Escrivá and Opus Dei

The books published on Opus Dei and its founder are becoming numerous. We list here only works published in an English original or translation. Again, original publication year is given first (with original language), followed by year of first English edition. Fuller bibliographies are available in the works by Berglar and Le Tourneau.

Salvador Bernal, *A Profile of Msgr. Escrivá* (1976 in Spanish; 1977). This book illustrates the life of the founder with an abundance of citations from his writings and preaching.

François Gondrand, *At God's Pace* (1982 in French; 1989). A very readable account of the life of the founder and of the expansion of Opus Dei.

Peter Berglar, *Opus Dei: Life and Work of its Founder* (1983 in German; 1994). A more scholarly biography, based on a wide-ranging investigation of sources, which treats of historical, religious, and biographical aspects.

Dominique Le Tourneau, *What is Opus Dei?* (1985 in French; 1989). A brief but comprehensive treatment of the Work.

Dennis Helming, *Footprints in the Snow* (1986 in English). A pictorial introduction, by an American journalist, to the person and work of Blessed Josemaría Escrivá. Foreword by Malcolm Muggeridge.

Amadeo de Fuenmayor, Valentín Gómez–Iglesias, and José Luis Illanes, *The Canonical Path of Opus Dei* (1990 in Spanish; 1994). The three authors researched a vast number of documents, mostly unpublished, in order to define the characteristics of the path followed by the founder and his successor in reaching the definitive canonical status of Opus Dei: that of a personal prelature. It includes important excerpts from the founder's personal notes. The extensive appendix contains a number of documents in their original languages, including the statutes of the Prelature.